Two Mountaineering Classics in One Volume

DAVID ROBERTS

The Mountain of My Fear

Deborah:
A Wilderness Narrative

Foreword by Jon Krakauer

THE
MOUNTAINEERS

Published by
The Mountaineers
1001 SW Klickitat Way, Suite 201
Seattle, Washington 98134

© 1968, 1970, 1991 by David Roberts
Foreword © 1991 by Jon Krakauer

First edition: first printing 1991, second printing 1997

Published simultaneously in Great Britain by Cordee,
3a DeMontfort Street, Leicester, England, LE1 7HD

Manufactured in the United States of America

Cover photos: Background photo by Jon Krakauer. Inset photos of Mount Huntington and Mount Deborah by Bradford Washburn.
Photos on pages 89 and 285 by Bradford Washburn. Photos on page 93 and on pages 286 through 292 by Don Jensen. All other photographs by David Roberts.
Cover design by Helen Cherullo, with graphic technical assistance from Kristy Welch

Library of Congress Cataloging-in-Publication Data

Roberts, David, 1943-
    (Deborah)
    Deborah; and, The mountain of my fear : the early climbs / David
Roberts.
    P. cm.
  Reprint (1st work). Originally published: New York : Vanguard Press, 1970.
  Reprint (2nd work). Originally published: New York : Vanguard Press, 1968.
  ISBN 0-89886-270-1
    1. Mountaineering—Alaska—Deborah (Mount). 2. Mountaineering—
Alaska—Huntington (Mount). 3. Deborah, Mount (Alaska)—Description and
travel. 4. Huntington, Mount—Description and travel. 5. Roberts, David, 1943-
. 6. Jensen, Don. 7. Mountaineers—United States—Biography. 8. Jensen, Don.
I. Roberts, David, 1943- Mountain of my fear. 1991. II. Title.
GV199.42.A42D437 1991
    90-28126
796.5 ' 22097983--dc20
        CIP

▲ Contents

Foreword ▲ 5

Preface ▲ 9

DEBORAH: A WILDERNESS NARRATIVE ▲ 15

Interlude ▲ 205

THE MOUNTAIN OF MY FEAR ▲ 211

Epilogue ▲ 359

Glossary ▲ 365

Foreword ▲

In the literature of mountaineering, certifiable brilliance
is in short supply. Over the two centuries that men and
women have been writing about climbing, only a handful
of authors have created work that can honestly be called
great, work that can stand on its own as literature beyond
the forgiving confines of the mountaineering *genre*. Most
of those belonging to the pantheon are gifted full-time
writers who have done little more than dabble in climbing;
conversely, a smaller number are accomplished climbers
who have likewise dabbled in writing and managed, almost
as if by accident, to produce one or two extraordinary
pieces of work. There is one person, however, who has

made a significant mark both as a climber and as a writer, that man being David Roberts, the author of this volume.

At the age of twenty, three years after he took up climbing, Roberts and six Harvard buddies made the first direct ascent of Mount McKinley's huge, avalanche-swept Wickersham Wall—a route that, twenty-eight years later, has yet to be repeated. Following the McKinley climb, Roberts participated in more than a dozen additional Alaskan expeditions, in the course of which he blazed alpine ground in such now-legendary ranges as the Arrigetch Peaks, the Cathedral Spires, the Revelations, and the Ruth Gorge. A number of the first ascents Roberts bagged along the way—Shot Tower, for instance, and the southeast buttress of Mount Dickey—are indubitable classics, among the most beautiful lines on the North American continent.

But Roberts' most famous—and perhaps finest—Alaskan deed remains one of his earliest undertakings, the first ascent of a route he, Matt Hale, Don Jensen, and Ed Bernd put up in 1965: the west face of Mount Huntington. Their remarkable climb became the subject of *The Mountain of My Fear*.

It was Roberts' first book. He wrote it as a first-year graduate student, in nine feverish days. Against all likelihood, it turned out to be one of the best mountaineering books ever written. A critic for *The Atlantic Monthly* praised *The Mountain of My Fear* as "Exceptional for the young author's subtle, unsentimental attempt to define the motives that drive men to climb mountains." W. H. Auden, the great English poet, selected an excerpt from the book for inclusion in a collection of his favorite writing titled *A Certain World*. Auden thought so much of Roberts' prose, in fact, that the poet later wrote a glowing review of Roberts' second book, *Deborah*, for *The New York Times*. Never, before or since, has an author of climbing books been taken so seriously.

The publication of *The Mountain of My Fear*, in 1968, and *Deborah,* in 1970, changed the face of the literature of mountaineering. Roberts' trademark was—and is—unflinching honesty. He tells it like it is. He also tells it beautifully, in a distinctive, flawless voice that leaves the rest of us who write about the sport feeling an uncomfortable mix of admiration and bald envy.

In the review section of the 1990 *American Alpine Journal*, Steve Roper critiques the latest book by a famous British climber and finds it wanting. "I dream of perfection, I suppose," he complains. "Not everyone can write like David Roberts, but why can't he at least have a few writers hot on his tail?" The truth in Roper's lament is unfortunate, but undeniable. We should be especially grateful, therefore, that The Mountaineers have reissued *The Mountain of My Fear* and *Deborah* in this single volume. It's been long overdue.

JON KRAKAUER

Preface ▲

The Mountain of My Fear was my first book, written in the spring of 1966, eight months after our expedition to Mount Huntington. During that lull, I toiled through a lonely first year of graduate school at the University of Denver, far from my climbing friends, not sure that I wanted to climb ever again. I was enmeshed in a tangle of disturbing emotions, the legacy of our costly victory. For the first and only time in my writing life, I felt obsessed with a need to put the story down on paper. It seemed of paramount urgency to explain our climb to the world—as I then, with a twenty-two-year-old's brash earnestness, might have phrased my mission. I wrote the book in a white heat, a chapter a day, too impatient for second thoughts or serious revision.

The act had its cathartic effect, though it would be decades before I came to terms with the more recondite qualms and guilts that Huntington had worked under my skin. This purgative deed allowed me to climb— and soon, to climb hard—again.

I sent my manuscript to a publisher, where it landed in the "slush pile." At the time, I had no idea what the odds were against an unsolicited manuscript's swimming to the surface. Two publishers rejected the book, and then, one day a year after I had written it, I pulled out of my mail box the most joyous piece of news a writer can ever receive: my first acceptance. An editor from Vanguard Press in New York said they would like to publish *The Mountain of My Fear.*

Although I was enrolled in the writing program at Denver, I had not shown my Huntington manuscript to any of my professors. I had failed, in fact, even to mention it to them. When they learned that my book was going to be published, they were miffed at my secrecy. But it was an innocent, not a smug, concealment. In creative writing classes, I was submitting precious villanelles and maudlin short stories to the strictures of my peers and pundits. It never occurred to me that my teachers might be willing to read a non-fiction account of a mountain climb.

By the time Vanguard accepted my first book, I was writing my second. *Deborah,* in fact, became my M.A. thesis. *The Mountain of My Fear* had been written under the influence of a kind of romantic existentialism and, in its giddier flights, of the prose of Faulkner. When I started *Deborah*, I was in counter-reaction—thanks, in large part, to the credo of my thesis adviser, John Williams, a cranky professor and underrated novelist, who later won the National Book Award for *Augustus*. Williams preached that the proper tone for prose is dry and plain, so that the story itself comes to the fore. By 1967 I was a disciple, and as I wrote *Deborah* I kept the impulses that had produced the frenziedly poetic passages of my first book under tight restraint.

If *The Mountain of My Fear* burst forth in a cathartic flood, *Deborah* seemed to emerge from a process of slow, incremental brooding. It had been three years since our expedition to the Hayes Range, and I had had plenty of time to puzzle over its dark severities. Now I was consumed not with telling our story to the world, but with discovering just what had happened between Don Jensen and me during our forty-two days alone together, and why.

I have always preferred *Deborah* to *The Mountain of My Fear*, but of my friends who have read both works, most make the opposite choice; *Deborah* has always been the less popular of the two books. It may be simply that the account of a long, grinding failure cannot compete with a story of triumph and death. Or perhaps, as one of my closest mountaineering friends told me, Deborah seems to have been such a relentlessly miserable expedition that it is hard to enjoy the telling of it.

Reprinting the two books in a single volume creates

a sequential dilemma. Although I wrote *Deborah* after *The Mountain of My Fear*, our Deborah expedition took place a year before the Huntington climb. The only solution is to let historical chronology outweigh authorial: thus *Deborah* appears here first.

Rereading both books more than twenty years later, I am struck by how intensely serious we were in those days. My God, I muse now, we were just college kids! Yet, while our roommates were playing bridge and chasing girls at mixers, Don and I, like vision-tormented pilgrims, schemed esoteric assaults on a wasteland of ice and rock five thousand miles away.

Yet I feel nostalgic for that intensity. Humorless we must have seemed to those bridge-playing friends, shy and fanatic to women who might have dared show an interest in us, recklessly foolhardy to our worried parents. We had found, as people almost never find, something to do together that was so compelling we could go for months at a time without any of the more mundane pleasures of the world. On those unexplored Alaska glaciers, we felt like scholars of an arcane discipline who had come upon a hoard of unsuspected treasure. There was far too much to do and never enough time to begin it.

The deepest despair I have ever felt, as well as the most piercing happiness, has come in the mountains— a fair portion of each on Deborah and Huntington. In my later years as a writer, I have been lucky enough to travel widely, often on fine adventures: rafting an unknown river in New Guinea, climbing to prehistoric

burial caves in Mali, prowling through Iceland in search
of saga sites. But none of these latter-day exploits has
had quite the intensity of those early climbing expeditions. And looking back, at age forty-seven, I have
to confess that nothing I have done in my life has made
me nearly so proud as my best climbs in Alaska.

▲

DEBORAH
A WILDERNESS
NARRATIVE

▲

1 ▲

I first met Don Jensen at the beginning of our sophomore year at Harvard. We had both joined the mountaineering club our freshman year, but had never gone
on the same week-end trip until the first rock-climbing
outing in October, 1962. I had heard of Don—other
members of the club had told me what a strong, enthusiastic climber he was. But it was something of a surprise to meet him. That Friday afternoon, I had lugged
my gear over to the entry of Lowell House, where the
cars would pick us up. With the other beginners, I
stood for a few moments in an awkward silence. Then

one of them stepped aggressively toward me, stretching out an eager hand: "Hi! I'm Don Jensen."

I shook hands and introduced myself. I was surprised because he seemed so boyishly friendly. I had imagined some cool, hard athlete. I could see that Don was powerful, about my height but much heavier, built like a football player. His black hair and solid face were strong and masculine. But his face was also young, and terribly sincere. I was used to the Harvard "style," in which one affects a biting wit and a cold heart; instead, Don reminded me of friends in Colorado, where I had grown up. We talked about climbing for a while. He was from California; as he talked, I could see that already, three weeks into the term, he was nostalgic for the Sierra Nevada. He told me about a twenty-day trip he had taken alone, following the divide southward. I had never been out for that long, let alone by myself; I suggested that he must have got lonely. On the contrary, he had found the several people he had run into a disappointment. Once he had seen a large group of Sierra Club hikers, and had deliberately skirted them so that he would not have to talk to them.

Don and I both lived in Dunster House, so that fall we saw each other often. We ate lunch and dinner together frequently, talking about little else than climbing. It was, for each of us, the primary pleasure in life. I was majoring in mathematics, with vague plans of a career in research and teaching. Don, with the same vague plans, was struggling with philosophy. But in our spare time I dreamed about the Rockies, Don about the

Sierras. A dozen times I went up to Don's room, to find maps spread on the floor, the corners held down with Kant and Wittgenstein and Aristotle. And whenever Don came up to my room, I insisted on hauling out my muddy three-by-five snapshots of Colorado peaks.

With another friend, we planned a Christmas trip climbing in the Crestones, in southern Colorado. Don flew home for Christmas, then back to Denver, where I met him at the airport. I had never seen him in such good spirits. He didn't really like the East; this land of unlimited sky and sun—anywhere from Nebraska to Oregon—was his spiritual habitat.

The three of us had a fine six-day trip, the longest I had ever taken in the winter. The weather was perfect each day. We camped on the frozen bed of a river at 12,000 feet, crowded snugly into a three-man tent we had rented. We found running water by chopping through the ice. It got bitterly cold each night (perhaps twenty below), but we were up before dawn to get a good start on the peaks. We climbed two of them, both over 14,000 feet, and had to stop short of the summit of a third when our friend got sick. On the sixth day we hiked back out to our car. It was a wonderfully happy trip, and we dreaded going back to Harvard. For the first time, I think, I felt an alliance with Don that went beyond friendship: we began to feel the cooperative excitement of a good team. But I also noticed, for the first time, two things that would cause trouble between us later: often, at night, we ran out of things to talk about; in addition, I loved conversations but Don preferred to think by himself. The other disparity had to do with a kind of emotional endurance: at the end of the six days I felt satisfied, without much desire to climb any more right away; but Don saw peaks and ridges surrounding our camp that we hadn't had time to climb, and he felt as if he had cheated himself by not arranging for at least a few more days there. Don could never see a mountain, even an ugly mountain or an easy one, without feeling a duty to climb it. Instead, I chose the ones I was most interested in and tended to ignore the rest.

Back at school, we faced papers and finals. I managed to get through them but Don procrastinated on his papers and began to panic; he took NōDōz to stay awake but couldn't concentrate. He began to look rundown: he gained weight, and his tough, youthful face grew haggard. At last he got everything finished but he knew he had done badly. What was worse, he saw how much of a drain on his health school could be; with the attitude of any true outdoorsman, Don valued his physical well-being above his mental achievements.

He began the spring semester of 1963 with a determination to do better. But everything went badly from the start. More and more he turned to his maps and thoughts of the stark, splendid mountains of California. He had never spent much time in them in the winter; our Christmas trip had obviously sown the seeds of restlessness. Moreover, in February I was invited by the older, more experienced members of the mountaineering club to go on an expedition to Mount

McKinley, in Alaska; I felt extremely flattered, because the others had climbed all over the western United States, and in the Canadian Rockies and Coast Range; one had even been on McKinley before. Don, though, was not invited. It seemed unfair to me, because we were equally skillful; if anything, Don had more experience on snow. But I was also selfishly pleased to be the only sophomore chosen. Don generously claimed that he was glad for my sake and that being left out made little difference to him; but his disappointment was evident.

Shortly after that, he decided to drop out of school for the semester. I was surprised and tried to joke him out of it. But he had carefully made up his mind before telling anyone. He was going to go home—not to his parents' house near San Francisco but to the little town of Big Pine, on the eastern slope of the Sierras. I knew this was only a few miles from his favorite mountains, the Palisades, so I kidded him about being a hedonist. But he had a perfect rationalization: he was planning to take Professor Riesman's course on social structures in America when he returned the next fall; hence he would do field research on the natives of Big Pine. He described the complicated web of cliques and prejudices he had noticed there before. I tried to picture Don, camped just outside town all spring in the little orange tent he had just made for himself, sneaking in during the day to interview old ladies. But he could not be joked out of it; he had made up his mind.

He had almost run out of money. He stopped going

to classes but he could not pull himself together and actually leave. I think he was a little afraid that he was letting his parents down and, with them, all the high-school friends who had expected so much of him when he first went to Harvard. He stopped eating, for the most part, to save money; for about a week he staggered about in a ravenous daze. At last he was kicked out of his room in Dunster House, so he moved to the mountaineering clubroom, a damp closet in the basement of Lowell House. I felt sorry for him, but he was so ludicrous that I couldn't help laughing at him. I would sneak bread and rolls out of the dining hall for him; one evening I smuggled him into a beer-and-sandwiches reception with the master. Having shipped most of his clothes home, he had to go to the reception wearing a dirty shirt, a borrowed coat, grass-stained Levis, and his climbing boots. The master was surprised to see him at all, and especially in such a state, but he maintained decorum. The master's wife nervously watched as Don wolfed down sandwich after sandwich.

The day before he left, I bought some bread and cheese and we had a picnic in a Cambridge park. We called the little lunch the "Don C. Jensen Memorial Farewell Dinner." For once during these last few weeks, Don was in fine humor; we laughed at every remark, releasing tensions and covering the genuine sadness we felt at saying good-by to each other. There was a warm, wet breeze; it seemed the first day of spring. We promised each other all sorts of climbs together in the vague future. After the picnic, I saw Don to the bus depot.

He wrote me one or two letters from Big Pine. Needless to say, he was spending every moment in the Palisades, descending to town only to get food. In rapturous terms he described holding down his tent, alone, during a week-long blizzard that had threatened to tear it loose. He was reading Goethe, he said, and learning more than he ever could have in school. He described a natural echoing rock he had discovered; in good weather he would go out and shout to it for hours on end, carrying on eloquent conversations with it.

That spring I was preoccupied with planning for McKinley. We were going to attempt its Wickersham Wall, or north face, by a rather audacious route straight up the middle of it. This was the last side of McKinley that no one had climbed, and the Wall was one of the two or three biggest cliffs in the world, rising more than 14,000 vertical feet from bottom to top. I had never even seen such a mountain. Privately, I felt sure we were too ambitious and I anticipated the summer with a kind of fear. But I didn't show the others my reluctance and the more I got involved in the work, the more enthusiastic I grew. At the Spring Dinner meeting, I was elected the club's vice-president.

Then, a few weeks before we were to start for Alaska, one of the expedition's six members dropped out. We frantically looked around for another experienced climber who could go on such short notice. I urged the others to ask Don. None of them knew Don well; one of them had scarcely met him. But as I described Don's talents, they were gradually won over.

The next problem was to contact Don. We quickly found out that he had last been seen trudging back into the Palisades. We felt frustrated; in desperation we sent a telegram to General Delivery in Big Pine. A few days later Don happened to come out for supplies and got the telegram. At once he called us, agreeing to go. In a matter of days he got together all the gear he would need and arranged a ride to Alaska. We would meet him in McKinley Park.

School let out in June. We packed supplies nonstop at a friend's house in New York, then drove nonstop to Alaska, over the forty-eight hundred miles of dreary road. Six days later we arrived at the little railroad stop of McKinley Park (a full hundred miles away from the mountain) in a dismal rain; that afternoon Don showed up, soaking wet, from a three-day climb he had gone on while waiting for us. I was especially glad to see him. He looked so much healthier than when he had left Harvard that I could hardly believe only two months had gone by.

The expedition went smoothly. In thirty-five days we hiked in to the Peters Glacier, climbed our route without a serious mishap, traversed over the mountain, climbed both its summits, descended the easy route, and hiked out. Unknown to us, we had caused a national scare for a few days in July, when we were reported missing. Of course we didn't know we were "missing"; we had simply been ahead of schedule. It had been a difficult climb and a tiring trip, and we were all glad to get back; but the adventure had been closer to a lark than an ordeal. There were enough of us so that we never grew lonely and so that no personal antagonisms built up too high. At times some of us got angry at one another, but it never lasted.

Don and I had not climbed together very much on the expedition because the older members wisely insisted on splitting up, so that one of them always climbed with one of us. On the few occasions when Don and I shared a rope, I noticed the return of the "team" feeling we had discovered in Colorado, a feeling I hadn't developed with any of the others. On the last stretch of the hike out, Don and I had roped together to cross the McKinley River; both of us, I think, felt that that was fitting to our sense of comradeship.

In the fall of 1963, Don was back at Harvard. He had been moved from Dunster House to Claverly, the overflow hall, which was the least popular place to live. I first saw him that September carrying his refrigerator out of Dunster House. He put it down and we shook hands, much differently than we had the first time. We both felt proud of our summer; in fact, most of our friends at Harvard had heard about our climb and had congratulated us the first moment they saw us.

Don and I climbed together often during the fall weekends. We played touch football in the afternoons and sometimes worked out together, running a circuit of bridges over the Charles River or exercising in the fieldhouse. We planned another Christmas trip to

Colorado; at first it was designed as a six- or seven-day trip, like the one before, but Don talked me into using every minute of our vacation that we could, even Christmas and New Year's Day. By driving straight through to Colorado and back, we could arrange an eleven-day trip.

By now Don was treasurer of the club and I was vice-president. Most of the veteran members, our McKinley friends, had graduated. So Don and I talked four of the less experienced club members into going with us. We were planning to visit the Needle Mountains, near Durango, in southwestern Colorado. No one had ever been there in the winter.

At last Christmas came. The six of us managed to get out to my home in Boulder, where we packed supplies frantically all night. In the morning the other four drove to Silverton, while Don and I flew to Durango. From the air we could see our mountains, gleaming with new snow. We hitchhiked from Durango to Silverton. It was a warm winter day and the blazing sun and dry air exhilarated us. We talked about the other four and agreed that we would have to split up, just as our more experienced friends on McKinley had split up to climb with us.

We met the others after dark in a bar in Silverton. That night we camped outside town. It got very cold, but the morning was clear and warm. We set off down the snow-covered railroad tracks, all of us excited, two days before Christmas. But it took three days, through bad brush and occasionally deep snow, to reach our mountains. Don and I watched, a little nervously, for signs of discouragement among the others: the signs were there. In the next two days we climbed three different peaks among the six of us. But already some of the others were getting edgy; the youngest and least experienced of them, a sophomore named Matt Hale, was apparently altitude-sick, for he could eat almost nothing.

The sixth day dawned on a windy blizzard. We had planned to move camp that day, but only Don and I felt like going out in the storm. At last he and I decided to go ahead, leaving the others to follow the next day. As the weather improved, Don and I stopped on the top of the pass leading to the new basin. We felt a little guilty for deserting the others; but we felt a wonderful freedom to be able to climb together again without worrying about anyone else. As it turned out, two of the others hiked out the next day, fed up with the climbing. The other two, including Matt, who was genuinely sick, climbed over the pass to catch up with Don and me. But they had to stop at nightfall, exhausted, short of our camp. The next day they too decided to hike out, since there wasn't time left to accomplish anything by joining us.

So for the last five days Don and I saw no one else. This worried us, but on the third day we spotted tracks among the trees in the valley far below us and guessed that the others had hiked on out. During those first three days we made three superb climbs, one a first ascent. The weather held good and we used every available moment of the daylight. We slept soundly through the long, cold nights; when we had to hike out at last we were very sad that our perfect days had to end; that, once again, Harvard and finals were all we had to look forward to. On the three climbs we had adapted our styles of climbing to each other in nearly perfect synchronization. We had begun to feel the instinctive awareness of each other's movements, even when out of sight, and the confidence in each other that can make roped climbing one of the most sensitive means of communication.

We hiked back up the railroad tracks on the eleventh day and arrived in Silverton around noon. There we met four irritable and depressed climbers. Only Matt, who was still sick and unable to eat much, offered us any congratulations on the climbs we had done. Again Don and I felt guilty, but as we separated from the others to go back to Durango, we felt relieved for the second time to get away from the atmosphere of discouragement that surrounded them. Flying back to Denver that night, Don and I could glimpse the white mountains under a pale moon. We were tired and happy. After a while, Don fell asleep. I sat in the dark, staring out of the window of the plane, full of a wonderful feeling of companionship. This was only the beginning, I thought. We were a great team; no mountain could stop us. And somewhere out there in the dark, beyond the hills of Colorado, beyond thousands of miles of prairie and forest, was Alaska . . . .

2 ▲

When we got back, Don went through the same experience with finals that he had the year before. If anything, it was worse this time. We were both planning to go on the club's annual four-day trip in the White Mountains of New Hampshire during term break; but on the day before we were to go, the day of his last final, Don got sick. He looked terrible. We persuaded him to go to the infirmary. When a doctor took his temperature, it came out 94°. The doctor told Don, "Either this thermomenter's broken or you're dead."

So Don spent the break in bed. He recovered quickly

and the doctors never did decide what had made him sick. The spring semester of 1964 began; for a month there was little pressure and Don was able to relax somewhat. But he'd missed his last final when he got sick and had to make it up in April. The burden of it hung over him and he began to dread it out of all proportion to its importance. He remembered the year before; events seemed to be repeating the same pattern. But he thought that if he quit again he would never be allowed to finish at Harvard, so he doggedly tried to stick it out.

Meanwhile, Don and I had decided to organize an expedition for the following summer. In the spring, some older club members invited us to join them on a rather casual summer trip to the Andes. We looked over maps and pictures with them, discussed finances, and went home to talk it over with each other. After a while we agreed to turn down the invitation; we wanted something tougher, and we wanted to plan it by ourselves.

Besides, our finances pretty much restricted us to North America. The obvious choice was somewhere in Alaska again. Don and I spent long evenings in the clubroom, poring over journals, searching for pictures of Alaskan mountains. Tentatively we considered Mount St. Elias and Mount Foraker, both giants like McKinley. But we weren't enthusiastic about either. One evening I came upon a picture of Mount Deborah, a mountain in the Hayes Range we had both vaguely heard of. The picture was spectacular; an apparently sheer face swept from a pointed summit down to a broad, banded glacier. On either side were knife-sharp ridges, studded with ice flutings and seamed with dark rock. "Don, look at this!" I said.

We quickly read the article, which described the first ascent of Deborah, in 1954, by three famous mountaineers, one of whom had been on the legendary first ascent of the Eigerwand, in the Alps, way back in 1938. With growing excitement we realized that none of the parts of the mountain visible in the picture had been touched: the trio had attacked the only "reasonable" side of Deborah, out of sight to the west. Even so, they had found it an exacting climb. The article said, "It was our unanimous conclusion that Deborah was the most sensational ice climb any of us had ever undertaken."

Almost at that moment we decided on Deborah for our expedition. We argued for a few minutes about the route to try. I liked the northwest ridge; Don was intrigued by the east ridge. After a while we agreed on Don's choice, partly because it was on the exact opposite side from the route of the first ascent. It did not matter much to us that Deborah had been climbed; for all practical purposes, we would be climbing an entirely new mountain. It didn't take long to verify that no other attempts, except the first ascent, had ever been made on Deborah; that, in fact, virtually no one had been anywhere between Deborah and the gigantic Mount Hayes, twenty miles to the east. This would obviously be a very difficult climb, probably harder than the Wickersham Wall; but this was what we wanted.

We ordered the maps of the area and planned our schedule. It looked as if we could walk in from the Denali Highway, a dirt road forty miles to the south. And Deborah was surrounded by lesser mountains, only one of which had been climbed. If we could arrange enough time, we could climb peaks all over the range, perhaps even Mount Hayes itself, as well as Deborah.

The next thought was the make-up of the party. We had hoped some of the younger club members would be ready for such an expedition; but our Christmas climb made us dubious. Matt Hale had seemed the only one with the right spirit, but the altitude had made him quite sick and he had never climbed beyond the eastern United States before the Christmas trip. The Hayes Range would be no place to get sick or to lose enthusiasm. Somewhat reluctantly, we decided not to ask Matt.

We were hesitant about inviting someone we didn't know. The rest of our McKinley friends had other plans or jobs. Finally we wrote a letter to an outstanding older climber who had been recommended to us. He wrote back to say that he would be in Boston soon and would like to talk with us. When he came, Don and I tried to share our enthusiasm about Deborah with him. He looked at the maps and pictures for a very long time, without saying anything. Don and I felt awkward and wondered if the man thought we were too rash. He made, in fact, a remark to the effect that this kind of climb had not yet been done in Alaska; but we couldn't tell whether it was in approval or chastisement. At last he left, saying he would have to think it over. A few weeks later he sent a postcard indicating he had decided not to go with us.

Don and I felt let down. We had almost begun to count on the extra member. Listlessly, we talked over other choices and reconsidered Matt. Time was growing short. Above all, we didn't want to go with someone with whom we might not get along well, or with someone who would not be able to keep up his drive for a long period of time.

One day Don said, "Dave, I've been thinking this over." He paused, characteristically, to ensure my attention. "What do you think of just the two of us—a two-man expedition?"

I was surprised. But I felt an immediate impulse in favor of the idea, and I suppose the impulse was, in the long run, the basis on which I decided. We both knew that it went against all the rules. But so, in a sense, did the route itself. With contagious enthusiasm, Don began to list the advantages. It would make the expedition truly our own; we would do all the climbing, all of the load-hauling, make all the decisions, and succeed or fail on our own efforts alone. Don and I remembered the frustration of having to carry loads over previous sections of the route on McKinley while someone else was exploring above. True, if we had an accident on Deborah, we could be in serious trouble; but with only two of us, there was less chance of an accident. We could rent a radio to give ourselves an added safety factor. It would be lonely—but it would be so beautiful, so truly adventurous. Finally, of course, it would mean we could stop worrying about finding a third and fourth member.

So we decided; and once we had, we never wavered. Our friends and the older club members were all skeptical; some even told us we were foolhardy. We tried to be polite and explain our reasons, most of which were, after all, rationalizations. Back of all our other feelings, we had developed a sense of common purpose that told us this was what we owed each other, that a two-man expedition was the only "right" expression for our partnership. We had got along so well at Christmas, after we had escaped from the others. Deborah would be like that, we guessed—longer and more trying, of course, but essentially amicable.

Yet even as we decided, we began to notice the weaknesses in our friendship. Don was feeling more and more oppressed by school; every paper was an agony, and he could scarcely concentrate. In addition, he complained often to me, in somewhat paranoid terms, about his problems. I found "getting through" easy, so I tended to be unsympathetic; the more Don complained, the more irritated I grew. I realized that I had never been sympathetic to this problem of Don's; but the year before, I had been able to laugh at it; this year I couldn't. Don transferred his feelings about everything connected with Harvard to New England itself. He claimed that people in the West were basically friendlier and more human. I began to develop a real hostility toward his feelings, because I liked Harvard and the East. So instead of listening, I would argue with Don, trying to show him how ridiculous his ideas were; and, when that failed, I would cruelly make fun of them. Whatever the cause really was, Don was certainly unhappy, and his physical condition suffered with his mental one.

At the same time, Don threw himself into planning for Deborah. He studied maps for hours, made a catalogue of the whole range, and made a careful drawing of the east ridge of Deborah in elaborate detail. I lacked the patience for such tedium. I preferred to spend most of my free time playing tennis or baseball, or dating, or climbing on the weekends. Don actually stayed home from several weekend climbing trips in order to plan for Deborah. He began visibly to resent my unconcern. I claimed, in defense, that he planned so elaborately only to escape studying; there was a germ of truth in this, but it was an ungenerous remark.

We came to a temporary impasse on the question of how much time to devote to Deborah. I thought twenty days would be enough; Don was sure that would be inadequate. He would have liked to spend the whole summer in the Hayes Range. I remembered how anxious I had been to get back after a month on McKinley, and doubted that I could enjoy the Hayes Range for a whole summer. At last we compromised on two months, with seventy-two days' food, allowing a margin. We would airdrop forty-four days' food below Deborah, the other twenty-eight days' worth in a high basin just west of Mount Hayes. Since we would not pick up the second airdrop until after we had used up the first, there was a good chance the second might be buried by the snows of the intervening weeks. But we could think of no alternative.

Most of this planning was Don's; I let him figure out the details, then generally agreed to them. But Don was obviously disappointed in my lack of interest. We tried to split up the jobs by ability. I corresponded to arrange for a pilot to drop our supplies, and I handled most of the food buying. We were both financially cramped, so we had to skimp wherever we could. Fortunately, we arranged to drive someone else's truck to Alaska, so we had free transportation. I managed to get free candy bars and rope in exchange for possible testimonials. We made our own snowshoes, and Don (who was extremely resourceful in this respect) made a bivouac tent, down vests, special clothing attachments, and some extra-long ice pitons, barbed like harpoons, for the extremely rotten ice we knew to expect.

I much preferred climbing to making ice pitons; hence I went on the club's trip nearly every weekend. But I also thought it important that we get into as good shape as possible before we tried anything so difficult as Deborah. With more practice than Don was getting, my climbing quickly got better than his. I climbed often with Matt, and found that I liked rock climbing with him better than with Don. Matt was impatient and quick, like myself; Don was slow and thorough. On one unfortunate weekend, the three of us climbed together on the same rope. At one point, Don couldn't climb a section that Matt and I had both managed. We felt embarrassed; at the same time, I got annoyed as Don made excuses about the heat. But it was obvious that he was not feeling well. What I ignored was the fact that Don simply could not get into good shape as long as his school situation was so distasteful—the East genuinely oppressed him. What he ignored was the silliness of his own rationalizations about this problem.

Our rift deepened. We had to meet often to talk about plans; but whereas in March the hostilities would develop as we talked, in April and May the hostility was there to begin with. I found it hard even to talk to Don. His slow, deliberate way made me terribly impatient; on the other hand, he began to distrust my impatience and felt that he had to be careful and thorough to cover up for what I should overlook in my haste. At the same time, I was turning more and more toward Matt for friendship.

Don and I both knew how badly things were going. Yet we persisted in planning for Deborah almost with a kind of fatalism. It was I who tended to provoke the arguments between us; I knew vaguely that I was using Don simply as a release for hostilities I felt toward a hundred different things, but I could not change the fact. Yet it was obvious the expedition would be unpleasant, maybe even a disaster, if we continued this way. In a friendlier moment I told Don that I thought the problems would tend to vanish once we were actually climbing. But he was not so sure. Later he told me that he had come close to calling it all off; he had talked it over with his roommates, who had suggested that. But perhaps out of the same mixture of loyalty and fatalism that I felt, Don didn't call it off. Instead, he wrote me a long letter. He gave it to me one day and asked me to read it. It was absurd, I thought, that things had come to this, that we could not even talk out our problems. But I read the letter. In it Don said, in part, "As we are committed to each other to climb Mt. Deborah as a team, fruitless arguments must be eliminated . . . I am sure we have sufficient experience in this sort of climbing. I am also confident that we can rise to the occasion. . . . We are undefeatable. . . . It is immensely important that we understand and respect each other and his judgment." As little as I wanted to admit it, I was moved. For one thing, I had not realized that Don understood my feelings, because he tended to disguise his perception of them. For another, I was moved by the tone of the letter: Don's affection for me showed plainly; it made me nostalgic for the easier days of our friendship, when we talked indefinitely about mountains all over the world we would climb together.

Although I did not give Don the answer he probably hoped for, things seemed to improve somewhat after that. Gradually I got more involved in the planning, as the shortness of our time demanded it. Then came Harvard's reading period, in May, at the end of which we would take finals. I got my studying done, but Don almost threw up his hands in despair. He could not do both things at once, and Deborah was more important.

During the last, hectic days, we spent almost all our time in the clubroom. While Don made equipment, I packed all our food into plastic bags and boxes for the airdrop. For compactness and lightness, and to save money, we had planned a minimum of food: less than two pounds per man per day. But we reasoned, on the basis of our Christmas trip, that this would be plenty to keep us going.

During the last week we stayed up most of the nights, working virtually without rest. Matt dropped by often to chat with us. He seemed to be sorry he wasn't going himself, yet I think he was convinced that Don and I were going to get along so poorly that the expedition would be very little fun. We took breaks from the packing only to go to finals and meals. On my birthday I spent a few hours with a girl from Radcliffe. Don said he didn't mind; but he must have thought it a little frivolous. As I walked my date back to her dorm, in the warm sun of a late spring afternoon, we talked about classes and friends and the next year; Deborah seemed impossibly remote. It was then that I realized how I was approaching the expedition: as an arduous adventure to get through with, a thing to be conquered, a place to visit for the sake of wonder and beauty, but from which to return when it began to wear thin. If I had thought carefully, I might then have seen that for Don the expedition was just the opposite: an adventure to be lived as long as possible, a place to go where he could be at home and relax, almost like home itself. If I had understood that, perhaps I could have understood what lay behind many of the intense antagonisms we were to go through on Deborah. But perhaps even then we couldn't have prevented them.

At last, at noon one day in early June, we were ready to go. We had a last ritual beer together, then climbed, exhausted, into our truck, and started driving westward.

3 ▲

A few miles out of Boston we ran out of gas. Fortunately, we had just passed a service station and it didn't take long to get moving again. We were hoping to drive straight through to Alaska, since we had planned to meet our pilot on June 10, less than six days away. At first the driving was pleasant, and we could relax from the frantic pace of packing. Don seemed to cheer up the moment we left New England, and to grow happier and happier the farther west we got. We took turns driving every three hours or so. All our gear was packed in the back of the pickup, which barely held it; to sleep, we had to lie half curled up on the seat. It wasn't very comfortable, but at first we could have slept anywhere.

The turnpikes took us quickly through the night, across New York, Ohio, and Indiana. Then we circled Chicago and headed northward into Wisconsin. It was a fine, sunny day; we felt particularly cheerful and benevolently gave a hitchhiker a short ride. In an area called the Wisconsin Dells, we drove off on dirt side roads to reach one of the strange sandstone towers that dot the flat countryside there. For a delightful hour we climbed various routes on the crumbly rock, roping up for the harder ones. Hardly practice for Deborah, but it was a welcome interlude in the monotonous driving.

It was Sunday. That night, just before midnight, we were driving into the outskirts of Minneapolis. I pulled out to pass a car dragging a boat on a trailer. Two jolly-looking men in the car yelled something at us and I yelled back as I pulled in front of them. They immediately pulled out and passed us back; the man on the right-hand side leaned out the window to shout something. Then they pulled off on the shoulder of the road. I thought they were trying to tell us there was something wrong with our tires or the load, so I pulled off just ahead of them and started to get out. But Don, who had been looking back, said, "Hold it!" I turned to look, and saw the man who had yelled running up toward our truck; as he got near, we could hear him screaming obscenities. Don locked the door an instant before the man grabbed the handle. In the dark I saw a furious, brutish face screaming at us. The man started kicking the side of the truck. I put the truck in gear and shot off, spraying gravel behind. Don, watching, saw the man run back to the car and jump in.

For about ten miles they chased us. Neither of our vehicles could go faster than fifty, so we stayed just ahead of them. But we couldn't lose them. Eventually we had to stop at a red light where cars were lined up in front of us. Moments later, the men appeared behind us. Again the maniac jumped out. We had the doors locked, but couldn't move. I started blowing the horn. The man jerked fiercely on the door, yelling with almost berserk fury, while Don sat there helpless. Then the man began hitting the window with his fist. Just as it shattered, the light changed and I could start off again.

They chased us through the darkened residential streets of Minneapolis. I ran red lights and stop signs, afraid to pause, driving recklessly. We looked desperately for an open store or a gas station. Don kept peering back and reported them always just behind us. At last we saw a lighted gas station. I careened toward it as Don opened the window and yelled, "Call the police! Call the police!"

A stupefied attendant looked up and froze. The men with the boat started to follow us into the station, then swerved and took off down a side street. Breathlessly, we told the attendant what had happened and used his phone to call the police. They sounded slightly skeptical but promised to look for the men. Don and I were still irrationally afraid they would return. After half an hour, we started on. The window was shattered but still held together. The door was slightly dented.

We left Minneapolis and headed into the dark again, wondering what we had done to provoke the men. Perhaps they had just been on the way home, drunk and belligerent after a Sunday outing. Laughing nervously, we told each other that we had better get up to Deborah in a hurry—driving was too dangerous. In the early morning darkness, after the excitement, neither of us could sleep. We began to feel quite happy; the dark was comfortable, and we were glad to be alone, moving away from people, toward mountains and vast stretches of barren tundra and subarctic nights without darkness.

The countryside grew more and more desolate. We loved it: the open, dusty land spoke of the true West to us. The next morning found us crossing North Dakota. We got to the border station in the afternoon. The customs man asked us if we were carrying any alcoholic beverages. "No," I said, just as Don also started to answer. We looked at each other. The customs man eyes us sharply. "Just a half pint of brandy," I admitted; with a sinking feeling I could imagine digging through all our carefully packed boxes to find it. "For medicinal purposes, of course," the man said. "Have a good trip, boys."

So we were in Canada. If anything, Saskatchewan looked bleaker than North Dakota. We drove mile after monotonous mile, beginning to feel tired and listless. But the weather grew splendid again. In the afternoon we approached the Canadian Rockies; for an hour we gazed at the shimmering white peaks in the distance, picking out glaciers and summits among them. We tried to identify the highest ones: that looked like Alberta, and perhaps the other one, on the left, was Edith Cavell. All at once we noticed that one of the glaciers seemed to be moving before our eyes. Sheepishly, we realized that we'd been looking at a bank of clouds, not a mountain range.

From Calgary we headed north to Edmonton, the last big city on our route. There we bought final supplies for the Alaska Highway. Don pointed out how friendly the people were compared with Easterners; my disagreement provoked a short argument.

Soon after leaving Edmonton, we began to feel the toll of continuous driving. It was hard to sleep well on the seat; every bend in the road jostled the sleeper. We developed a kind of paranoia about having to take our turns driving; when we slept, we dreamed about going off the road. Several times Don woke up with a start and lunged for the wheel to save us.

Moreover, as we got more tired, we felt we had to spend all our spare time sleeping, so the driver seldom had the other to talk to. But the nondriver would be afraid the absence of conversation would make the driver sleepy, so he would try to stay awake, chatting, as long as he could. Typically, for instance, if I was driving, Don would lie down, saying, "I'm just going to doze off for a while." I would murmur an O.K. A few minutes later Don would say sleepily, "Feel free to wake me up if you get sleepy." I would answer, "It's all right, I'm wide awake," even though I was wondering how much longer I could keep my eyes open. "You go ahead and catch some sleep," I would continue, "you'll have to drive soon enough." At last Don would relax and fall asleep. After what always seemed to him only two or three minutes, I would pull over. As Don woke up, I would say, "Your turn." He would ask, suspiciously glancing at the mileage, "How far did you make?" Then he would groggily get behind the wheel while I tried to sleep, and the roles would be reversed.

At midnight, under a spectacular display of aurora, we reached Dawson Creek, where the Alaska Highway begins—twelve hundred miles of dirt road winding through British Columbia and the Yukon. Until now we had been able to average fifty mph, but henceforth we hovered around thirty. The standard two-hundred-mile shift was too long now; we had trouble covering a hundred miles at a stretch. We took NōDōz tablets, but they actually seemed to put us to sleep; perhaps whenever we took them we relaxed, counting on the stimulation.

The next day we stopped at Liard Hot Springs, five hundred miles along the highway, and soaked for an hour in the steamy baths. Don seemed unusually morose. We had been under tension for the last two days. On the way back to the truck, he insisted that we take the driving more slowly and stop to sleep part of each night. There was no point getting to Alaska exhausted, he said, and driving when we were sleepy was dangerous. This was true, but I was secretly glad Don had admitted the strain before I had. I pretended that the driving didn't bother me. I was extremely impatient to get to Alaska; so I argued that we had to meet our pilot on time. We drove on, but the argument waxed bitterly. All our hostilities came out; we accused each other of things that had nothing to do with the driving. Don was truly exhausted and seemed close to tears. In reaction, I grew as cold and heartless as I could; I said that if Don couldn't take the pace, I would drive all the way myself. The argument ended without a compromise, and we sat in silent hostility for hours. This was different from our arguments at Harvard; here we could not get away from each other. It was the first hint of what the bad moments of the expedition itself would be like. We sat in the same small, contained space, just as later, during storms, we would lie in our tent, only a few feet away from each other, with no one else to talk to, wordlessly furious at each other.

But now and then we could relax and enjoy the trip. Though we had not driven together the year before, each of us remembered hundreds of spots along the road. Much of the little conversation we did have dwelt on these memories; we could discuss for fifteen minutes whether or not a given mountain had had more snow on it the year before. We bought a huge piece of cheap steak in Whitehorse and cooked it beside a swamp along the road: for a while it was just like a picnic. I gave in to Don one night and we spread our sleeping bags on the ground for a good five-hour nap.

I was driving just before sunset, on our sixth day out of Boston, as we neared the border of Alaska. The sun was setting straight ahead of us in a prolonged blaze of orange: it was hard to see the road, but the evening was dazzlingly beautiful. Don kept waking up to admire the sight. For the first time we really felt we were in the north country: it was after 10:00 P.M., and the sun was taking hours to set as it obliquely angled toward the horizon. The long drive was almost over, and we could forget some of the disagreements that had made us quarrel.

In the early morning of June 12, we reached Marvin Warbelow's house and airstrip, a few hundred miles into Alaska. We knew him only by correspondence. He was glad to meet us, hadn't worried about time, and wasn't in any rush to do the airdrop. A dark-haired, folksy man of about forty, he loved to talk; he had grown up in Minnesota, but that was too crowded for him—he intended never to leave Alaska. His equally talkative wife claimed that Marvin was so antisocial that he'd only worn a suit once in his life, at his own wedding. Don took to him immediately; I liked him but had reservations because his lack of haste seemed inefficient to me.

In a final burst of activity, we double-boxed all our supplies for the airdrop. Don was to fly with Warbelow as soon as the weather allowed; meanwhile I would drive to Fairbanks to pick up our portable radio. We got the packing done in a few hours. Don and I drove to an airport that evening to meet Warbelow, who was

South-Central Alaska

going to look the weather over. When he got there, he said they would have to wait. He flew Don back to his airstrip with him while I drove to Fairbanks. Before I left, I had pestered Warbelow for a guess when he could fly. In true Alaskan bush-pilot tradition, he was noncommittal. Later he observed to Don, "Your friend's a mighty impatient fellow, isn't he?"

On the drive to Fairbanks, I felt a relief to be alone for a change. I stopped the truck on the bridge over the Tanana River, which was in flood, and got out. I was standing only about fifty miles north of the Hayes Range but Deborah was hidden by thick clouds. The river thundered under the bridge, carrying huge trees with it like little twigs. The river made me imagine Deborah. For a moment I felt a heavy foreboding about the whole thing. Here we were, before the trip had even begun, already glad to get away from each other for a while. Nothing could have seemed further from the easy camaraderie we had felt before McKinley.

But it was a fruitless speculation. I reached Fairbanks the next morning and quickly picked up the radio and last-minute supplies. Now there was nothing to do but wait for Don, who would take the bus to Fairbanks as soon as he had finished the airdrop. On the second bus, I got a note from him: they couldn't fly because the bad weather was still prevailing. There was no telling how long they would have to wait.

A friend I had written to arranged for me to stay in a dormitory at the University of Alaska. I had only my climbing clothes, but I could take a shower and sleep in a clean bed; the change was welcome. As impatient as ever, still I looked forward to the rest. My only duty was to meet the bus every day. And every day Don failed to show up. I spent long hours, especially around midnight, when the light was soft and mysterious, lying on the campus grass, reading. Had it been clear, I could have seen Deborah from there, nearly a hundred miles away; but the mountain was always lost in clouds. During the day I listened to records on a phonograph in the library or browsed through the stores of Fairbanks. I wrote a high-spirited letter to the Radcliffe girl and a letter to Matt, telling him that already Don and I had had serious arguments—I also asked Matt if he would like to plan a trip in the Colorado Rockies, in late August, when I got back.

Nothing could have seemed less like a prelude to an expedition. Don, waiting at Warbelow's, was enjoying the rest immensely. He hiked off one night and made a bold solo ascent of a difficult unclimbed, unnamed peak. For the first time that year he felt he was getting into good shape.

I waited five days. At last, on June 17, Don arrived; Warbelow and he had just done the airdrop that morning. He was unrestrainably excited about the mountains —they were spectacular beyond all our dreams. But Deborah! In a grave voice, Don warned me, "We're in for something incredible, Dave."

We packed up what we would be carrying on the hike-in: all the equipment that we would need to get to base camp, eight days' food, and everything, like the radio, that was too valuable to have risked in the drop. We left Fairbanks and drove all night again to reach the Denali Highway. It was a clear, cool day; at 3:00 A.M. we saw no other cars on the road. We reached Susitna Lodge, the only house for forty miles, around six in the morning. The owner was just getting up. Explaining who we were, we asked him to drive us about ten miles farther down the road, then bring the truck back to his lodge, where it would be picked up later. The man, himself a bush pilot and big-game guide, might have thought we were crazy if he hadn't often felt the same sort of urge we did, hadn't seen Deborah from the air, and hadn't grown to love all the country surrounding it. "Just the two of you, eh?" he said, bemused. We had coffee; then he drove us the ten miles down the road. He parked on the shoulder, helped us lift our seventy-five-pound packs out of the truck, wished us luck, and drove off.

4 ▲

We faced about a forty-mile hike in. For the first fifteen
miles we would cross level tundra, swamp, and gravel
bar to reach the mouth of the West Fork Glacier. Then
we had to ascend the glacier twenty-five miles until at
last we would round a corner of Mount Deborah and
overlook our airdrop site, which would become base
camp. Don said that the Deborah drop had gone off
well; Warbelow had had just enough room to circle
over the glacier while Don pushed the boxes out from
only about sixty feet up. But the second drop, west of
Mount Hayes, hadn't gone so smoothly. The basin was
so narrow that Warbelow couldn't circle within it; in

fact, he doubted that he would have tried the drop at all, given a second chance. At last they had had to throw supplies out from about three thousand feet above the glacier, attached to a parachute. Don had seen the parachute fall but never quite saw it land, and couldn't be exactly sure where it had come to rest. This was a crucial disadvantage, for a month later the supplies might well be buried under new snow.

It was seven-thirty in the morning of June 18, a fine, warm day. We put on our heavy packs, groaning competitively under the loads. Without a glance back, Don started off through the spongy grass on the side of the road; I followed him. The mosquitoes were scarce, and for several miles the muskeg we walked on stayed decently dry. We crossed several shining brooks, taking off our boots to wade them barefoot. Instead of a nuisance, the glacial water was a refreshing shock. We were both, apparently, in good shape and went for hours without a rest. And it took hours for the pleasure of hiking to wear off, hours before our shoulders noticed the loads or our legs the pace. Around noon, the sky clouded up, threatening rain. The ground had gradually been getting wetter, which slowed our pace. We had to look for drier, slightly raised ridges of ground and often had to detour around large swamps. We could no longer hope to keep our feet dry but waded obliviously through the ankle-deep ooze. Our feet made sloppy sucking noises and splattered our pants with mud. It was hard work and we could average only about one mile an hour.

I was getting not only tired, but sleepy, since I had

done most of the driving through the previous night. We stopped for a rest on a dry log, facing a particularly large swamp, through which we could see no easy route. After a few minutes Don got up. "I'll just go ahead a little to look things over," he said. I answered that I'd follow in a minute or two. The sun was out again; I felt too warm and comfortable to move.

I fell asleep. When I woke, I couldn't tell if it was thirty seconds or half an hour later. Don was nowhere in sight. The sleep had disoriented me. I got to my feet, looking around; for a moment I couldn't remember which way we'd been going. Then I recognized the swamp. I put on my pack and started off. For a while I could see a faint track of Don's steps through the water and weeds, but I soon lost it. I stopped and shouted Don's name. There was no answer. It seemed silly, but I felt the edge of panic and I felt terribly lonely. I could imagine Don stopping to wait for me ahead, while I, going a different direction, went past him and on toward the glacier. Don might go back to look for me, might even return all the way to the road, while I wandered around the snout of the glacier, shouting and searching. What an absurd beginning that would be! I hurried on, stopping to shout every now and then. To get around the swamp, I had to go somewhat out of the line we had been following before. For the first time I appreciated how huge the country was and how lost a single person inevitably was in it.

Perhaps twenty minutes later I heard an answer to one of my shouts. With great relief I followed it until,

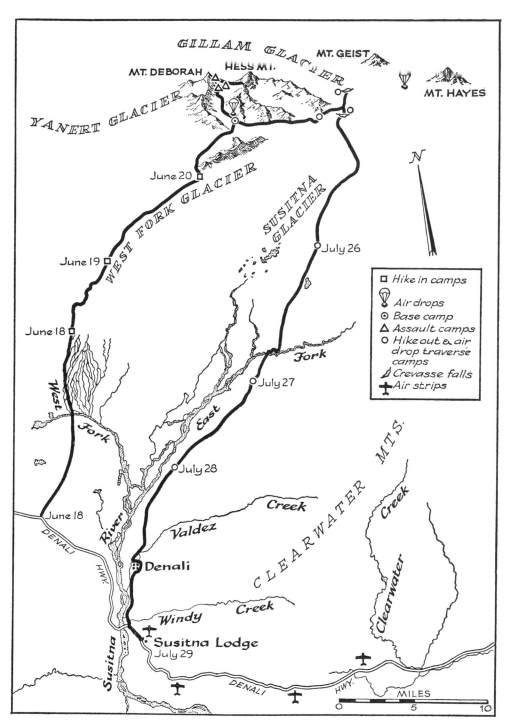

Route of the Expedition

quite far off, I saw Don standing beside a tree. He looked so tiny; the tree could have been any of a thousand; there was no way of singling it out in this landmarkless country. Don waited for me, a bit impatient perhaps. I joined him with a sheepish feeling; but we decided to be more careful from now on about splitting up.

At last the tundra sloped downward to the broad sandbar of the West Fork River. We could see, stretching into the distance, five miles of perfectly flat sand, through which wove the many braids of the river. At 3:00 P.M. we put down our packs before the first of the many little streams and ate a breakfast from our food box. We spread our sleeping pads, then napped for three hours. Afterwards, we started on. The weather was clearing, and the late afternoon sun highlighted the rugged mountains ahead of us. The sand was the easiest going yet; we could make a steady three miles an hour. The nap had refreshed us, and once again moving was a pleasure. A crust of ice lay on some of the river bed, allowing us to cross many of the little streams without even getting our boots wet.

After an hour we spotted some animals, running away from us, about half a mile ahead. Stopping to look carefully, we saw that they were grizzlies. Every so often the largest one would stop abruptly, turn, and rear toweringly on its hind legs to look back at us. Apparently they were a mother and two cubs, the worst possible combination. But they showed no signs of turning on us. Even half a mile away, we could see the awesomely powerful muscles in the mother's back ripple as she ran. We remembered that the bush pilot had told us we should carry a gun in this terrain. As we walked, we kept an eye on the grizzlies until they were too remote to see; meanwhile we talked about methods of defense: Could we stand back to back warding them off with ice axes? Or dodge their rushes, like touch-football players? We felt naked and vulnerable, without a tree for miles around; but perhaps the very openness had made the grizzlies see us from a distance and flee instead of attacking.

We stopped at 10:20 P.M., with the end of the glacier only a mile ahead. We had covered about fifteen miles this first day and felt tired and satisfied. In the placid twilight we gathered sticks and built a comfortable fire. As we had learned from McKinley, nothing could dispel the loneliness of the huge flatlands like a fire, especially at dusk. We cooked in great leisure, drying our boots before the flames. For the first time since Christmas I felt the wonderful, easy companionship that Don and I had discovered then. The first day had gone well, without a harsh word between us. The darkening sky was still clear and we had forgotten about the grizzlies. I recognized the still-strong habits of civilization: the sudden urge for an ice-cream cone or the baseball scores, the reliance on clocks and surrounding noise for mental security, so that the silence and changelessness of this spot where we were camped seemed bleak and alien. But I was happy, too: Deborah, after all the preparation, was becoming a reality.

Instead of the tent, we set up only our plastic rain fly, propping it up like an open tent with our packs. We got into our sleeping bags and quickly fell asleep.

During the night I awoke to the sound of big drops of rain hitting the fly. Somehow, in a matter of hours, a storm had moved in. I fumbled for Don's watch, which we kept between us; since it was still the middle of the night, I crawled farther under the plastic roof and fell asleep again. In the gray light of morning I woke to find it still raining, steadily and hard. I felt depressed. We decided to wait till the rain showed signs of stopping; I welcomed the chance to rest. My shoulders ached from the pack, and I was developing slightly sore hips from the rubbing of the waist loop.

For hours, while Don continued to sleep, I lay awake watching the rain. We could stay completely dry; hence it was fascinating to see the water falling directly above our heads, to watch it splash on the plastic, then trickle toward the ground. There were several little pools of water where the sheet sagged; I would pick a particular drop and try to guess which pool it would end up in. Sometimes there was real suspense as a little bead of water poised above a crucial junction, resisted nudges, and at last hurtled down the plastic slope. I tried to imagine the drop of water with a mind of its own; but there was such random abandon to its motion that I could not. I tried to imagine all the drops that had fallen here, in all the millennia before this day, with no one to watch them, or all the drops that were falling now beyond my vision, on Deborah itself, for instance.

The effort depressed me further; there was such a mind-less vastness to the rain, as to this country, that I, with purposes and memories, felt ineffectual and silly by comparison. I read a book for a while but went back to watching the rain because it seemed more interesting

In the middle of the day Don discovered that he'd left his boots out in the rain, beside the coals of last night's fire. He dashed out to get them, then brought them back under the fly, lamenting that they were soaked through. We ate lunch slowly, waiting for the rain to ease up. At last, around 4:30 P.M., it stopped. It seemed an unusual time to start out but we did so anyway. The sky was gloomy and overcast; in the dim light the rubble-strewn snout of the glacier loomed heavily above us. So much crushed rock had collected there on top of the ice that a few weeds, and one scrawny tree, grew out of it. In a few years the tree would probably plunge, uprooted, off the edge of the glacier; but no one would be there to see such a major event.

We followed the western edge of the glacier for two miles, as the slope of a low mountain gradually pinched us in. For a while we had a good caribou or sheep trail to follow, but it gradually got lost in the rocks. At last we climbed onto the glacier. For about a mile we wound our way through piles of shattered rock, occasionally scraping through to the hard ice underneath. We came to only one obstacle, a swift glacial stream that cut a deep channel down the glacier. There was no question of wading it, because the bottom would be polished ice.

We wandered up and down the edge for a while until Don found a bed where the stream undercut the near bank. He took off his pack and jumped easily down and across. I handed him the packs, then jumped myself. Of course we were not "stuck" on the glacier now, but the irreversibility of our jump pleased us. We knew we would be on glaciers for a long time, that we would have no more wood fires, and, soon, no more running water. But these deprivations were steps in our initiation, steps toward Deborah.

Soon we reached the bare tongue of ice marked on the map. The night was getting darker, but we could easily see where we were going. It was pleasant walking, very slightly uphill. The hard ice had a rough surface, like asphalt. To relieve the monotony, it was pocked everywhere with thimble-sized holes filled with crystal-clear water. Little channels of running water threaded their ways toward the end of the glacier, and here and there a small crevasse lay open.

After about seven hours, we decided to camp. For the first time, we pitched our tent, the small orange tent that Don had designed and made himself. Cooking dinner inside reminded us at once of Christmas, and of McKinley; it was much cozier than lying in the open. We were camped at the only big bend in the glacier. We had made good progress and hoped to reach base camp in another day or two. Again we had got along well, without even the threat of an argument. We slept soundly.

Early the next afternoon we were off again. The

weather was clearing gradually, and for a while we made fast progress. But soon we came to the nevé line, above which the snow had not yet melted down to bare ice. It was wet stuff; we got soaked to our knees in hidden pools of slush. We trudged over to a moraine, where we could follow the long ridge of rock debris that the glacier was imperceptibly carrying downhill. This kept us dry, except where here and there we had to wade a gap of slush; but it was much slower going. We stopped for lunch after a few hours, then continued on our homemade snowshoes, deserting the moraine. As we got higher, the snow turned drier and deeper. Soon we decided to rope up, since the snow might be hiding crevasses. After that we traveled a hundred and fifty feet apart, keeping the rope taut between us.

All the clouds had vanished, and the sun, reflected by snow on all sides, made the glacier actually seem hot. We sweated and put on sunburn cream. The going was extremely monotonous; on both sides we were enclosed by steep, intricate peaks. Although they seemed only a few hundred yards away, we could see from the map that the glacier itself was two miles wide. In demonstration of this trick of scale, we seemed to be walking on a treadmill, so that it took forever for the walls to recede beside us. Ahead we could look at a wall of rock where the glacier split into two forks. There we would take a short cut, the left-hand fork which led past the southeast ridge of Deborah to an easy gap overlooking the airdrop basin. But only after seven hours did we reach the junction. Meanwhile the south face of Deborah had come into view, a sheer five-thousand-foot wall of ominous blue-black rock. Even from six miles away, the wall jutted high into the sky. Don had warned me about the sight, but I was still overwhelmed by my first glimpse of Deborah.

By the time we had reached the junction the sun had set, the glacier had cooled off, and the pale twilight again decorated the mountains with gloomy shadows. We were tired and decided to camp. It would take another day to reach the airdrop. In seven hours of steady hiking we had covered only nine miles.

A breeze sprang up, chilling us as it dried the sweat on our bodies. We pitched the tent quickly and put the rain fly over it, in case it should storm during the night. We were camped near a slushy pool; for the last time we were able to collect water for cooking. After that night, for weeks, we would be melting snow for all our water.

I went to bed feeling depressed and a little bit lonely. The encompassing solitude, the lack of things to say, the contrast of emptiness around us—we had not really felt these on McKinley. The day's work had been dull and arduous. But dinner itself was, as always, a pleasure, and I managed to sleep well afterward.

We got a good start the next morning. The going was the same, slow and monotonous, but the slope gradually steepened as we neared the southeast gap. Soon we came upon the tracks of some animal, apparently a bear. Don had seen them from the air, apparently fresh, six days before; now they were faded, having melted and broadened into the snow. They led, very purposefully, up to our gap; we followed them. It seemed incredible that a bear should have been so far up on the glacier; what could he have eaten, and where was he headed? On the other hand, what sense would a bear have made of our footprints?

After three hours we reached the gap. Stepping through it, we came at once into sight of the immense and frightening east wall of Deborah, at the far end of which we could see the precipitous line of plastered ice that marked our route, the east ridge. As I wrote in my diary that night, "Descriptions fail. It is going to be tough." We could also see, only a mile away, our airdrop, a scattering of boxes on the flat snow.

Our first argument had been brewing. The pretext was a trifle: I got annoyed because Don had used the phrase "well-behaved" four or five times to describe the glacier's lack of crevasses. Absurdly, then, as we walked the last mile to base camp, under the stupendous shadow of Deborah, we irritably argued the merits of the word "well-behaved." What had really provoked the quarrel, I suppose, was the boredom of the hiking. I had started to notice some of Don's mannerisms and, for lack of a better preoccupation, had picked on one of them to vent my frustrations. It was the first time that I recognized a trait of my own, which seemed to me in analysis almost diabolical. I could not stand for things to go well for too long a stretch; it was as if I needed a regular exercise of hostility. Don realized this need in me but could not understand it. Later it would intensify and work itself out in unexpected guises.

But reaching the boxes diverted our attention. We gathered them up, pleased to find almost no damage from impact and nothing lost. In the afternoon we pitched our tent there, at 6300 feet, two miles south of the east ridge of Deborah. Beside the tent were stacked ten boxes, each containing food for the two of us for four days. We were alone and self-sufficient; we could not use the radio until we reached the ridge at 9400 feet, for it required a direct line to Fairbanks. All our climbing equipment, including three thousand feet of fixed rope, eighty pitons, and hammers and carabiners and slings and stirrups, was piled there with us. We also had a few paperback books, the newspapers we had stuffed the airdrop boxes with, full of two-week-old news, our diaries and a few pencils, and, in with the food, a half pint of "victory brandy"—actually, an apricot liqueur we had bought on the last day in Cambridge.

We planned to shift to a nighttime schedule, to take advantage of slightly colder temperatures and crisper, safer snow. That night we would start hauling supplies to the top of the basin, directly under the dark mountain wall. I got into the tent to read. Don had found that the long aluminum pole we had dropped in to mark base camp made a natural trumpet. For an hour he blurted wild peals toward Deborah, which echoed them magnificently. The basin, which for aeons had overheard only the clatter of an occasional falling rock, or the rumble of an avalanche, or the whine of wind or the murmur of falling snow, became for a brief hour an auditorium for stranger cries than any animal had ever made. Don loved it; he was home at last.

5 ▲

That night, the first of summer, we set out with hopes not only of relaying loads but of starting the climbing itself. As we had found before, however, the distances were deceiving. It took us two hours just to get to the head of our basin. The snow was crisp and dry, but we had to find a path through a series of large crevasses that blocked the way. In the dull light of night the glacier looked featureless until we were almost upon the crevasses. It was no trouble to avoid the open ones; what scared us was the possibility of a thinly covered, hidden one through which we might suddenly plunge.

However, we had no trouble that night. At an altitude of 7500 feet, just under the towering wall, we dumped our little cache of supplies.

Two thousand feet above us was a shelf of snow, or col, where the east ridge dipped lowest between Deborah and nearby Mount Hess. It was on the col that we planned to place our advance camp, from which the final assault could proceed. But it was clear to us that simply getting to the col would be quite a problem. To go straight up would have been to climb a steep wall of snow and rock, often swept by avalanches. Even if we could climb this headwall, it would be hellish to carry supplies up it. The alternative was to climb the shoulder of Mount Hess, actually reaching a point a full thousand feet above the intended col, then to descend toward Deborah along the ridge until we reached the col. But this, too, was a tricky proposition. That night we decided only to haul another load up to the point we had reached, which would become Camp I.

The trip back was quick, but we found the second trip grueling. We set a fast pace because we wanted to keep warm. But when we reached the cache spot again, a stiff wind met us. We would have liked to rest, but as soon as we sat down we started shivering; hence we turned back right away toward base camp. Both loads had taken us a full six hours, which was rather discouraging progress. But base camp cheered us up. Soon the sun rose and it grew comfortably warm. We moved our rubber pads outside the tent, where we could sun-bathe on them while we cooked dinner. The incongruities of a

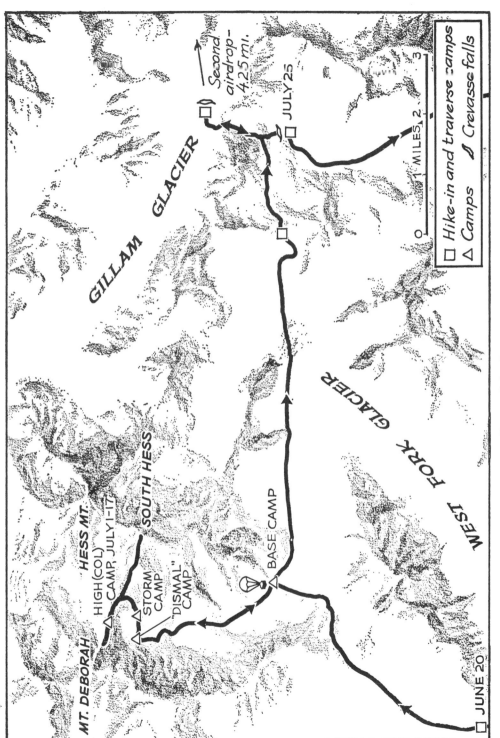

Route of the Attempt

night-climbing schedule were familiar to us from Mc-Kinley; so was the hot glacial sun, which could grow even stiflingly hot during the day. Thus this pleasant basking seemed to us one of the privileges we earned by working at night. Had we been told that this was to be the last truly warm day we would have on the whole expedition, we would not have believed it. So far, after all, the weather had been good; except for the day of rain, we had had basically clear skies. It was much the same sort of weather we had enjoyed on McKinley.

That evening, the sky began to cloud up. We had managed, before the sun set behind the huge east wall of Deborah, around 2:00 P.M., to dry our boots for the first time in four days. But by 9:00 P.M., when we were ready to set out, a mist had descended; a warm wind blew rainy snow across the basin, and our boots got wet immediately when we began hiking. We managed, with very heavy loads, to carry everything else we would need for the route; thus we could abandon base camp in favor of Camp I. We left eight days' food and some gasoline at base camp: provisions for the traverse to our second airdrop, later, with a slight margin for safety.

We moved very slowly up the basin, uneasy because of the mushy snow surface. It was obviously too miserable to explore higher, so we pitched the tent at our cache and got inside. The site had an immediately depressing effect on me. I felt at the bottom of a chasm formed by the surrounding walls. We would only get a few hours' sunlight on a clear day, and we had a cramped view of things. But despite all the shelter of the huge walls around it, the place was almost continuously swept by winds. We had spent only a few hours there that night when I wrote in my diary, "It is a gloomy spot, a place we would call dismal if we had to spend too much time in it."

Instead of letting up, the storm increased. For eighteen hours high winds shook the tent. We dozed fitfully, to the sound of wind rippling the nylon walls. For a while it was relaxing to have only to eat, sleep, and read. Even at midnight it was light enough to read inside the tent. We had counted on this; only in the second airdrop had we bothered with flashlights or candles. Of course, we had to go outside occasionally to relieve ourselves; in the strong winds it was a bitter task. On the night of the 23rd, just as the winds seemed to be letting up, snow began falling. It continued monotonously for another eighteen hours. We could watch the snow level rise slowly along the side of the tent. During the afternoon of June 24, the winds returned. This was a genuine Alaskan storm, taking days to blow itself out. I settled down to read some Fielding and some Hemingway. Passages in the books, especially eating episodes, made me nostalgic for civilization. I reflected that this was only the eighth day of the expedition; it was a bad sign, to be nostalgic already. But I couldn't help it. Don and I were getting along all right, in a negative way. We had little to talk about: we tried one literary conversation, without much heart in it. Don, I knew, was thinking about the mountain, plotting a way to move supplies efficiently and to get us into the best possible position when the storm ended. We might have talked about this; but I was responding to the gloom of the place by ignoring it and didn't want to think about Deborah until we had started climbing on it.

By evening the winds were roaring at high speed again. Don was getting tired of lying down, so he dressed and went out to shovel the snow away from the tent. It took him two hours to do a thorough job because of the winds: occasional gusts nearly knocked him over. When he came back in, his beard and eyelashes were frosted with snow and he dragged snow into the tent with him. He had noticed that a waterfall we had seen earlier, spilling down the east wall, had frozen up.

We slept some more. Gradually the wind died, but the snow continued to fall. About a foot of it had accumulated since we had got there. At last, around noon on the 25th, it started to clear. We were anxious to get out of the tent and start climbing; I, especially, got impatient with the unchanging routine of storm days.

By afternoon it was completely clear. The wall was breathtakingly laced with new snow. We photographed everything in sight, waiting impatiently for night, when the climbing would be safest. The air rang with the thunder of avalanches on the huge east wall, as the new snow was swept off. After the long storm, it looked as if a spell of good weather would be ours. But by the evening the mist had returned and a light snow was falling again. Our spirits took a big drop.

However, it was colder than usual (25°), so we

decided to climb anyway. Eagerly we got dressed and stuffed twenty-five pounds of climbing gear into each of our packs. Instead of snowshoes we put on crampons, since the snow had frozen enough to give their long spikes good purchase. Don started up a steep snow slope toward Mount Hess. I felt as impatient as ever, but excited in a new way. For the first time we weren't carrying back-breaking loads, and for the first time we would really be climbing. With luck, we would reach the col that night. We hadn't lost a serious amount of time during the storm; we were still on schedule.

The snow soon became mixed with rock. I took the lead from Don, who was tired after a long spell of kicking steps. The going was easy; only here and there did we even have to use our hands. But to our dismay, as we touched the rock for the first time, we found it loose and shattered: a blue-gray schist, much like the rotten rock we had encountered on McKinley. In a short while we were out of the rock section. On smooth, steep snow above, we first grew aware of the drop beneath us. The slope was disconcerting, for it was certainly steep enough to avalanche; indeed, on either side of us it had already avalanched. Besides, the texture of it was bad: loose, granular snow often shallowly overlay smooth ice.

As we ascended, the mist had been getting thinner, as if we were near the top of a cloud. We had the feeling we were about to break into clear sky. Don took the lead. He went slowly, chopping steps methodically. After only a few hundred steps he paused, apparently tired. I took the lead again and scrambled over some steep rocks that led to the base of our main obstacle, a large, vertical ice cliff. So far we had not been belaying each other but climbing simultaneously, a rope-length apart. But as Don came up to me, I noticed that he slipped and caught himself. Alarmed (for the slope was easy, if steep), I put him on belay. He came up very slowly, slipping a few more times. When he got to me, I said, "Is there anything the matter? How do you feel?"

"Out of it," he said. "Sleepy . . . and cold."

"How about your balance?"

"That's not too good either." He was looking away from my face. "I don't know what the problem is."

I wanted to go on but I said, "Probably we'd better go down."

Don seemed to agree. I began to build a platform of rocks on which to leave our loads. Suddenly Don said fiercely, "We can't go down, Dave! We've got to make the col. We're losing too much time. I've got to drive myself."

The words startled me. They were so unlike Don, so irrational. Gradually I talked him out of going on, telling him not to feel guilty. He started shivering from the cold. We left our loads on the little shelf I had constructed, tied to a piton I had been able to hammer into the crumbly rock. We were still in mist, but we could see the outlines of the col, at about the same height as we were, toward the northwest. I had brought the radio up. It was possible we were now, just barely, in a direct line with Fairbanks. Before we started down, I tried it. All we heard was static. But we weren't disappointed. Rather than trust the expensive radio to the cache, I carried it with me on the descent.

All the way down, I belayed Don from above. Even on easy places he seemed to be going terribly slowly. At last I lost my patience and asked him to hurry up. He said to me, annoyed, that he felt as if he were racing down the slope. I was disturbed that his sense of time had been so upset. I was sure he was taking four or five times as long as I was, and I attributed it to whatever was making him feel bad. It was only days later, when Don insisted he had been going as fast as I that day, that we realized how differently we had viewed the descent. Don was genuinely astonished that I could have thought he was going four times as slowly as I. When the incident came up, later, in the middle of an argument, each of us was sure he was right. Only gradually did such discrepancies make us start to wonder—what had really happened? How long had it really taken Don? How sick had he acted? Had I exaggerated it, or he underplayed it, or both? On a larger expedition, the truth could never seem so subjective. For the two of us, this uncertainty would subtly add to the fantastic other-worldliness of Deborah. Gradually it would become another danger to guard against. Gradually we would lose a certain sense of our own identities and begin to think more exclusively in terms of reaction to each other.

But as we got lower, Don improved and seemed to

speed up. By the time we had reached camp again he felt fine, though still sleepy. He slept solidly for more than ten hours when we got back.

It was a disappointing beginning. We were still not even near the col. The ice cliff above our highest point didn't look too hard, but it could take a long time. I wondered that I didn't feel more annoyed at Don for halting our progress. But if he was sick, it was nothing to trifle with. And I had almost enjoyed, perhaps in a condescending way, being solicitous toward him, though I knew he would feel in debt to me, in the wrong, resentful way, for it. Perhaps I had been tired myself and was glad of the chance to turn around without having to take the blame for it. I had noticed feeling tired recently—maybe it was the immobility of the storms, or had something to do with our food. But my appetite was fine; in fact, I was ravenously hungry now.

Drearily, it was snowing again. We were bound to spend at least a few more days in this dismal camp. Caches like the one we had made above were unstable; so, for that matter, was the whole dangerous slope we had ascended. There was so much of the climbing left to do. But when we got up high, where mountain climbers belonged, we would do better. Anyway the storms could not last forever: it was bound to clear.

6 ▲

That night, June 26, we woke around eight-thirty. Within an hour we had cooked breakfast and were ready to go. But as we walked around outside the tent, gathering supplies to pack, Don began to feel the same symptoms that had made him shaky the night before. We talked over whether or not we should go. We couldn't decide; Don didn't want to hold us up and I was impatient to be climbing, but neither of us wanted to waste a night's effort. At last I suggested a test: we would run about fifty yards through the deep snow at top speed and see how Don felt after it. Wallowing absurdly, we made our little dash. Don didn't feel very good after it, but neither did I. We hemmed and hawed some more and at last decided to go back to bed.

It seemed just as well, for it began to snow again and a moderately brisk wind swept the glacier. We admitted to ourselves that the weather had been worse than usual; but we felt guilty for not seizing the few opportunities we had had. The depression of the dark camp began to infect both of us. We determined to make a strong push the next day. Since the temperature seemed to vary little between day and night, we decided to start in the afternoon instead of in the evening.

With this resolve, we set out at 1:30 P.M., carrying fifty-five to sixty-pound loads. At first we thought we had made a mistake, for the snow was wet and sloppy. As we were climbing the first of the rock, we heard a rumble and saw a small avalanche headed toward us. Leading, I yelled to Don and jabbed the point of my axe into the slope, then crouched, hanging onto it. Some of the slide hit me but I held on; it missed Don below. I felt a tug, which must have come from the weight of the snow catching the rope. I looked down and saw that Don had held his ground. We shouted to each other to confirm that we were all right. Then we continued, nervous about the slopes above. Gradually, though, the snow got colder and safer as the sun left the mountain. Don was feeling strong and we made excellent time.

When we reached the highest point of our previous effort, we found the cache intact. We left our heavy packs attached to the piton, then carried ice-climbing equipment up a little higher to attack the cliff. Almost at once, we realized we had underestimated its severity. The ice was rock hard, and the slope subtly steepened until it was actually vertical. Don chopped the steps on the first pitch. When he reached the end of the rope, he drove a metal screw into the ice for an anchor and brought me up. I made a route-finding mistake by continuing straight up. I had hoped to cross a short steep section head on, but when I got there it bulged out at me, actually overhanging. It would have been far too risky to try it while Don was attached to the mountain only by a flimsy screw and two thousand feet of unbroken slope yawned below us. But for a while I chopped at the ice furiously, swearing out loud as I got more frustrated. Don shouted, "Take it easy, Dave, this is no place to get mad." Sheepishly, I realized what a foolish spectacle it was, cursing a cliff of ice simply for being there, with no one within fifty miles of us in any direction. *That was the old Don!* I thought with gratitude: the sane, careful, competent Don. I put in an ice screw and belayed Don while he chopped a diagonal traverse to the left. It was awkward and difficult, but he did it adroitly. Still, it took a long time for the whole pitch, and I grew uncomfortably cold, standing on my little niche of ice. The mist had lowered just beneath us and the sun was setting beyond Deborah in the northwest: a soft, rosy light spangled the ice all around us. Facing out, I could occasionally let go of the rope with one hand to take pictures. Don rounded a corner, out of sight. For a long time I could only hear him chopping and watch the little chips of ice dance dizzyingly down the slope into the darkness. At last Don shouted, "On belay!" and I could follow. Only by chopping vigorously as I led the next pitch did I get warm. Don's stance was right below me; the chips I knocked loose bounced down on him. The sun had set by now, and he soon got even colder than I had. I could actually see him shivering, and his voice shook with the cold when he talked. But I was on a 60° slope and had to fashion each step carefully. At the top of my pitch, I found that an ice screw would not hold. Instead, I hammered in the first of Don's special aluminum daggers. It was a godsend, the solidest anchor we had yet found on the mountain. We were only about forty feet below the top of the cliff, but the last stretch was the steepest of all. Don led it very nicely. At the top he had to pause on his ice steps while he reached high with his axe to scrape away a lip of rotten snow. At last he was up. I followed him and dashed up another short pitch on steep snow. We were approaching exhaustion, having gone for twelve hours straight without food or a drop of water.

We turned back to descend. On the way down we attached light manila ropes to the screws and dagger, as handlines for the next time we should have to climb the cliff. When we got to the bottom of the ice, where we had left out packs, we could relax somewhat and eat our lunches. We emptied our packs, stashing our supplies in the cache, which was reaching formidable size. Again I had brought the radio. On a hunch I decided to try it again. Turning it on, we were amazed to hear at once clear voices chatting casually. I tried to broadcast; the receiving person heard something but could not make out my words. We soon realized that we were speaking to someone not in Fairbanks, but in Anchorage, almost two hundred miles to the south. Because of the distance, we could not broadcast clearly, it seemed. I tried to get across the words "O.K." and "Portable Seven" (our number), but at last I gave up and signed off with a doubtlessly unintelligible "thank you." The one-sided conversation excited us but also somehow disappointed us; perhaps overhearing someone talk about banal, urban matters while we were perched on an unexplored mountain in the dark of early morning was too much of a contrast.

The candy bars and lemon drops we had for lunch seemed a precious gift; but we got cold quickly and had to start descending before we felt rested. All the way down, the snow was beautifully firm, making the going as easy as we could have wished. Perhaps the cold was a sign of improving weather, we thought. We staggered back to our tent at 6:00 A.M., after sixteen and a half hours of hard climbing, certainly our most demanding day yet on the expedition. We had climbed some difficult pitches of ice; but we were still a long way from the col. That night we hoped to leave our "dismal" camp for good, carrying the tent up and over the ice cliff, pushing for the col, even if it meant another long day. As it always seemed when there was a lot of work to do, we were getting along well. We were too tired to have disagreements. When we got back to camp, it was all we could do to cook dinner and slide into our bags for a blissful sleep.

It was snowing when we awoke. Looking out of the tent, we could see only a very short distance. We stayed put, discouraged, although after our long push we needed a rest. We read and dozed through the night, constantly checking the weather. The steady snow continued to fall. Sometime the next day, I went outside to relieve myself. I happened to notice the tracks of some small animal passing camp. The line of tiny steps went straight by our food cache, without deviating, within three feet of the corner of the tent, and on toward the headwall of Deborah and, perhaps, some instinctive rendezvous. I had thought that we were the only animals that could live in such an inhospitable place; but here had passed some docile creature, making less sound than we could hear, with no curiosity about us or desire for our food. On the other hand, perhaps the animal was trapped and weak, wandering blindly in these cold recesses in a last attempt to find its way off the glacier. We never saw the animal itself.

At 10:00 P.M. on the 29th, we resolved to leave camp. In the confusing mist, we packed up our tent and the last of the supplies that we would need above. We left our snowshoes there; we were worried that we would lose them under the snows that might fall before we got back, but they would have only been an extra burden above. As we left camp, I glanced back. All that marked where we had lived were the crossed snowshoes, stuck upright, and soggy copies of *Joseph An-*

drews and *The Snows of Kiliminjaro* lying there, strangely out of place, on the snow.

We could follow our tracks, but the condition of the snow was very bad. In addition, the blindfold of the mist disconcerted us. It soon became evident that it would be dangerous to climb above; we could hear small avalanches hissing invisibly all around us. But we hated the prospect of returning to camp in the gloomy basin, of wasting our previous efforts.

At last we pitched the tent on a 30° slope beneath the beginning of the rock, between two open crevasses. It was a hazardous site, and we were determined to spend as little time there as possible. We had only a day's food left with us and some odds and ends we could stretch for another day, having carried all the rest up to the cache. We faced the unhappy prospect of having to climb up to the cache simply to bring food back down, food it had taken a considerable effort to carry so high. Moreover, we knew that the steps in the ice cliff, which had cost us so many hours to cut, might well have melted smooth into the cliff, so that we would have to do the chopping all over again.

Thus we camped very discouraged that night, and nervous as well. Sometime the next day we suddenly heard the unmistakable sound of a nearby avalanche. Holding our breaths, we listened as it got louder. We were powerless; we didn't even get out of our sleeping bags. The sound increased, then stopped. Looking out of the tent, we saw that the avalanche had passed by about thirty yards above us. The camp site was no good; but, as the avalanche proved, neither was climbing, so long as the snow continued to fall. And it showed no signs of stopping.

We spent the next night, the last of June, in the same spot. We had eaten the last day's food and were down to the odds and ends. We made a delicious concoction with extra-thick tomato soup and concentrated bacon, but after we had eaten it we were still hungry. Reading had paled. I drew a chessboard in the back of my diary, made little chessmen out of paper, and we played a game. But I played enough better than Don so that the game wasn't much fun.

We would have to climb that night, if only to retrieve food. Deborah itself seemed to be floating away from us; so many unforeseen obstacles had been thrust up in front of us, and the snow, mindlessly monotonous, fell and fell.

In the same kind of weather we packed up and started off at 9:30 P.M. on July 1. But the snow was in good shape, and we traveled fast. It took only two hours to reach the cache. I was leading; just as I got to our supplies, the rope dragging behind me dislodged a rock. I heard it roll down the slope, so I yelled to Don, "Rock!" But it wasn't enough warning. Don ducked, but the rock hit him sharply in the left elbow. He gave a cry of pain and knelt, cradling his arm. Fortunately, the rock had only bruised him, but it was a very painful bruise and hampered him for the rest of the night. I offered to lead all the pitches of the ice cliff, to make it easier for Don.

We picked up a few things from the cache, most importantly the radio and a food box, good for four days. Even the sight of the box reawakened our hunger.

Just at that moment we reached the top of the clouds and broke free of the storm. Like a shipwreck in shallow water, Deborah gleamed in the midnight sun. Even Don, despite the bruise, felt rejuvenated. We had another pleasant surprise: the steps in the ice cliff had filled with loose snow but had retained their shape; it would take no rechopping to use them. The ropes we had left made the going easy, even with our substantial loads. Above the ice we found deep snow, much deeper than the first time we had been there four days earlier. I led the first new pitch, stamping steps quickly in the steep snow. It seemed almost easy enough to justify both of us climbing at the same time; but, after a discussion, we decided it would be wise to continue to belay. We were still on a 45° slope, with the nearly vertical ice cliff now below us.

Don was feeling better, so he started ahead on the next pitch. About forty feet above me, without warning, a hole in the snow appeared under his feet, and he disappeared. I gave him a quick belay, but snow inside the crevasse apparently stopped him first. He yelled that he was O.K.—he had only fallen about fifteen feet. But we were both startled; we wouldn't have believed, until now, that crevasses could exist in the middle of a steep slope—was no part of the mountain safe from them? I tied my end of the rope to my axe and took our spare axe and an extra rope up near the edge of the

Above: The 6000-foot north face of Deborah. East ridge on the left. The triangle indicates col camp, and the end of the solid line indicates the highest point reached. *Below:* Looming beyond Mt. Hess, the east face of Deborah, also 6000 feet high. The east ridge is the thin ribbon at the right edge of the face.

Above: Don Jensen on the third day of the hike-in on the West Fork Glacier. Deborah is not yet in sight. **Left:** Jensen eating lunch before the backdrop of the east ridge, on the ascent of South Hess.

Above: Jensen chopping an ice traverse on the ice cliffs between the Dismal Camp and the col camp. The sun has just risen (1:30 A.M.) in the north. *Right:* Jensen at the top of the second pitch (rotten rock) on the east ridge.

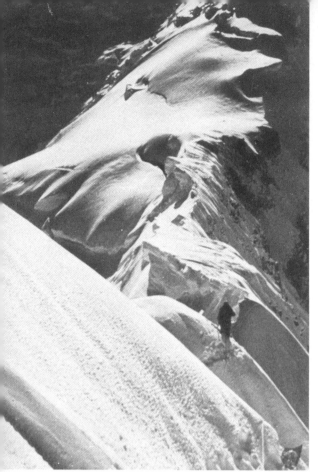

Left: On the east ridge. Looking back, one can see the col camp and climbers' tracks leading across the knife-edged ridge toward the first cliffs (Jensen seconding). *Below:* The camp on the col, looking north, before the storms hit.

The east ridge of Deborah.

Above: Jensen seconding on the east ridge below a detached cornice. In the background, crevasses on the Gillam Glacier. *Below:* Roberts wading the East Fork of the Susitna, at the point at which the climbers finally found a crossing.

crevasse. I threw the rope in. Don tied his pack to it, but I couldn't haul it out. So I retrieved the rope, tied loops in it for footholds and handholds, and lowered it again to Don. He managed to climb up the loops until he was almost out, then helped me pull out his pack. Within an hour we were ready to go again.

When we continued, we were nervous: besides the crevasses, we had avalanches to worry about, and we had to keep our eyes out for the best route. Here and there we could see darker shadings in the snow, where the empty space of a crevasse apparently lurked under a snow bridge like the one Don had broken through. In addition, we noticed when we looked back that it was impossible, except by our tracks, to see where we had come from. If even a light snowfall covered our tracks, then it might be impossible to find the top of the ice cliff, to which the highest fixed rope was attached. How we wished we had brought some of the usual light bamboo stakes to mark the route. But we had a few long aluminum pickets, which we hoped eventually to use for anchors on Deborah; for lack of anything better, we stuck them in the snow every two hundred feet or so, to mark where we had gone.

In the early morning, about 5:00 A.M., we reached the ridge itself, at 10,200 feet. Immediately, we stepped into the warm sunshine. At last we felt we were near Deborah. Besides, the ridge down to the col looked easy. After a comfortable lunch, during which we exchanged enthusiastic predictions, we started down toward it. Just as we were almost there, we suddenly came to a large drop-off, a vertical ice cliff. We couldn't possibly have seen it from above. It was much too high to jump down, and we had no good anchors left to set up a rappel, by which we might have left a rope to slide down and climb back up. Moreover, the cliff stretched, unbroken, across the whole ridge. Finally we had wearily to retrace all our steps back to the point where we had first reached the ridge, detour some forty feet to the north, off the opposite side of the ridge, and hike down a parallel path. As soon as we left the crest of the ridge, we found very deep powder. Our snowshoes would have come in handy here. Instead, we wallowed downward in the hot sunshine, up to our thighs in snow.

But this time we had found an easy route. At 7:00 A.M. we reached the col, a flat shelf of snow that narrowed toward our route. Plastered with new snow, the east ridge of Deborah looked incredibly difficult, but inviting. We set up the tent and made a little cache of supplies beside it. At last we had escaped the pallor of our low, gloomy camps. Before we could start on the route, however, we would have to hike back to the cache at least twice to pick up all our supplies. We were now quite a bit behind schedule but we had twenty days' food to try to get up our route. The weather looked as if it might hold good for a while. Perhaps, as we had found on McKinley, the higher we got, the better the weather would get.

As soon as camp was set up, I tried the radio. It worked perfectly. In clear tones we could hear the people in Fairbanks; they indicated that we came through clearly too. The radio receiver was connectible to the telephone system, so we could call anyone we wanted. We tried a few friends in Fairbanks; then Don decided to call his parents in California. We couldn't quite believe it, and his parents certainly couldn't, but the call went through, and soon Don was chatting with them as casually as if he had called from a corner phone booth in the same town.

We were in tremendous spirits. The radio gave us both a boost; it was as if someone else had dropped by to break up the monotony of our companionship. We felt safer, too, though it was a largely irrational sense of security. The weather was perfect; for the first time, we would be able to watch the sun set and rise from the door of our camp. On the first day we noticed that the sun actually set and rose three times each day: first, it would rise from the horizon in the north, about 1:30 A.M.; then it would set behind the ridge of Mount Hess, which we had just descended, at about eight, reappearing two hours later. Around two in the afternoon, it would set behind the high crest of Deborah, rising just before five; after that we would get golden sunshine from the northwest until the true sunset, around 11:00 P.M. What place could have been more exciting to live in?

We broke open the food box and cooked a breakfast. With huge appetites we gulped down the food. The work and our enthusiasm, no doubt, were making us hungrier than usual. But there was no danger of our getting fat: if anything, I thought Don looked leaner than before. We were in good shape, as the recent sixteen-and-a-half-hour effort had proved. We couldn't wait to turn loose our energies on Deborah.

7 ▲

Within a matter of hours the sky began to cloud up again. We lost the edge of exhilaration and optimism we had begun to feel. By early afternoon the mist had closed in and it had begun to snow. It snowed for forty hours straight. We wondered whether it was impossible to get more than eight consecutive hours' sunshine here; we had had no more than that for the last ten days. We lay lethargically in the tent, constantly aware, with every meal we ate, that our chances of success were shrinking. We would have been willing to stay until we could climb Deborah or know that we couldn't, but our food supply put an absolute limit on our time.

We had reached the col the morning of July 2. That evening, we decided, we would go despite the weather. But at 9:00 P.M., when we got up to leave, the storm was raging. It was 20°—cold enough to numb us, but warm enough so that we felt the painful sting of wetness in the wind, which ripped furiously across the col. There was almost no visibility; particles of ice flayed our faces when we tried to look into the wind. As we stood there, getting bitterly cold, attempting to pack up and put on crampons, it became obvious that we couldn't accomplish anything that night. Shouting to each other over the wind, we called off the effort. I went back inside the tent; Don, eager for exercise, built a snow wall around the tent. The job took hours; he kept yelling to me to inform me of his progress.

After Don came in, we went to sleep for a little while. The snow wall seemed to divert the wind somewhat. But the storm blew just as hard all day on the 3rd. The storm days fouled up our schedule, because we got too much sleep. During them there was nothing by which to mark time except Don's watch. We played a few more chess games and read a while. Little things began to get on my nerves; I got angry at Don because he sometimes lost interest in our chess games. At first I hid my annoyance, simply saying, "Your move," to remind him when he forgot. Then I lost my patience and told him the game was no fun unless he paid attention. Don apologized but added that the game wasn't much fun for him anyway. We decided not to play any more.

This was unfortunate, because it was one of the few things we could do together during the storms. Our conversations either died insipidly or led to arguments. I felt so frustrated by the weather that I had to get angry at something; Don was the nearest object and the only one capable of response.

The only events during the storm days that we could look forward to were meals. When we had finished one, we would set the time for the next, usually five or six hours later. Lunches we could spread out over the hours as we liked; but breakfasts and dinners had to be cooked. When the time arrived, one of us would curl up or sit up to make room for the stove. To compensate for this inconvenience, the other had to get the food and snow for the pots. When the wind was blowing, this could be a grim job: the fine snow shot inside the tent, and a hand scooping or groping outside would grow painfully numb. At last it got to be such a nuisance that we kept the food box inside all the time, even though it meant that it was hard to find room for our legs. The most comfortable position was to keep our legs slightly bent; but every now and then we had to straighten them. The ends of our sleeping bags were usually touching each other. If one of us felt his legs cramped, he began to think the other was taking up more than his share of space. It took the greatest restraint not to complain about it. When we eventually did, it took the form of aggravating politeness: "Do you have any more room down there?" "Could you move over just a little? My feet are against the wall." Gradually, for me at least—and I think for Don too—the nuisances encouraged a subtle defensiveness. I was always sure Don was more comfortable than I, sometimes at the expense of my own comfort. For instance, a few days earlier I had tried to broach a conversation about food—did we have enough, and did it seem enough, day by day? Don, I thought, had discouraged the talk. Now I began to look forward to meals inordinately; sometimes I daydreamed about food, simply to pass the time until the next meal, and I read sometimes only for the sake of filling up the same time. I tried not to look at the watch too often but couldn't help doing so eight or nine times a day. But Don seemed unaffected by these problems. Therefore I decided my hunger was only psychological, a function of boredom. So I kept quiet. We played a kind of gamesmanship when eating time neared (though I didn't realize until later that it was also gamesmanship for Don). Typically, our conversation would take this form:

"Don . . . it's about five-twenty."

"Hmm . . . what time did we say for dinner?"

"Five-thirty, I think."

"You hungry?"

"Well, not terribly. I could eat, though."

"That's about how I feel."

"Well, what do you think?"

"Just let me finish this short story first."

In the back of both our minds was the necessity of stretching the three meals over a full twenty-four hours. That was what made sleeping so attractive: the time passed fastest then. I remember waking several mornings, when my first thought was not *How is the weather?* but *Is it time for breakfast yet?*

Another nuisance of being tent-bound was that the inside of the tent gradually got wetter and wetter. Our breath would condense on the walls and sleeping bags, and the warmth of our bodies, even through the rubber pads, would cause small pools of water to form on the floor of the tent. We tried to sponge the walls and floor regularly, but we couldn't keep the bags dry. Gradually not only their covers, but the goose down inside grew damp, then wet; correspondingly, the bags kept us less warm. Often our feet or knees got cold. In normal weather we would have had enough sunshine to dry the bags out.

At last the storm exhausted itself. During the day of July 4, small patches of blue appeared among the clouds. We prepared to go that night. We were surprised to realize that it was already the fourth of July —in our predictions we had thought it possible to have reached the summit by then. Instead, we were three thousand feet below it and had not even begun the real climbing. I recalled last year's fourth of July, when we had sat in warm, clear weather outside a camp on McKinley, giving each other haircuts and already talking about reaching the summit in another week.

That night we set out. To the north, clouds boiled over the Gillam Glacier, the tops of them just below us. It was cold and crisp underfoot, but the dampness of our clothes and the long, logy hours in the tent made us get cold easily. We moved fast to try to warm up but never really succeeded. Our tracks had completely vanished. We had been counting on this; but we were alarmed when, on the far side of the ridge, we could find no trace of the aluminum stakes either. Everything looked the same, and we had only a vague memory of where we had placed the stakes. It would have been pointless to dig for them; it could have taken a week to find one.

We had counted pitches on the way up; now we counted them backwards, trying to hit the right altitude, always fearful, besides, of the hidden crevasses. The new snow seemed dangerous for avalanches as well.

At last I caught sight of a faint mark in the snow. When we approached, we saw with great relief that it was the upper two or three inches of the lowest aluminum stake. It was the only one left showing at all! I belayed from the stake while Don descended to try to find the highest fixed rope, buried somewhere just above the invisible ice cliff. He could only go to what seemed the top of the cliff, then dig in the snow with his axe. Thanks to his good memory, he found the rope fairly quickly. We descended the ice pitches rapidly, though even there the ropes were completely buried. Fortunately, the ice steps were still solid. Some of the ice-screw anchors had melted loose, but the long daggers were still frozen in.

We found the cache in good shape. We packed up some climbing equipment and three of the precious food boxes, good for twelve days. On the way back up we marked the route again and carefully measured the distance to the ridge.

At our high point, around 10,000 feet, we heard a soft whirring sound. We looked up in time to see a single, tiny bird flash by us. We were completely surprised; it was the first living thing we had seen for days, and it was even higher than the lichens on the rock seemed to grow.

As we descended to the col, the clouds that had been gathering below rose and engulfed us. In a few moments it was snowing again. The pattern was so familiar that we felt little disappointment; instead, as we crawled back into the comparative warmth of the tent, we felt relieved that we had been able to get the vital food boxes up before a new storm hit.

Until now the wind had been predominantly from the north. This time a strong gale from the south swept over the col, drifting the snow in a whole set of different places. Our protective snow wall did no good: it even seemed to help the drift collect. Our tent was the only object that stuck above the flat crest of the col, so the snow drifted easily around it anyway. At 2:30 P.M. the snow had reached a point halfway up the walls of the tent. Don went outside and thoroughly shoveled away the drift. We were alarmed when, only four hours later, the drift had reached the previous level. This time I went out. It took more than an hour to dig out the tent. As the blinding wind, filled with snow, roared across the ridge, I had the feeling of being lost in a desert. I couldn't even glimpse Deborah. All that existed were the tent, the snow, and the shovel.

Four hours later we had to do the job again. We had never seen snow like this, that could drift so quickly. It was making what should have been a rest day hard work. One of us would have to stay awake now, watching the dark snowline slowly rise on the side of the tent.

At 2:30 A.M. we finished the third shoveling job. We were both tired and sleepy. We settled in again to wait. The monotonous roar of the wind was hypnotic, and it was almost dark inside.

Apparently, we both fell asleep. When I awoke, I was aware of the wall of the tent sagging heavily about an inch from my face. It was almost pitch dark inside and strangely quiet. I tried to force myself to be alert, but I felt a strong desire to fall asleep again. Looking up, I could see only a thin strip of light, just along the ridge pole, at the top of the tent.

Instantly I realized what had happened. "Don!" I said, "Wake up!" The air seemed to be stale and stuffy. I tried to sit up, but the wall got in my way. Eeriest of all was the quiet. Don awoke. "We're almost buried," I said urgently. I managed to reach Don's watch. It was 9:30 A.M., seven hours after our last shoveling.

Don offered to get dressed. Only one of us could move at a time. Awkwardly, he pulled on his pants and boots. Then he slid out of his bag. He started pounding the door of the tent back, at first with his hands, then with his shoulder in lunges, like the football lineman he had been in high school. With intense relief we saw that the snow gave behind the door, though it did not fall away.

At last Don had enough room to open the door. Snow fell in at once when he did, but I grabbed the door behind him as he slithered out. He managed to fight his way up and out of the little trench he had formed. I could barely hear him swear as he got out; later he described to me the frightening sight of a smooth, wind-lashed plain of snow, out of which protruded only an orange, horizontal pole. Had the snow covered that last bit, we might never have awakened.

We had carefully placed the shovel, and Don found it quickly. With a vengeance he dug away the drift. It took hours. As he gradually uncovered the tent, he saw that the strong poles had been bent out of shape by the weight of the snow.

Before he got the tent completely dug out, Don decided that the only thing to do was to move the tent. I agreed with him and got dressed to go out and help him. The wind was blowing bitterly, but we managed to pull the tent loose. We had left everything inside it, to make it simple to move. We climbed out of the hole we had been in, pulled the tent out, and repitched it nearby.

The move seemed a great improvement, for we had only a minor drifting problem after that. We were still tired from the exertion: contrary to our usual feeling during storms, we wanted to rest instead of to get moving. In the evening I had to go out, first for a bowel movement and second, to get a new food box. I dreaded the first task. The wind had slackened not at all. I dashed out during a lull that was gone immediately and walked a distance from the tent. I pulled my pants down quickly and squatted. It was utterly miserable: the blowing snow got inside my pants and blew up under my shirt. Shivering, I pulled up my pants.

Now I had to find the pile of supplies, which was totally buried. Fortunately, we had been careful to locate it to the exact foot with respect to the tent. We had moved the tent, but its hole, rapidly filling with snow, was still visible. I started digging. It was hard work but warmed me up. Astonishingly, I got to the food box only when I was seven or eight feet down, having dug a pit deeper than my height. That much snow had drifted there in less than two days! I pulled a food box out and returned, very tired and wet, to the tent. Later Don went out and moved the whole pile of supplies, putting them nearer the tent, stacked tighter.

Before the drifting problem we had had trouble with the radio. It had broadcast all right, but we had had difficulty understanding what Fairbanks was saying. We had assumed it was weather interference because the radio had worked so well on the 2nd. Now, in our new site, we tried the radio again. This time neither the broadcasting nor the receiving worked well. We were quite upset; it couldn't be the battery, for we had a spare one that worked no better. We had been so careful of the damned thing: I had always carried it in the safest, softest spot in my pack; we had kept it absolutely dry, and we had warmed the batteries in our sleeping bags each time before trying the radio. Now it looked as if our only link with the outside world was cut off.

We lay in apathetic discouragement. The hunger was as strong as ever. At last we had admitted to each other that we *were* hungry. But we could not understand why; we thought we had enough calories and vitamins, especially for the storm days, when we usually did little work. Perhaps, Don suggested, we burned a lot of calories simply trying to keep warm in our soggy sleeping bags. Perhaps, I ventured, it was purely psychological but was affecting both of us. Whatever the cause, we definitely felt hungry. For a short while we sensed a friendly cooperation, partly because we had acknowledged the hunger, partly because of the close escape in the tent.

But it wore off. Our chances on Deborah seemed almost vanished. We had, stretching it, at most fourteen days' food left on the col. Our only hope was good weather and a dash for the summit. But we knew the route was too difficult for dashing. Still, there was always a chance. We developed a defensive feeling of pride. As I had written in my diary as early as the fourth, "We like to think others would have quit by now."

I had been having wish-fulfillment dreams. Typically, I would be a guest at a buffet dinner where every imaginable delicacy was heaped in inexhaustible piles on a huge table. There would be scores of other guests, people to talk to, all my home and Harvard friends, surrounding me. Don, though, was never there. But each time, as I started to eat, someone would interrupt me with a question. . . . Finally I would wake up and see the dull crisscross pattern of the orange tent wall above my face and know that nothing had changed, that it was still three hours until dinner.

I developed another problem, apparently related to the humidity. Even though we weren't drinking very much, I had to urinate every three or four hours. If I was asleep, I would dream about an indoor bathroom in some house to which I could pad, barefoot, in my pajamas. But something would always hinder me: perhaps I couldn't lift the seat to the toilet. . . . At last I would wake up, pull on my pants and boots, and dash out into the storm. I dreaded it, and having to do it every few hours seemed a terrible burden. I thought of an alternative. I would take a used plastic bag from our food box, urinate into it, tie off the top, then throw it out the door. Don didn't like the idea but bore it silently two or three times. He was worried about the bag leaking; so I agreed to place my eating bowl under it.

The process, disgusting as it would have seemed to me otherwise, was much more pleasant than going outside. But Don got fed up. He argued with me that it was an emergency procedure and that it was dangerous to resort to it before we were in a real emergency. Besides, he noticed the faint smell of urine in the air for a long time afterward, and the smell nauseated him slightly. After this complaint, I agreed not to use the plastic bags any more.

The weather improved the evening of July 7. We set

out at 9:30 P.M. for the last trip back to the cache. In the northwest, the sun was setting in a purple blaze of clouds. As I stopped to take a picture of it, I dropped a mitten. We watched it roll lazily away; three hundred feet below us, it stopped on a snow ledge. Don wanted to go on, but I insisted on retrieving it. Restraining his annoyance, Don climbed down with me, giving me a belay on the last part so that I could reach the mitten. We wasted forty-five minutes on this delay and much-needed energy.

When we got off the ridge to the south, we found a wind-slab crust everywhere. It looked extremely likely to avalanche. But there was no way to avoid it, and no anchor to place to make it safer. If an avalanche had broken off, we couldn't have stayed out of it, and it would have carried us three thousand feet, certainly to our deaths. Moreover, there was a danger that our line of tracks itself might cut off a slab of snow and start an avalanche. Accordingly, we tried to take big steps and avoided long horizontal traverses as much as possible.

Again the marking stakes were buried. Our careful measurements paid off though; we recognized lumps of snow and subtle contours and found the vicinity of the ice cliff. Then, just as before, we saw a few inches of the lowest stake protruding above the snow. This time the stake marked the top of the fixed rope itself.

Once more we found the ice steps covered with snow but still solid. We went briskly down the pitches, counting the hard part of the job done. But as we rounded the last corner above the cache, we saw no sign of it.

When we got to where the cache should have been, we could see that an avalanche had covered everything, even the identifying rocks just below it. For all we knew, our supplies had been swept away.

We tried to reorient, measuring our distance down from the lowest ice screw. There was nothing to do but probe with our ice-axe shafts for the cache. For a long time we had no luck. Here and there our probes hit rock, which meant that the snow wasn't deeper than the length of our axes. But it seemed hopeless. At last, as we were about to give up, I tried farther to the right and hit something soft. It was the last food box. Thanks to the piton, the whole cache had held. Relieved, we dug it out and packed it up.

As we climbed the ice cliff for the last time, we pulled out the fixed ropes. We would need them on the route itself, later. The screws came out easily, but the aluminum daggers were frozen in so solidly that we broke them off trying to get them out.

We dashed across the wind-slab slope, glad to be over it for the last time, and descended wearily to the col.

The inevitable storm arrived. We stayed put all the next day and the next night as well, sleeping and thinking about food. The wind was coming from a new direction, the southwest, but we had less of a drifting problem than before. Our hunger seemed to have increased in the last few days, perhaps because we had talked about it. We had devised a system for dividing the meal into equal halves, at first only for the sake of impartiality. The rule was that the one who divided the portion gave up the choice to the other. To even things out, each of us had to divide different items. But at breakfast, for instance, there were only three things that needed splitting; hence one of us had to split two of them. To make this fair, we exchanged jobs each day. This complicated system would have been absurd normally; but we watched each other distrustfully, and when we had to cut a piece of Logan bread or pour cereal out of a bag, we did so with painstaking care. At first we covered the ritual with nonchalance. Don would finish dividing and say, "O.K., take your pick. Which one looks bigger?"

I would answer, "I can't tell, they look about the same."

"Couldn't be much difference either way."

Reaching for the portion I had in my mind carefully weighed and found heavier, I would say, "I'll just take this one; it looks fine."

We tried to eat slowly, making the meal last. But when it was done, we were still hungry. Cramped in our bags, we would curl up and try to sleep; if sleep wouldn't come, we would reach for a damp paperback book, open it, and try to concentrate on the irrelevant words.

8 ▲

The weather cleared at noon on the 9th. By that evening, amazingly enough, it was still clear. Eagerly, we
got dressed to go; for the first time we would head toward Deborah, not away from it. We put on our canvas-
soled overboots for extra warmth and strapped our
crampons beneath them.

As Don led away from the tent, I felt a momentary
thrill. It was like starting all over; every inch of ground
was new again. As we neared Deborah, the flat platform we were on gradually narrowed, becoming first a
broad ridge and finally a knife-edge of snow. As the

ridge got narrower and we became increasingly aware of the sheer drop on either side, I had the feeling of walking out on a gangplank. For the last six rope-lengths, we belayed each other. It was not difficult going, but it was certainly spectacular. At places, we had only about a foot's width of safe snow: on the left we could see the cracks where avalanches had broken off and plunged to the floor of the West Fork Glacier; on the right, the tricky cornice overhung empty air and the Gillam Glacier. The belayer vaguely intended, if the leader fell off one side, to jump off the other. It might work as a last resort, though we weren't sure how to get back to the ridge after such a thing might happen. Fortunately, the snow was solid, and we had no troubles. All the same, we had to go slowly; inevitably the belayer got very cold as he stood in his steps, managing the rope.

We had crossed the knife-edge and reached the first rock cliff by midnight. As I hammered the first piton into a crack, I was dismayed to see the rock break away and crumble. It was fully as rotten as the stuff we had found on the way up to the ice cliff. By now we had expected this, but it proved discouraging anyway. We stood together, shivering, on the ledge just below the cliff. The first part of it was steeper than vertical. The rock was clearly difficult enough so that we might have to take off our overboots and, in places, our mittens. Somehow, in the cold, we could not bring ourselves to do it. We realized that if we were going to climb at all, it would have to be during the daytime, bad snow conditions or not. It was simply too cold at night; the cold itself made our climbing dangerous.

We left our supplies hanging from the piton I had hammered in, then returned to camp. We got back only four hours after we had left, feeling slightly annoyed that we hadn't been able to use more of our clear weather. But we knew we had made the right decision.

We planned to sleep briefly, then try to climb in the daytime. True to the familiar pattern, the skies clouded, the wind sprang up from the north, and it began to snow. We were pleased to have, if ever so slightly, started the route. But in the backs of our minds we already knew we were probably defeated. Still, we did not admit it to each other: we talked of "pushing" and of getting a break in the weather. But I wrote in my diary that morning, "At least we will be able to say we made a good try."

The treacherous snow began to drift against the tent in much the same way that it had when we were nearly buried. Don dug it out once; after that, the snow rapidly piled up to the midpoint of the walls, but it seemed to stabilize there. Uneasily, we started to relax. But it got warm during the day, and the drifted snow started to melt through the walls. We realized the only thing to do was to move the tent again. I dug it loose; then Don joined me to pull the tent to the other side of the supplies, where we repitched it at a slightly different angle. For some reason, which we were too grateful for to bother figuring out, the drifting problem vanished.

We took the back off the radio to try to figure out

what was wrong with it. What we found was an immensely complicated circuit of transistors. With very little mechanical aptitude, I couldn't hope to figure it out; Don, irked by my lack of patience, studied the diagram carefully and tried to check the connections. Our hands, cold and clumsy, couldn't handle the tiny parts very well. At one point, one of us broke a wire. I was ready to give up completely, but Don patiently figured out where it belonged and managed to reattach it. We put the thing back together, then tried broadcasting. The radio was virtually dead. When we tried to receive, we could only get faint static.

We slept listlessly. The storm continued without change; by now we were so accustomed to its sound that we might have felt uneasy in the silence of a clear day. In the middle of the night, while I was asleep, Don heard a different sound, a deeper rumble, and felt the tent shake. In a few moments it was over. It was so gentle that I didn't wake up, but Don thought it was probably an earthquake. After all, it had been only four months since the disastrous quake in Anchorage. Was this another hazard we were going to have to worry about? Suppose we were climbing on the rock wall when an earthquake hit—would it shake us off?

The strain we were feeling was subtle and undermining. We felt physically relaxed most of the time; so much so, that if the weather showed even a hint of improving, we began to feel guilty for not climbing. But for all our leisure, we were undergoing an enervating change. The food was most important; though we couldn't be sure of it, we were losing weight steadily. We thought about food even when we thought we were thinking about something else. A dozen times I told myself what fools we had been not to throw in a huge sack of oatmeal—it would have cost so little. Had the radio worked, we might conceivably have been able to call our pilot, Warbelow, asking him to drop some extra food to us on the col. But that was out of the question now. In our diaries, both of us began unconsciously to transfer the adjectives of enthusiasm— "wonderful," "beautiful," "great"—from the mountain and the scenery to our meals.

We had partly dropped the habit of arguing; we knew that we would get too angry at each other, regardless of the pretext. We tended to withdraw into ourselves, and our dreams began to use up the supply of imagination that we might once have shared in a good talk. My "banquet" dreams became more frequent and more believable; my "bathroom" dreams, more elaborate and fantastic. Don noticed a tendency in his own dreams away from the mountains, toward the familiar past of his home and friends; but always, he noted in his diary, with "some terrible new element—a combination of the nostalgic and the grotesque."

Outwardly, things were calm between us. But I felt the lack of communication poignantly. I had got into the habit of reacting to Don's mannerisms—to the way he cleaned his knife, or held his book, or even breathed. The temptation was to invent rationalizations: I told myself that I got mad at his deliberate way of spooning up his breakfast cereal because it was indicative of his methodicalness, which was indicative of a mental slowness, which was why he disliked and opposed my impatience. The chain of rationalizations almost always resulted, thus, in a defensive feeling; I was becoming, in the stagnation of our situation, both aggressive and paranoid. So I would try to keep from thinking about it; instead I would daydream about the pleasures of warmer, easier living. But all the while I could be working myself into a silent rage over the sound of Don's chewing as he ate a candy bar.

We had a brief flare-up on the 11th when Don decided to clean the stove at the precise time we had set for breakfast. Though I didn't say so, I suspected that Don had planned the cleaning simply to delay breakfast, which, he might think, would make it easier to wait for lunch. He probably felt indignant, in turn, at the fact that I wouldn't even bother with such things as cleaning the stove unless he suggested it.

For once the argument took a positive twist and evolved into a discussion about the future. In particular, we talked about the possibility that our second airdrop, over by Mount Hayes, had been lost under the nearly incessant snowfall of the last few weeks. We both imagined getting to the airdrop site, low on food, only to see a smooth, snow-covered basin. And we talked about the possibility of failure on Deborah. I remembered the first days, now more than a week past, that I had entertained the thought; it had seemed impossible, somehow beneath us, to fail. Now I was quite sure of it. But Don was unwilling to give up, and his attitude gave me a germ of new hope: if only we could get some good weather.

On the morning of the 12th, I looked out the tent door to see a pale mist, beneath which ominous clouds billowed in the north. But the wind had almost stopped blowing. We decided to give it a try, and would have been off by 4:00 A.M., except that Don discovered that a trickle of water had rolled off the tent wall and into his boots, where it had frozen to ice. We had to spend an extra two and a half hours thawing the ice over the stove. I was furiously impatient and even suggested, though I knew better, that Don should put on his boots, ice or no ice, so that we could get off. As in all our outbursts, dozens of other hostilities reached the surface; but, as in all our recent arguments, the bitter words had an important function for us as release. They allowed us to puncture what Don called the "sound barrier"— the hours of wordless antagonism when our nerves wound tighter and tighter. By the time Don's boots were dry, we felt friendly again—painfully friendly, like lovers after a quarrel. Our situation was, of course, something like that of lovers or married people, except that, instead of a bond of physical love, our bond was danger and the mountain. But our relationship was importantly different too. Frustratingly, we could not conciliate like lovers; we had to express our feelings in self-conscious terms that denied the real affection we felt for each other, in talk of "getting along" and "climbing well together." Thus, after all our arguments, a sense of embarrassment lingered with us, a desire to "make up," for which we could not find the right words.

We got moving by 6:30 A.M. At once, it looked as if the shape of the ridge had changed drastically. We attributed it at first to a confusion of memory, since our previous steps had been covered by snow. But Don thought of the possibility that the earthquake in the night had shifted the ridge slightly or broken off sections of it. A few days later our old steps miraculously reappeared, and we saw them lead right off the present edge of the ridge into space, rejoining the ridge a few hundred yards farther on. What would an airplane pilot flying over have made of that line of steps! It was an idle speculation: we had not seen an airplane since the first day of the expedition.

We reached the first rock cliff by 8:15 A.M. Though we had been going less than two hours, we decided to eat half our lunch there. At least there was a small platform of snow to sit on, and the cliff gave us some shelter. We each ate a candy bar, a few bites of dried sausage, and a lemon candy or two. The air felt warm, although a light, wet snow was falling. We took off our crampons and overboots so that the rubber soles of our boots could touch the rock. After lunch I started the first pitch as Don belayed me from our little platform. Rounding a corner to the left, I entered a steep chute of snow. Out of sight of Don, I soon found myself shoveling piles of snow away to get to the rock underneath. How absurd it seemed to be burrowing in the snow like a gopher, on the side of this mountain, which no one but us had ever really seen, much less cared about; to go short on food and patience simply to be allowed to paw through the snow in search of rock! But I was excited and happy; at last we were back to real climbing. With a foot on either side of the chute, gradually I could work my way up it. After a long time I was standing directly above Don, at the top of the little overhang that protected him. I shouted, and we flipped the rope out of the chute so that it ran straight up to me. I moved up for sixty feet more, hammering an almost worthless piton for "safety" at the hardest point and two more pitons for an anchor above. Don came up; he had been getting cold, standing there—now it was my turn to shiver. The rock above was even more rotten than what I had found on my lead—almost like frozen, chunky mud. But Don slowly and carefully worked his way up the last thirty feet. At last he was at the top of the cliff. He found an anchor and brought me up. We complimented each other for two and a half hours of work that had got us up a paltry 140 feet of the mountain. Still, it was as hard as anything we had done on McKinley the year before, and our fingers were still tingling with the feel of the rock. We ate the rest of our lunches. It was almost noon; we kept thinking about the knife-edged snow ridge softening in the warmth of the day. We had to go back. We stretched a single fixed rope all the way down to the snow platform. As we hurried back over the sharp ridge, we saw to the south, all along the massive wall of Deborah, little avalanches shooting downward, one or two each minute. By the time we got back to the tent we were tired and famished. Dinner was a bland "glop" of powdered egg and rice—but it had become our favorite because it was the largest.

The weather seemed to be getting steadily nicer. By now we knew better than to count on anything lasting, but we looked forward to whatever chance of working on the route we might get. There was still a faint hope for the summit. One rope-length for a day's work—it didn't seem much at all. But in good weather we would go much farther. Still, we had been tired when we got back, very tired. Perhaps it was all those days of inactivity; perhaps it was the lack of food. One thing was clear: we would soon need a new camp site on the ridge. It took too long to retrace all the old steps each day, and the farther we got, the more there would be to retrace. So far, however, we had hardly found a place where we could sit down, much less pitch a tent.

But we went to bed happy and slept soundly that night.

At 1:30 A.M. Don woke up to go outside. The mist had cleared completely; the crisp, startling blue of clear sky surrounded us. In the northeast the sun was just rising. It looked like the best day we had had in weeks. Don photographed the sunrise, trying to shake off the aura of a nightmare he had been having. In it someone, some close friend of his, had died or been in a violent accident; it was all fuzzy, elusive, disturbing.

We got started by 5:00 A.M. This time we attached

our crampons directly to our boots, leaving off the over-boots. The snow was in fine shape, frozen and crunchy. We moved together, without belaying, and nearly flew across the knife-edge. Exuberantly, we knew that we were working together as well as was possible. The fixed rope helped immensely on the rock cliff. In only an hour and a half we were as high as we had got the day before. Quickly we climbed three pitches of steep and somewhat treacherous snow, warily staying below the cornices. Twice we hammered the aluminum daggers that Don had made into the soft slope for protection; even they seemed not to hold very well, but they gave us some psychological security. To belay, we would stamp down a little pocket of snow, thrust the axe as far in as possible, then feed the rope around the head of the axe. Often we could sit down, which made the belaying much more comfortable. Still, there were no level spots, or even gentle ones, and certainly no places to pitch a tent.

As I belayed, facing outward, I saw a huge white mountain far in the distance to the southeast. We figured out that it was Mount Sanford, some 140 miles away. The air was so splendidly clear that we fancied we could see rivers meandering in the lowlands to the south. It was the first day of the whole expedition that we had been at a high altitude on a clear day. We could estimate in the gray-blue flatness where the road was that we had hiked in from twenty-five days before.

At the top of the third pitch I reached an isolated block of rock. Curiously, it was far more solid than any

of the rock below; the piton rang in the cold air as I
hammered it in. On the next pitch, while Don climbed
out of sight above, I felt wonderfully secure. Again the
route grew difficult. Don had to scramble up patches of
rock and snow until he reached a prong of rock, on the
north side of which he swung around. As he did so, he
was dizzily hanging over the vertical drop above the
Gillam, which we had never been able to look down before on account of the cornices. After this, he climbed
over a tower that was topped with a froth of snow, like
whipped cream, through which he dug a kind of canal.
On the tower's far side he had to drop into a deep gap
spanned by unstable snow, from which he clambered
onto rock. I yelled that he was out of rope. He went a
little farther and hammered in a mediocre piton. This
was exciting stuff! Nothing on McKinley had been so
spectacular. Don's pitch had been the hardest yet, and
it was still early in the day.

I climbed above, finishing the short, tricky cliff and
forging up a smooth snow slope to a big rock. When
Don came up, we stopped for lunch. For once we didn't
mind the meager amount of food. We were full of optimism and spoke almost breathlessly about our progress. It looked easier above. As we ate, we craned our
necks back to try to gauge how high we were on the
mountain. We knew the steepest part of the ridge was
yet to come, a frightening, nearly vertical 600-foot wall
of rotten black rock. And above that was a thousand
feet of steep ridge, festooned with the unbelievable
curls, loops, and blossoms of ice we had seen from our

tent. But it looked easier just above us, and our hearts leaped. For once we hurried through the lunch instead of trying to make it last. The sun was warm enough for comfort. This was what we had come to Alaska for!

Above, we had to go carefully, for the snow thinned in places to a bare skin over the ice beneath. Long sections of steps had to be chopped with the ice axe. The higher we got, the more empty space seemed to yawn below us. So far there had not been a single spot on the whole route where, had we fallen, we should have had a chance of stopping before the floor of the glacier, three thousand feet below. But to prevent that was what the rope, the pitons, the ice daggers, and all our skill were for.

Alternating leads, we climbed three quick pitches. At the top of a fourth, I reached rock again. We were tempted to go on but knew it was time to return; it was past noon, and the snow was melting. On the way down we were forced to go slowly, often having to improve the sun-weakened steps. We hadn't carried enough rope with us to string over all the route, but we placed fixed lines on the lowest five pitches.

As we neared the bottom we grew extremely tired. The snow on the knife-edge was very dangerous; much as we wanted to hurry over it, we had to go slowly, with gingerly steps. At last, at 5:00 P.M., we stumbled back to the tent, near exhaustion after twelve hours of hard climbing. Our throats were parched for lack of water, but we were tremendously happy. True, we had found no reasonable camp site yet, but the weather seemed to be getting even better; indeed, this was the first entirely clear day of the whole expedition. And we had done nine new pitches in a single day!

In the tent, we were overjoyed to find our sleeping bags drier than they had been in weeks. Lying down seemed a luxury again. We talked about whether or not we could keep up such a pace and whether such a pace might make the summit possible. Despite our enthusiasm, we really knew how unlikely success was. We had only about a week's food left on the col; with any safety margin at all, we could afford to climb, at most, three or four more days. We needed at least a day's food to get down to base camp, and a storm might besiege us at any time. But it wasn't in our hearts to waste such good weather.

From the best picture we had had, months before, we had hypothesized a camp site on a short, apparently level gap of ridge at 10,400 feet. We guessed that we had got almost that high already. Perhaps in the next effort we could reach the gap. If a camp could be placed there, then the following day we might move the tent, or Don's tiny bivouac tent, up there. And then, the day after, dash for the summit? But a "dash" over the hardest two thousand feet of the climb was out of the question. Still, with some unforeseeable break . . .

But the effort was hard on us. We fell asleep right after dinner, knowing that all too soon it would be morning again and that we would *have* to get an early start for the sake of good snow conditions. We almost wished for a storm, simply to rest. Best of all, though, with the good weather there had been hardly an ill word between us. That night we slept as sound as rocks —sounder, in fact, than the rocks on Deborah.

July 14 dawned even clearer than the day before. We got started at 6:10 A.M., impatient but still tired from the day before. When we reached the first cliff we decided, for the sake of speed, not to take off our crampons. This worked surprisingly well: the spikes held on the crumbly, wet rock at least as well as the rubber soles of our boots had. Above the cliff, we found the snow in splendid shape; in places our steps were like plaster casts. The cold nights, without precipitation, had allowed the snow to freeze hard. Don suggested that we climb continuously, a rope-length apart, without belaying. It was pretty difficult climbing not to belay, but we tried it. It worked perfectly; our instinctive understanding of each other, even when we were out of sight, paid off now. We were making remarkable speed. I felt a piercing joy—Don was the only one in the world with whom I could have climbed like this; in fact, there were few people anywhere who could do this as capably as we. If we did no more climbing the whole trip, we could remember this day with gratitude.

In the astonishingly short time of one hour and forty minutes from the tent, we had reached our previous high point. I led on. The little rock cliff was no trouble, but the snow above it suddenly changed in character from the solid stuff below. On a very steep, wrinkled slope, I traversed to the left. I had to climb almost on the cornice, and I prayed that it would hold. A powdery surface layer of snow brushed off at the touch; underneath, instead of firm snow or hard ice, I found a pocked and brittle lacework of ice, like a hideous honeycomb, that seemed limitlessly deep. The whole ridge was made more out of air than anything else. I placed an ice screw that seemed to offer a little security; when Don followed later, though, he picked it out of the slope with his fingers. The farther I got above Don, the more I felt as if I were walking on a kind of cloud that might suddenly collapse. Finally I put in a dagger, which, though it wouldn't have held a long fall, seemed better than nothing. If not the most difficult, this was the scariest pitch yet. When Don came up, we were suddenly isolated from the rock, with nothing but the honeycomb holding us to the mountain. But there was rock about forty feet above us; with infinite caution, Don led beyond me. For a little while the slope got very steep. I think I was holding my breath as I belayed. At last Don reached the rock where, after some searching, he could hammer in a piton. At once I felt better. Don found an ample, but narrow and downsloping, ledge from which to belay me. There we had half a lunch, a few minutes after 10:00 A.M. We were less than a pitch below the sharp plume that hid the level gap— our hoped-for camp site.

After we had eaten, I led on. Don had a fairly good rock piton for anchor. As I climbed the plume, it got steeper and steeper and smaller and smaller. Halfway up, I stuck my axe through the cornice into blank air on the right side. A few minutes later I did the same on the left side. This was appalling; the plume was corniced on both sides! I tried to hug the middle and ended up virtually crawling up it, almost like shinnying up a pole of horrible, empty, airy ice. Still, I was dying with curiosity to see over the top. A long stake I tried to place for protection went in and out like a toothpick in butter. Clumsily, but carefully, I inched to the top, then looked over.

In a glance that lasted a few moments, the expedition seemed to end. I stood silent, not quite able to believe what I saw. Both Don and I had thought about the little gap often, and it must have taken on in our imaginations something of the quality of a heavenly oasis. Perhaps we had even begun to think of it as a reward in itself, like the summit, an isle of safety in the middle of a vertical sea of danger. At best it would be a broad, flat platform, as big as a tennis court; if things went badly, perhaps only the size of a large mattress. But we could pitch a tent on a mattress.

What I saw, instead, was a serpentine wisp of snow, like the curl of a ribbon on edge. This time I could see the double cornice—the whole of the little bridge was undercut incredibly on both sides, so that it looked as if a strong wind might topple it. It was only ten feet below me and thirty feet long. The last ten feet of it were impossibly thin. Next, I saw the face of the mountain beyond. The crumbly brown rock towered, flat and crackless, a few degrees less than vertical. A thin, splotchy coating of ice overlay most of the rock. Where the rock overhung, great icicles grew. A few vertical columns of plastered snow, like frozen snakes, stuck to the coating of ice. And above, blocking out half the sky, was the terrible black cliff, the six-hundred-foot wall that we had once blithely, back in Cambridge, allowed three days to climb. At its upper rim, nearly a thousand feet above me, hovered monstrous chunks of ice, like aimed cannons at the top of a castle wall. As I watched, one broke off, fell most of the six hundred feet without touching anything, then smashed violently on a ledge to my left and bounced out of sight down the precipice.

I had never seen a mountain sight so numbing, so haunted with impossibility and danger. Don yelled up, "How does it look?" I almost laughed. I shouted back something inane, like "Not so good." Then I told Don that I would climb just over the plume to try to find a spot from which to bring him up. I pivoted over the top and started kicking steps down the back side of the little tower. Bizarrely, I felt safer at once, because the rope passed over the plume; if I fell, it might conceivably act like a piton. My feet broke through the steps, and I half slid down to the bridge. I walked out a few feet on it, just short of the point where it grew impossibly narrow. Then I tried to stand in the middle of the little gap, as I delicately stamped the snow down under my feet. It gave and gave; soon I was nearly shoulder deep in it. I could imagine myself imbedded in the ice-cream cone as the whole thing toppled off its pedestal. There was something desperately ludicrous about it. My axe could find nothing that gave any resistance. But it was safer than being on the other side of the plume when Don came up.

I yelled, "Off belay!" Don had trouble hearing me

and yelled back something indistinguishable. His voice seemed infinitely remote. At last we communicated by rope tuggings; then, as I gradually pulled in the rope, I could tell he was slowly climbing.

Don's head poked over the top of the plume. "Don't come any farther," I said. "It isn't safe." Don stood there, as transfixed as I had been; perhaps more so, for he saw me sitting like a pilot in a plunging airplane, in the cockpit of the bridge of snow. As he looked, the inevitable decision, without a word, passed between us. We could go no farther; Deborah's summit was unattainable. With another twenty days' food and some kind of equipment not yet invented and brazen skill, perhaps we could have gone on. With a handful of days left, a few puny fixed ropes, a few pitons made for rock that stayed in one piece, and some vestiges of sanity, we had to give up.

Of course we were sad. But as we turned to head down, we were almost lighthearted, too. The mountain had been fair to us; it had unequivocally said *Stop,* instead of leading us seductively on and on, forcing the decision of failure on us, so that we might suspect and blame only our weaknesses. The mountain had allowed us pride.

9 ▲

The descent was dangerous. The snow had melted to the point of sloppiness. We had to go slowly, but the longer we took, the longer the hot sun had to attack the snow. Near the bottom we grew tired again. Don was going first; each of our steps he methodically tried to reinforce or kick deeper. I got impatient and fumed silently. At last I said, "Can't you go a little faster?" He turned on me with angry words, telling me I should be aware of how bad the snow conditions were. His point was soon proved; twice my steps broke out under me, and I started sliding down the steep slope. Each time, I tried to dig the point of my axe in as a brake, but it took the fixed rope, which I held in my left hand, to stop me. The second time, the force of my fall pulled out one of the daggers to which the rope was attached; fortunately, the rope was anchored elsewhere and held. All the same, these were frightening experiences for both of us. Much as I hated to, I mumbled some kind of apology to Don for having hurried him. We got back to camp at 4:30 P.M. and threw down our packs; for the third day in a row we were near exhaustion. But we began to cheer up with dinner. Afterwards, we had a few sips of our misnamed "victory brandy"—Don suggested calling it "consolation brandy."

A curious sense of peace surrounded our next few days. We were discouraged, but our failure had only clinched suspicions that had been growing in us, unuttered, for weeks. On the whole, the defeat tended to banish anxieties rather than produce them. We talked about our effort in detail; as always, in the last few days, the talking put us at ease instead of on edge. We had no energy left for loud arguments.

The weather showed no signs of worsening. Oh, what we might have done with such a spell of perfect days earlier! But our minds kept returning to the unforgettable picture of the little gap of snow, the stark, active wall above—the Nemesis, as we had nicknamed it—and we wondered if anyone would ever climb our route.

We could afford two or three more days on the col. We might have spent them trying the Nemesis; but we could not imagine a more futile project. Instead, we decided to climb the unnamed peak to the east of us, the summit we had passed under getting to the col. It looked like an easy day's climb, up a gently inclining ridge with no rock on it at all. After Deborah, it would be a picnic. And, besides it was unclimbed: Mount Hess, a mile northeast of it, had been ascended once, more than a decade before, but no one had touched this peak, which was simply marked "11,780" on the map.

We had decided to double our rations temporarily, since we could no longer use them on the route. The next morning, July 15, we had our first double breakfast: it was a marvelous luxury. We were a little worried that it would be hard, after splurging, to get back to our inadequate daily supply, but we couldn't bring ourselves to push asceticism so far as to deny ourselves now. Surprisingly, though, we did not feel stuffed after we had eaten, even with the double meal. Perhaps our extreme exertions in the last three days had burned a huge number of calories.

We made a late start, around 8:00 A.M. The weather was still perfectly clear and windless. Everything seemed so easy by comparison with our recent climbing. At about 10,200 feet we stopped to take pictures and decided to unrope. But as Don was walking across the platform of snow, camera in hand, he fell into a hidden crevasse. Fortunately, he went only about fifteen feet in. I threw down the rope, and he climbed out by himself. He was worried most about the camera having gotten wet. We were chastened, though; if crevasses could be found even on the crest of a ridge, they could be found anywhere. We resolved not to unrope again on any terrain.

For a next few hours we carefully crossed several other hidden crevasses and imagined a dozen others. The climb was just varied enough to be interesting. It reminded me of the White Mountains in New Hampshire, or of Colorado, and I dwelt briefly on memories of climbing there, picturing other friends whom I poignantly missed now. Don was leading, just before noon, as we came to the summit ridge. I watched him climb the last bit of hard snow and step to the top. Immediately, he shouted about the view. I came up as quickly as I could.

The whole panorama of the Hayes Range had opened before us. Don had seen it once before, from the airplane, but I was looking at it for the first time. Biggest of all was Mount Hayes, stretching its massive white arms to the north and the south. Beyond it, in the eastern distance, we could glimpse the tops of the high peaks that stood at the far end of the range. Glaciers wove shining in and out of chains of unclimbed, unknown mountains. For the first time, fifteen miles away, I could see the basin where we had dropped our second load of supplies. Low clouds hugged the surface of the glacier, but the sharp peaks we intended to climb poked their heads above. None of them would make up for Deborah, but they would help. They were other, easier challenges; perhaps we could partly forget our failure among them. Twenty-eight days of food, too—we could almost taste it already. Still, we wondered about the storms. The glaciers and walls looked unusually snowy for this late in the summer. Would we be able to find that parachute?

It was only a short walk to the top. We felt relaxed and exuberant as we strolled across the nearly level ridge. A few feet short of the summit I gave us both a scare by falling up to my shoulders in a crevasse. They were everywhere! We carefully belayed the last stretch. The summit itself appeared to be a cornice; hence only one of us at a time stood on it. We left one of our aluminum stakes to mark our ascent, though we knew the snows of winter would quickly cover it. Then we retreated a few yards, sat down, and ate a double lunch.

This was the highest point we had reached on the expedition; the highest, in fact, we were going to reach. We sat close to each other, in almost total comfort; I remember reflecting that it was remarkable, after nearly thirty days together, that we could have even a moment of such perfect friendship. I looked at Don. His shaggy, black beard covered most of his face; what I could see of his skin was deeply tanned, despite all our days of storm. But his face looked thin, too, and there were marks of strain about his eyes. I wondered how much he had changed; I could not really remember what he had looked like before. I wondered if my face looked different, too, and if I had really lost any weight.

On the way down, we stopped just before we passed into Deborah's shadow to eat the last scraps of our lunches. As we were sitting there we heard a strange sound in the air, then recognized it as that of a plane. All at once a small Air Force jet, with red markings, soared over. It made a sweeping circle low over Deborah, then flew off. Had it seen our tracks? Or was the shape of Deborah intriguing enough in itself? The plane had made no sign of noticing us. We watched it disappear without regret.

We were back to our tent by 4:00 P.M. We tried the radio once more, thinking the weather might have made some difference; but it was completely dead. Inside the tent we cooked our double dinner at once, as we talked about getting our money back on the radio rental after the trip. We would have liked to throw the thing off a cliff, but it was too valuable; we would have to carry its six pounds of useless weight all the rest of the way. The dinner, bacon and sliced, fried beef and soup and rice and cheese, all mixed together, came close to satisfying us.

On the next day we rested. For all the troubles we had had on the col, we were reluctant to leave it. Moreover, carrying any more food than we had to back down seemed stupid. We worried a little about the descent because we had pulled the ropes off the steep ice cliff and had no way of finding it now. But on the climb of the 11,780-foot peak, we had looked for, and apparently found, another route down that avoided the ice cliff completely.

July 16 began clear again but grew cloudy toward afternoon. We lay reading but found the books of little interest. Don went outside to set up his bivouac tent; later I scanned the whole mountain carefully with binoculars. In the afternoon we walked over to the edge of the col, where there was a great prong of rock overlooking the West Fork Glacier. In a niche of rock, just in case we should ever come back, we left the extra fixed ropes and a bottle of cooking gas, in a plastic bag, as a little cache. From the prong I looked for some trace below of our snowshoes at the "dismal" camp, where we had left them. We would need them for traversing toward Mount Hayes. I saw something at about the right place but couldn't be sure that it wasn't a crevasse or a ball of snow.

We ate four meals that day, finishing with an extra breakfast. As we had feared, it was hard to cut back after our splurge. We had fondly imagined that the day of double meals would give our bodies a store of food to keep us satisfied for most of a week. By the next day, however, we were at least as hungry as before. By now we were sure the hunger could not be purely psychological. We had begun to find it easy to get tired; normally, by this stage of an expedition, we would have been in superb shape and would have taken strenuous days in stride.

The 17th began in a warm, wet storm. We put off our departure until the next morning. Now that we were not pushing, we began to sleep irregularly again. Both of us dreamed often and woke often. To his relief, Don's dreams seemed to have lost their aspects of horror; in one of them, he was back in California on a mild summer day, with some high school friends, eating a picnic in the country. I had another banquet dream, but this time I was the host, and friend after friend kept showing up and complimenting me on the food. Both Don and I felt heavy with nostalgia, but if we tried to talk about it, we tended to antagonize each other. Strangely enough, for all the nostalgia, we had felt almost no sexual urge, and our dreams never took an overtly sexual turn. Perhaps the craving for food had subsumed our less basic sexual needs. The other pleasures that we might normally have missed seemed similarly irrelevant. For instance, I had always wished, on shorter trips, that I could hear classical music, and I had always been able to entertain myself for hours by "playing" records in my mind. On other trips I had dreamed about composing, or about spending an afternoon with Beethoven. But on Deborah, after the first few days, I missed music not at all, nor did it take any place in my dreams. My fantasies were filled with conversations, as were my dreams—endless, lyrical, warm-hearted conversations (though Don, of course, was never a participant). He and I, apparently, could not talk well enough together. On the 17th we had a long argument about mannerisms, each of us trying to justify why the other's habits were unpleasant or annoying. It was our first drawn-out verbal fight in quite a while; much as we needed it, it saddened both of us.

I sensed that the wonderful cohesion of the last few days was coming to an end. In the absence of danger, hard work, and the suspense of discovery, our getting along was less vital. Whenever life was easy or dull, it was hardest—the tiny fears and resentments began to chafe us again. Nor did we have a clear goal ahead of us any more. The traverse to the other basin would be plodding work, and we felt real anxieties about finding our airdrop.

The wind sprang up overnight and blew the wet storm off. We got up at 3:00 A.M. on the 18th to pack up the camp, which we had occupied for nearly three weeks. As we started off at 5:40 A.M., we both looked back at the route, then at the col; the bare snow surprised me, and I felt a pang of regret. The sixty-pound packs were an unwelcome burden; for days we had been allowed to forget what a heavy load felt like. Still, we made it back to the crossing of the ridge in only an hour. On the south side, we traversed in the gray light of morning, roughly in the line that we had followed on the way up, then two pitches farther, rounding a corner. From there we descended a steep snow slope. At the bottom it grew icy in patches. We had to belay for six rope-lengths; with the heavy packs, it was a real nuisance. We quickly got cold belaying, and our calves and ankles began to ache from the constant effort of cramponing the slope. At last we reached the gentler glacier and for a while made fine speed downward. We were walking, most of the time, on the lumpy debris of dozens of avalanches. Because of this obvious proof of the danger of the slope in the daytime, we were anxious to get down fast. By 9:30 A.M. we had rejoined our ascent route, just at the spot where we had dangerously camped between avalanche tracks on the last day of June. From here it was a short distance to the "dismal" camp site, but all at once the going got very rough. We began plunging thigh-deep with each step. Even though we were going downhill, it became a terrible effort. At each step we had almost to roll out of the previous one, then step back up to the surface, only to have the next foot plunge all the way in again. With the heavy packs it became nearly intolerable. I stretched a crotch muscle painfully on a long step, and one of Don's ankles seemed to bother him. It took two more hours to travel the short distance to our snowshoes. We were quite happy to find them, buried except for their tips in the snow. We flopped down on our packs and ate the last bits of our lunches.

We put on our snowshoes and started back to base camp. The snow was sloppily wet, but at least we could stay on the surface, which made it easy trudging. By 1:00 P.M. we were back at base camp. We found the three food boxes and the long cache-marking pole just as we had left them. Obviously no one, man or animal, had happened by since we had left base camp almost a month before. We pitched our tent in the same spot that we had used originally and put a plastic sheet over the top in case it should snow or (for it was possible in this miserable warmth) rain. Glancing up at the col and the sharp ridge beyond, we felt removed from our weeks of combat not by hours, but by days; not by three thousand feet, but by a whole world.

For a few moments we took some interest in rereading the wadded and soggy newspapers with which we had stuffed the boxes for dropping. Political maneuvers, pictures of movie stars, baseball scores—they all seemed dead and trivial. This reaction might have been strange in view of our nostalgia for the outside world. But we were beginning to sense vague apprehensions about getting back, too—unanalyzable but real, for both of us.

As Don was inside the tent cooking dinner and I was scooping snow into the pots outside, I discovered a handful of brown rice and little chunks of meat scattered in the snow. For a moment an insane picture of Don throwing away our precious food flashed through my mind. Then I realized that it must have been an extra bit of one of our first dinners, at the end of June, which we had not been able to eat and had thrown out. Extra food! The thought was obscene. I considered scooping up the rice, but it looked spoiled. I called Don's attention to it. We both stared at the food, appalled by our former wastefulness, wondering how the rations could ever have seemed so ample.

In the tent, we prepared for sleep. We felt an unfamiliar sense of freedom because our tent needed no maintaining, no shoveling loose from the drifts, and because we could walk around safely outside. But with the ease came the inevitable lethargy and depression. As I crawled into my sleeping bag, something floating in the stuffy air caught my eye. It was a mosquito, blown up on the glacier by a stray wind perhaps. It wandered weakly, air-starved, around the tent, then lighted on my hand. I watched it as, oblivious to the nearness of its food or too near death to manage a bite, it stood there, motionless. Then the mosquito tried its wings, wobbled in the air, and fell to the floor of the tent. I flicked it out the door with my finger.

10 ▲

The summer was shortening; August would be upon us in another two weeks. On the col, we had noticed the gradually longer and darker nights. Now that we were low again, beneath the shadow of the mountain, and now that we had to return to a schedule of moving at night, the darkness seemed to be daily spreading and deepening. It was no longer possible to read at midnight in the tent; even at 10:00 P.M. or 2:00 A.M. it was a strain on our eyes. A few days earlier, near midnight, I had seen a twinkle of light on the tundra, far to the south. It was so faint that I had great trouble pointing it out to Don, but at last he verified it. Perhaps, we thought, it might be the hunting lodge where we had left our truck. That was the nearest dwelling we knew of. To the north, from our high camp, we had never seen the slightest sign of animate life, not even a bird or a bear. Still, we had always preferred to look north rather than south because that was where the sun set and most of the storms came from, and because it was where we had never been.

We had determined not to waste a single day on the glaciers, even during storms, because we would be doing mere load-hauling and could not afford to use up our food too quickly. But we were so tired from the muscle-straining descent that when July 19 began in a wet snowstorm, we declared a rest day. We had a few new books to read: I managed to use up the day with a Steinbeck novel, but Don could not get involved in reading.

We wanted to carry all our supplies in one load, but when we figured out the weight of everything, it dictated 85-pound packs. Reluctantly, we agreed to relay the equipment in two loads. I became aware of what seemed at the time an absurd paradox: the more we ate, the lighter our loads would be. For instance, by waiting one storm day, we had cut out three pounds of food.

The storm continued all day. We stayed dry only by virtue of the plastic sheet over the tent. By nightfall it had begun to clear, and we noticed a welcome drop in the temperature. We got off by 10:30 P.M., packing up only about thirty-five pounds of gear each. In the gloomy twilight we laced on our snowshoes, roped up, and set off. Because of an unusual cold (we recorded 24°), the snow surface of the glacier was nicely frozen —most of the way it was like walking a sidewalk. We found the going almost pleasant, though the loss of visual detail in the night made our hike hypnotically monotonous. In a little more than an hour we had covered three miles, reaching a low point at 5600 feet, where the glacier branched in four directions. We stopped at a sunken hole, the size of a tiny lake, that had filled with melt water. After a tricky approach on snowshoes, we managed to fill our water bottles and drink heartily. It was the first water we had seen since the third day of the expedition, the first since then that we had drunk without having to melt it from snow. As we sat, drinking and resting, we caught sight of two pale stars in the sky, the first we had seen on the whole trip. The glacier was wrapped in an eerie silence that seemed to urge us to get moving again.

I started off in the lead. The glacier sloped imperceptibly uphill, and we noticed that it seemed harder to keep up our fast pace. There was nothing for me to do but stare wearily ahead; nothing for Don but to keep the rope stretched between us and to avoid stepping on it. But gradually, as in the slow-motion sequence of some dreams, the scenery changed and the gray light turned brighter. We began to see the other side of Mount Hess and to catch glimpses of the precipice we had overlooked from the summit of our unnamed peak,

"11,780." Ahead of us, getting closer by achingly small stages, was a rim of snow, the pass to the Susitna Glacier. We would try only to get to the foot of it today. Two days later, perhaps, we would cross it: after that, cross another pass to the Gillam Glacier, and yet another, the steepest of all, to the basin of our airdrop. All the while we would be hiking east within the range toward Mount Hayes.

We had hoped to go all the way to the foot of the pass before eating, but our resolve faltered, and we stopped for half a lunch at a blank spot on the snow. Afterward, as we neared the pass, we discovered several huge crevasses, invisible from below, that stretched across our path. Patiently we skirted them. When we had reached an altitude of seven thousand feet, just three hundred feet below the pass, we stopped and dumped our loads. The pile of supplies looked ludicrously small; getting it there, however, had been the object of the whole day's work. We dashed back to our eating spot, where we had the rest of lunch. It was gone in no time, and we were still hungry. We talked about the food. Both of us felt that three meals a day didn't give us enough energy or incentive for a day's work. We decided to increase our intake permanently to four meals. We would follow the same rotation, but eat, for instance, a breakfast after dinner. It was a hard choice because it meant the twelve days' food that we had would last only nine. But all it had to do was get us to our airdrop—then we could eat like kings. Unless . . . the "unless" hung in our minds: unless the airdrop was buried beyond discovery. Then the nine days' food would have to get us out as well, and from that basin it could take six, or even seven days.

We got up and started back. The sun was coming up; for a while we amused ourselves with the new sights. But the monotony wore its way back into our minds, and we grew tired. We stopped for water again at the hole, then hurried on. Following Don, I stared glumly at the snow in front of my feet. Here and there I saw dark specks on the snow; they proved to be dead or weakly crawling mosquitoes. There was not a single one with much life in it. A little farther on, I saw a larger black mark on the snow, like a rock. It turned out to be a dead bird, a finch perhaps. It was cupped in a little pocket of ice as if it had hit with great impact. More likely, though, the dark lump of its body had melted the pocket into the glacier. Superstitiously, I avoided touching it.

Don was impatient to keep moving, so we started on. The last mile was the worst. I kept playing mental games to delay my boredom, but every step seemed to be sapping strength from a last reserve. At 5:30 A.M. we were back. We had covered twelve miles in seven hours, and our legs and shoulders ached from the strain. Perhaps it was the change from a routine of difficult climbing that made us so tired; still, both Don and I remembered days in California or Colorado when twelve gentle miles had been simply a pleasant hike.

Then, for all our tiredness, we slept poorly. It took

both of us hours to doze off, and we always felt only inches deep in sleep. We woke often and stayed awake from about 3:00 P.M. on. The more we tried to sleep in the afternoon, the harder it came. Worse yet, as long as we were awake, we felt hungry. At last, around 8:00 P.M., we both fell into deep sleep. I happened to awake shortly after midnight and peered drowsily at the watch. Every instinct urged me to go back to sleep, but I pulled myself together and woke Don. We didn't get off until 2:00 A.M. We felt sleepy and grouchy. The going wasn't bad at first, but we were aggravated by sore muscles and by the beginnings of heel blisters from the snowshoe bindings. With nothing else to concentrate on, the little pains grew in our minds and put us on edge. If I occasionally stepped on the rope, Don, leading, would feel a slight tug. Normally it wouldn't have bothered him, but it was an annoyance now, so that he would stop and look around, even though he knew what it was. I would wave the rope and mutter, "Sorry," which inevitably set loose a counterannoyance in me.

We had half a lunch at the water hole, spending the time in irritated silence. As we started off after lunch, I let Don lead again, since I felt too lethargic to set the pace. Reaching the low point, I glanced to the right, where the West Fork Glacier stretched south toward the lowlands. We were less than a day from the track of our hike in. It would only take four or five days to get out that way. All at once I realized that I felt more urge to hike out than to go on. Perhaps once we got to

the new basin I would feel like climbing again. But
there were so many uncertainties: not only the chance
that the airdrop was buried, but the chance that the last
pass leading to it might be too steep, on the far side, to
descend safely. And what was wrong with us? We had
increased our water intake, in case it was dehydration;
for the same reason we had started taking salt tablets.
But we seemed to be feeling worse every day. Above
all, I was sick of Don. It was an effort now not to get
mad all the time, not to let the irritations erupt. As I
watched his sturdy form plodding ahead of me, I
thought how much I would have preferred that it be
someone else—someone I could talk to better or climb
with more amicably.

The "escape route" to my right seemed to tug at my
emotions. But I would not admit it to Don, or even to
myself. We had agreed on the whole expedition, not
just on Deborah. I didn't want to be the one to
"crump." Besides, it was a momentary urge that had
come to me while I was feeling bad. There was, after
all, nothing except an accident that could force us out
now. And an accident seemed impossible on such dull,
level terrain. The only remote possibility was a fall into
a crevasse; but we hadn't had any trouble on the whole
glacier with crevasses—only up on the mountain. Besides, an accident was likely to involve both of us. Illness, perhaps—maybe we were catching some disease.
But there were almost no germs up here; even the mosquitoes could not survive. It would take something like
appendicitis to force us out. I imagined Don hurt, or

too sick to move. The radio was worthless; it would mean I would have to hike out alone, leaving Don with food and the tent. As much as I was fed up with Don, the loneliness of a solitary hike out seemed much worse. And what if it were the other way around, with Don hiking out while I waited? That loneliness would be even more terrible.

I decided to stop dwelling on such morbid possibilities. As we began the long uphill hike, we slowed down. Soon we were nearly staggering. Even so, I found Don's pace too fast, so I asked to go first. When I led, our progress was pathetic. I would wander listlessly for a few hundred steps, then stop and crouch, arms on my knees, for breath and rest. Don was annoyed by the frequent stops, but he needed rests himself. In addition, the snow was warm again (it was 33° all night), and our snowshoes kicked up a skim of slush. When we reached the cache at seven thousand feet, it was all we could do to set up the tent and crawl inside, where we could begin cooking a precious dinner.

I expected to sleep well on account of my tiredness, but I woke after a few hours and could not get back to sleep. I still felt enervated. At 3:00 P.M. I took three quarters of a sleeping pill. It did no good; I stayed awake, uninterested in anything, with a stale taste in my mouth. At last, around eight, I fell asleep. We both awoke around 11:00 P.M. The last thing either of us wanted to do was to go outside, pack up loads, and set out again. Don had slept poorly too during the day, and he especially was in favor of sleeping some more. From a feeling of duty, however, I talked him into climbing.

While we cooked breakfast, we mentally divided the load, as we had each of the last few days, so that it would be easier to pack once we got outside. The worse we had been feeling, the more important it seemed to us to make sure we divided the weight evenly. We had a pretty good idea what a given item weighed, but each of us tried to overestimate the weight if he planned to carry the item himself and underestimate otherwise. The pound was not a fine enough unit; we haggled over ounces. The ritual took on the same absurd importance that our food division had. In the backs of our minds we knew it was silly; at the same time each of us thought the other was doing his best to cheat him. We vacillated between the roles of accuser ("Come on now, the stove's easily two and a half pounds") and martyr ("It's all right, I'll take it anyway"). For a while I labored under the obsession that Don, since he was forty pounds heavier than I, should carry more weight; I might eventually have voiced the complaint had I not suddenly realized that, by the same argument, he needed more food than I.

We got started that morning, July 22, in the dark just after midnight. The temperature seemed stuck at a treacherous 33° or 34°; the snow was in deplorable condition, and the last steep section below the pass seemed ready to avalanche. Climbing in crampons was a welcome switch, however. At the top of the pass we got the momentary pleasure of a new view. But the Susitna Glacier below was shrouded in mist, and we could see very little of it. I started down the other side. It was a steep slope, longer than the West Fork side, laced with loose rock, gravel, and, where the gravel was particularly rotten, a kind of mud. As I descended, the rope pulled loose a fairly large rock. I tried to dodge, but it rolled down and hit me in the side. Infuriated more than hurt, I yelled illogically at Don to watch what he was doing. He yelled back that he didn't know what I was talking about.

At the bottom of the slope we conferred about which direction to head next. We could see almost nothing. The map offered a few clues; Don set off for a prong of rock we could glimpse in the dim mist. I was feeling terrible. I had to take frequent rests. Don felt all right by now, but I was overcome by a feeling of lassitude. At last I told him I didn't think I could go much farther and still have the energy left to get back over the pass to our tent. He seemed irked but consented to turning around. We cached our loads and started back.

We found a less rocky route back up to the pass and stumbled over it down to camp, arriving at seven in the morning. In the six and a half hours, we had managed to move our loads the pitiful distance of one mile. After breakfast we each took a sleeping pill.

This time our insomnia vanished. Instead, we slept for twenty-two hours straight. During this phenomenal period we were in a steady, drugged, dreamless stupor. We awoke feeling much better, if still logy; but the sleep, the longest either of us had ever had in our lives, seemed but another proof that something was wrong.

We ate a breakfast, waited a short while, then ate another. Even though we had accomplished no work during the twenty-two-hour sleep, we felt, irrationally, that we had got ahead of our food schedule by going so long without eating.

We were ready to go at 12:30 P.M. Both of us moved lackadaisically as we packed up the camp. Once we got going, Don began to feel better, but I remained listless and tired. We reached the spot where we had left our previous loads by 2:30 P.M. Don had noticed that his watch seemed to stop occasionally; several times he had had to shake it to start it. We wondered if it had lost any time yet—without it, it was impossible to tell the hour, except vaguely at night. We ate a full lunch, sitting on our previous loads. It was a fairly nice day, much clearer than the misty night when we had last been there. We could easily see where the pass to the Gillam lay, about a mile to the northeast of us. I was reluctant to move; only resting and eating seemed interesting to me. I voiced some of my fears to Don about reaching the airdrop and not finding it; he listened in patient but hostile silence. The admission of my fears gave Don more assurance in the opposite direction and more determination, perhaps, to oppose me. After I had spoken, he tried calmly to answer my objections, but we could not agree. Later, he wrote in his diary, "To me Dave's fears seemed ridiculous."

We added the cache to our loads, which made our packs weigh about 75 pounds each, perhaps the most we had carried yet. Fortunately, the glacier seemed in no worse shape in the afternoon than it had in the middle of the night: the temperature still hovered around 34°. We slogged upwards toward the 7200-foot pass. Two or three times Don stuck a foot in a crevasse hole, but each time it was easy to pull the foot out and step across. I began to feel a little better and took the lead for the last stretch below the summit of the pass.

On the pass we rested. A sharp wind whipping across it dried the sweat on our bodies quickly and began to chill us. But we were thrilled; to the north, clouds reeled in and out among half a dozen handsome mountains, three of which were possible objectives for us, once we reached the airdrop. Everything around the Gillam Glacier looked bold and clean in contrast to the dirty gray of the Susitna's walls. The floor of the glacier, five hundred feet below, looked clean and smooth. Best of all, across the glacier, like troops surrounding a general, the walls of dark blue schist seemed to center on a shining cliff of whitish-brown rock: no doubt the rare, solid granite found here and there in the ranges of Alaska. What climbing we could do on good rock like that!

We changed to crampons and descended to the floor of the Gillam. As soon as we reached level snow, at 6700 feet, we stopped and pitched camp. Toward evening it began to snow lightly, so we put the plastic fly over the tent. We felt better during dinner, almost relaxed and friendly. We were less than three miles from the last pass; even though it was a very high pass

(9100 feet), we had hopes of getting to it the next day. After dinner we would be down to six days' food at four meals a day, or eight days' food at three a day. We did not want to cut back again; even four meals was far too little to keep us satisfied for twenty-four hours.

The daytime schedule seemed to agree with us much better; stalking across the flat, soundless glacier at night had always been unpleasant. Besides, we were sleeping more regularly now; that night, indeed, we slept very soundly.

11 ▲

We woke comfortably late the next morning and daw-
dled over breakfast. When we looked out, we saw that
a beautiful day had dawned on the Gillam Glacier; it
was virtually windless, and a strong sun warmed us and
dried the tent and sleeping bags. We were packed up by
12:30 P.M. As soon as we had put on our snowshoes
and hefted our packs, we looked over all the glacier,
which was blindingly white with sun. The snow looked
perfectly smooth, but here and there we could see pale,
diagonal hollows that suggested crevasses. Don led off.
Only fifty yards from camp he stuck his foot into a cre-

vasse. He yelled back to me, "Give me a belay." I put my axe in the snow and knelt, as he gingerly stepped across. Then we were both moving again.

Perhaps sixty yards farther, Don suddenly plunged into a crevasse and stuck, shoulder-deep. Immediately I thrust my axe into the snow and took in slack. Then I waited for Don to crawl out. I was not terribly worried: I had belayed a few crevasse plunges like this on McKinley, and Don had belayed me in one near the summit of our 11,780-foot peak. I even grew slightly impatient as Don seemed to thrash around helplessly.

But then he yelled, "I'm choking!" I was alarmed; I imagined the pack strap or the edge of the crevasse cutting off Don's wind.

I waited a few more seconds, but it was obvious Don couldn't get out. Perhaps rashly, I took off my pack, untied myself from the rope, tied the rope to my axe, and thrust it in again for an anchor. It didn't seem solid enough, so I quickly took our spare ice axe from my pack and tied the rope to that too. Then I walked quickly up to Don. I could not really see the crevasse at all, but I could see that Don was wedged pretty deeply in it. His hands clawed at the snow, but he said that his snowshoed feet were dangling loose. He was not actually choking, but he was in a cramped situation. The heavy pack seemed to be the obvious problem: its straps were constricting his arms and upper body. I reached out and carefully tried to pull the pack up and back. Don screamed, "Stop! It's the only thing holding me up!" His voice was full of panic. My pulling had made him slip a little farther into the crevasse so that all but his head was below the surface. Don sensed, as his feet waved in space, that the crevasse was huge. He warned me that I was too close to the edge. I backed up about five feet. For a moment I stood there, unable to do anything.

Suddeny Don plunged into the hole. The anchoring axes ripped loose and were dragged across the snow as Don fell within the crevasse. I grabbed the rope, but it was wet and whipped violently through my hands. I heard Don's yell, sharp and loud at first, trail away and fade into the frightening depth. All at once the rope stopped. About sixty feet of it had disappeared into the hole.

An excruciating silence surrounded me. With a kind of dread, I yelled Don's name. There was no answer. I yelled twice more, waiting in the silence, and then I heard a weak, thin shout: "I . . . I'm alive." The words were a great relief, but a scare as well: how badly was he hurt? I yelled, "Are you all right?" After another pause, his voice trickled back: "I think my right thumb is broken! I hit my head and it's bleeding and my right leg is hurt!"

I ran back to reanchor the rope. From my pack I got our snow shovel, dug a pit in the wet snow, tied one of the axes to the rope again, and buried the axe in the pit, stamping down the snow on top. Perhaps in a little while the snow would freeze, making the anchor solid. Through my mind flashed all kinds of thoughts, reminders of warnings before the expedition about the dangers of going with only two men, fears of never getting Don out, the thought of his blood spilling, a curse for the worthless radio.

When the snow had broken around him, Don's first impressions had been of bouncing against ice and of breaking through ice: he was not aware of screaming. He expected to feel the jerk of the rope at any moment, but it had not come. Then suddenly he had been falling fast, free; he somehow supposed that I was falling with him, and he instinctively anticipated death. Once before, in an ice-gully avalanche in New Hampshire, Don had fallen eight hundred feet—but he had been knocked out that time and had remembered only the beginning. This time he stayed conscious throughout the terrible fall.

At last there was a crushing stop, followed by piles of ice and snow falling on top of him in the darkness. Then it was still. The fear of being buried was foremost. He fought his way loose from the ice; some of the blocks were heavy, but he was able to move them and scramble out. He realized that, miraculously, he had landed on his back, wedged between two walls of ice, with the heavy pack under him to break his fall. His hands hurt, his leg felt sharply painful, and his head rang from a blow. He became aware of my shouting, the sound weak and distant, and yelled an answer upwards. As his eyes grew used to the dark, he could see where he was.

The inside of the crevasse was like a huge cavern. The only light came from the small hole, appallingly far above, and from a dim seam in the ceiling that ran in a straight line through the hole: the continuation of the thinly covered crevasse. The bottom was narrow, and the walls pressed in on him, but about thirty feet above him the space bulged to the incredible width of a large room. Above that, the walls narrowed again, arching over him like a gothic roof. Don began to glimpse huge chunks of ice, like the ones that had fallen and shattered with him on the way down, stuck to the ceiling like wasps' nests.

When I had got the anchor buried, I returned to the edge of the crevasse and shouted again to Don. With great presence of mind, he realized how possible it would be for me to fall in too, and shouted, "Dave! Be careful! Don't come near!"

His voice was so urgent that I immediately backed up to a distance of twenty feet from the little hole. But it was much harder to hear each other now. We were shouting at the tops of our lungs; had there been any wind, we could never have heard each other.

Fortunately, Don's bleeding had stopped. Struggling loose from the debris had reassured him that he wasn't seriously hurt; in fact, the thumb seemed only badly sprained instead of broken. Industriously, he got his crampons loose from his pack and put them on in place of his snowshoes. He still had his axe; chopping steps and wedging upward between the walls, he got to a place where he could see better. At once, he discovered the real nature of the subsurface glacier: corridors and chambers, at all depths, shot off in every direction. The whole thing was hideously hollow. At first Don had thought he might climb out; now he realized it would be impossible. But he had a furious desire to get out. He had put on his mittens but was getting cold anyway. Around him, on all sides, water was dripping and trickling: it was impossible to stay dry.

Don became obsessed with warning me away from the edge. If I fell in too, there would be no chance for either of us to get out. I stood still, outside; I could see only the small hole and had little idea in which direction the crevasse ran. Don, on the other hand, could tell which way it ran but had no idea where I was. With a confused series of shouts we managed to orient with respect to each other.

We both realized Don's pack had to come out first. We could not afford to leave it there. He could not wear it on the way out; I would have to haul it up. It would not be safe at all for Don to untie from the rope; I might never be able to feed the end back down to him. But it was the only rope we had. I racked my brain for an alternative. There was some nylon cord in the repair kit, which was in my pack. I ran back and got it out—it was not nearly long enough. Then I remembered our slings and stirrups, nylon loops and ladders we had brought for the technical climbing on Deborah. I dug them out, untied all the knots, found some spare boot laces, and finally tied everything together in one long strand. When it was done, I threw the end into the hole and lowered it. Don yelled that it reached.

He had taken his pack apart. Now he tied his sleeping bag onto the end of the line, and I pulled it up. But as the load neared the top, the line cut into the bad snow at the edge of the crevasse. Just below the top, the load caught under the edge. I jerked and flipped the line, to no avail. Don saw the problem but could think of no solution.

It became obvious that I had somehow to knock loose the rotten snow from the edge. But I didn't dare get near the hole, and Don would be standing beneath all the debris I might knock down. I could imagine only one way to do it.

I checked the rope's buried anchor again: it seemed solidly frozen in. I pulled and jerked on the rope, but it wouldn't budge. With one of the nylon slings I had left, I tied a loop around my waist, then tied a sliding knot to the main rope with it. When I pulled, the knot would hold tight; but when I let up, the knot would slide. Don, meanwhile, had found a relatively shielded place to hide. I inched toward the hole, carrying an axe and the shovel. If the edge broke, I should fall in only a few feet: then I might be able to scramble back out. I got no closer than I had to, but finally I was within two feet of the dangerous edge. The rope was stretched tight behind me. I squatted and reached out with my axe. The stuff broke loose easily and plunged noisily into the crevasse. As the hole enlarged, I slipped the knot tighter and waddled back a foot or so. Some of the snow had to be dug loose; some fell at the blow of the axe. It was awkward work but it was profitable. At last I had dug back to bare, hard ice. The rope would not cut into it. Leaning over, I peered into the awesome cavern. At first I could see only darkness; moments later, I glimpsed the faint outline of Don below, much more distant than I had even imagined.

I retreated from the hole and resumed hauling Don's sleeping bag; this time it came easily. One by one, I fished out the pieces of Don's load. With each, we grew more optimistic. The pack frame itself was hardest—its sharp corners caught on the ice; but at last I shook it loose and jerked it out.

Now there was only Don himself to get out. There was no possibility of hauling him. He would have to use the sliding knots on stirrups, which would support his feet, to climb the rope itself. I dangled some stirrups into the hole for him. He yelled when he got them. Then I retreated to the anchor, added my weight to the solidity of the frozen snow, and waited.

Slowly, painfully, Don ascended the rope. Everything was wet, so he had to tie an extra, tighter loop in the knots. This made them tend to jam, and he had to claw them loose several times. He was shivering now, soaking wet, and tired; in addition, his sprained fingers made handling the knots clumsy and painful. But from time to time he shouted his progress, and each time his voice sounded stronger and closer.

The weather was still perfect, but the sun had traveled far into the western part of the sky A full four hours had elapsed since Don had fallen in. The peaks, as intriguing as ever, towered out of the smooth, apparently harmless surface of the glacier.

▲ 165

At last Don's head poked out of the hole. I cheered him on, but I was struck by the shaky tiredness I could see in his face. He crawled out of the hole and sat gasping on the edge. I came up to him, full of a strong impulse of loyalty, and put my arm around his shoulders, telling him he had done a good job. We ate a few bites of lunch—the minute the emergency was over, it seemed, our appetites returned.

We decided simply to backtrack the hundred yards to the camp site and pitch the tent again. I gathered the pieces of Don's pack and loaded it up. We staggered back to the fresh platform, very careful as we recrossed the first crevasse. In the subtle light of afternoon, looking back eastward toward the mountains we had been trying to reach, we could see faint blue line after faint blue line intersecting our potential path, parallel marks indicating a dozen farther crevasses like the one Don had fallen into.

I repitched the tent while Don rested. Inside, we looked at his injuries. He was badly bruised, especially on the right thigh; his head was bruised, with a small cut showing through blood-matted hair; half his fingers were sprained, the thumb badly. But it was a blessing there was no injury worse than that. Gradually, Don warmed up as his clothes dried out. We cooked dinner and ate, with a sense of peace and reprieve. Afterward, as it grew dark, we each took a sleeping pill; within a few minutes we were deep in slumber.

12 ▲

In the morning, when we awoke, we found the watch had stopped. We set it arbitrarily and started breakfast. Don was stiff and sore from his injuries, but the sleep had done him good. In my mind there was no question now but that we had to hike out to civilization. I was pretty sure Don would agree; even so, I was reluctant to bring up the matter. Finally I did. To my surprise, Don was set on going on.

We argued for more than an hour. I listed all the reasons for my decision. First, we were down to five days' food (perhaps seven, if we stretched it), and the hike out, we thought, would take about five days. If we went two days farther toward the airdrop basin, we might be forced into a seven-day hike out on only three days' food. And we had encountered only one of the obviously many hideous crevasses on this glacier. I argued that we had been very lucky to get Don out alive and that nothing would keep us from falling into another crevasse. The snow conditions, as we had found, were no better at night. Moreover, part of the hike-out route, to the south down the Susitna Glacier and River, was off our maps, since we hadn't anticipated it: who could say what obstacles we might run into? The radio was worthless, we were constantly hungry, and Don was bruised all over.

Despite all this, Don was determined to push on. He did not want it to be his accident and his injuries that stopped us. We could hike up the glacier on its southern edge, he argued, where the crevasses would be small enough to be safe. He was as eager as ever to climb the peaks ahead, and he was willing to go without food a few days, if need be, so long as we could definitely ascertain whether or not our airdrop was buried.

Don's stand put me in a strange situation. I was torn between admiration for and fear of him: at once he seemed terribly brave and terribly foolish. I remembered his insistence, early on the expedition, on going ahead the night he had been feeling dizzy and losing his balance. I wondered now if he wasn't expressing the same kind of overreaction: if so, it seemed a kind of madness. My inner voice, with its calculation of risks and complications, seemed to be speaking pure common sense, while Don's was fanatic. At the same time I could not help wondering if I was quitting on him, panicking prematurely. After all, before the accident I had been the one who was anxious for the trip to be over. I remembered the urge toward the safe south I had felt that dreary night, a week before, hauling loads across the West Fork Glacier. Perhaps I was "crumping"; perhaps I was not good enough for Don.

Our argument was uncommonly restrained, and for once we seemed objective and frank, as if a residue of respect for each other had settled out of the recent accident. I admitted that I was afraid of the glacier; Don granted that he didn't look forward to getting back to California. But I was possessed with a feeling that Don had gone slightly crazy, or that the crevasse fall had done something to him. I even fancied that the blow on his head had distorted his reason. At one point, as we were arguing about food, he said, "I'd almost rather starve here than go out now." Each symptom of fanaticism, like this one, made me look at Don in a more curious light. Yet I could not bear to attack his motives, as I had before, so soon after his ordeal in the crevasse. Don interpreted my reluctance to force the decision as a cowardice about taking the responsibility for it, which it may partly have been; all the same, I wanted the decision to be both of ours, so that we could not recriminate later.

Gradually, with heavy heart, Don saw that I was firmly set on hiking out. He could not be as staunchly in favor of going ahead—he naturally recoiled at the thought of falling into another crevasse. At last he gave in and agreed with me. I tried not to gloat over the relief I felt, and Don concealed his bitterness. We got dressed and packed up the camp in a marvelous spirit of reconciliation, a spell of grace over our life of antagonism. When we were ready to leave, we called it 2:00 P.M. With wistful glances back at the mountains we would never reach, still holding out their clean arms to us under a warm sun, we started trudging back up the pass to the Susitna Glacier.

My spirits, as always when the doubts and fears that had gnawed inside me were resolved, rose to exuberance. At first Don could not share my feeling, but his disappointment softened. On the climb to the pass we made up four or five verses, to the tune of "The Cowboy's Lament" ("As I walked out in the streets of Laredo"), about the crevasse accident. Instead of funeral roses, we pictured sacrificial piles of our favorite foods all over the glacier. One verse seemed particularly poignant:

> *It was once with my ice axe I used to go dashing,*
> *Once in my crampons I used to go gay,*
> *First over to Deborah, then down to the Gillam,*
> *But I've broken my thumb, and I'm dying today.*

At the top of the pass, we stopped to rest and gathered our last look to the north. Our marks on the snow eloquently told our story. Below us was a flat rectangular patch, where the tent had been pitched. From it a short track led straight east until it abruptly ended in a little hole. There were stray marks around the hole, but the snow lay untouched beyond.

We turned and headed down the Susitna Glacier. For a mile I led, here and there picking out our tracks from two days before, where they still showed under an inch of new snow. At the corner, the tracks turned west toward the pass we had crossed from the West Fork Glacier. We continued straight down the Susitna. We had only about a thousand feet of altitude still to drop before we would reach the nevé line, below which all the snow had melted, leaving bare ice, with the crevasses exposed and safe. But there were still quite a few crevasses to cross. I led for another half mile, through what seemed to be the worst of it. I was nervous about the hidden cracks and stuck my foot through a couple of snow bridges. However, the crevasses didn't look as big as the ones on the Gillam. Still, Don belayed me over any stretch that looked dubious, and we carefully skirted the obvious crevasses. It was slow going. As we seemed to enter a comparatively safe plateau, Don took the lead. The snow was soft and wet, scalloped with confusing sun cups. At about 4:00 P.M. he stopped to ponder an apparent pair of crevasses that nearly touched end to end. At the other end of the rope, I kept the line almost taut between us. Don started to cross what he thought was a little island of snow between the crevasses. Suddenly the island collapsed. I saw Don disappear and plunged the axe in immediately, crouching for the shock. A little pull came but it didn't budge me. I supposed Don had fallen about five feet and waited for him to scramble out. But there was no sign of him. Without getting up, I yelled, "Are you all right?" After a moment I heard his weak, distant voice, tinged with something like hysteria: "I've stopped bleeding, I think!"

With a gust of weariness and fear, I thought, "Not again!" I shouted, "How far in are you?"

Don's voice came back, "Thirty feet . . . there's blood all over in here. I've got to get out of here quick!" He sounded beaten, as if a vital string in him had broken.

When the island had collapsed, he had fallen slightly backward into the crevasse. The nylon rope had stretched and cut back into the near bank, allowing Don to fall as far as thirty feet. But this time the walls were only three or four feet apart. He had smashed his face brutally on a shelf of ice halfway down.

Outside, I imagined having to go through all the emergency procedure of evacuation again and hurriedly got out our hauling line. But Don, seeing that he could climb out by himself, took off his pack and snowshoes and put on his crampons. This was difficult, wedged as he was between the close walls. The crevasse, at a lower altitude than the one on the Gillam, was dripping and running with water. With the energy of panic, Don forced his way up and out of the crevasse, chimneying between the icy walls. As soon as I realized what he was doing, I pulled the rope in to try to aid him. Within a few minutes he had reached the surface.

I hurried over to help him. He looked scared and exhausted, on the verge of tears. His lower face was covered with blood; I winced at the sight of it. He was in an agony of pain. I made him sit down and got some codeine from the medical kit, which he managed to swallow. We got the bleeding mostly stopped. It was fairly warm, but Don was shivering uncontrollably in his soaked clothes. I helped him take off his shirt and put my own jacket on him. Don apologized for getting blood on it; I told him not to be silly, but I felt suddenly defenseless before his pathetic concern.

I changed to crampons; as Don gave me a nominal belay with one hand, I slithered down into the crevasse to get his pack. The ice on which Don had cut his face was actually sharp to the touch. The wetness was oppressive, and as I got farther into the crevasse, the darkness added to a sense of claustrophobia. I found Don's pack at a place where the walls were not much wider than my body, and tied the rope to it. Don's blood was visible on both walls of the crevasse; I felt an irrational fear of getting it on me. There was a rank smell of stale air and blood in the gloomy, wet cavern. I felt the same panicky urge to get out that Don must have felt. Quickly I chimneyed back to the top of the crevasse; then I sat, wedged feet and back, between the walls of ice, and tried to pull the pack up in one piece. It took an extreme effort, but at last I got the thing up and shoved it over the edge onto the snow. Then I crawled out of the hole myself.

Don was obviously in some kind of shock. The bleeding had essentially stopped, but his chin was a raw, ragged mess, and he could hardly talk. Despite the down jacket, he was shivering miserably. We decided to set up camp on the spot. I pitched the tent and got the stove and food out of our packs. Still, it was 7:30 P.M. before we were settled inside. The codeine had helped numb the pain, but Don was still in great suffering. He had sprained all the fingers on his left hand, so that he could barely use them. The knuckles were scraped raw. At last he could get into his sleeping bag and begin to warm up. I started the stove, which helped warm the tent, and melted snow for hot water with which to bathe Don's cuts. I daubed at the lacerations on his face with some wet cotton, but it only made the blood flow again. With pained words, Don complained of cuts inside his mouth too. I tried to look, and saw gouges on the inside of his lower cheek. Blood was getting all over the tent.

Just when we seemed to be getting the cuts clean, Don closed his mouth, and we heard a soft hissing sound as he breathed. "What's that?" he asked. With alarm, I saw bubbles of air in the blood on his chin. Checking his mouth, I found that the cut went all the way through the cheek below the lip. We both felt nauseated, but I tried to cheer him up by telling him that such things happened all the time. Finally Don settled into his bag, where he could hold a piece of cotton to his mouth to clot the blood. I cooked dinner. When it was ready, Don tried to eat, at my insistence. He found that by cutting the food into small pieces he could feed them into his mouth, chew them delicately, and swallow. This was crucial, even if it took him an hour and a half to finish a meal.

He took another pill for the pain. He seemed numb and sluggish, but he was taking the injury bravely. We divided a sleeping pill between us, Don taking three quarters and I a quarter. We would have taken more, but we felt we had to get up in the early morning, just on the chance that it might be colder and safer then. Ideally, we would have rested there the next day. But we did not have enough food and would have to push on. We had only made about two miles that day, much less than we had planned. We were down to four days' food, and we still had a mile of this treacherous glacier to cross and forty-five miles of wilderness beyond.

As I lay awake in the gathering dark, I heard Don's breathing grow deep and even. It was a blessing that he was able to sleep. Since the moment he had apologized for getting blood on my jacket, I had felt an inarticulate impulse of love for him. He had been so courageous; already he was showing signs of taking this accident, too, in stride. But I could not sleep. I imagined the morning's trek through the last of the crevasses. They were fiendish; there was no way to find them or tell how big they were: the axe could not probe far enough. And there was no way to belay across them safely. Even now, as we camped between a pair of them, I sensed the others crowding around our tent, like wolves in the night, waiting for us.

13 ▲

I awoke with the gray light of morning, at what our unreliable watch said was 4:00 A.M. The day was July 26, our thirty-eighth in a row on glaciers or mountain walls. It was already getting late; I was impatient to be off. The weather was still clear. Miraculously, it seemed substantially colder outside than it had the afternoon before. We cooked breakfast and ate it as quickly as Don's cuts would allow. Again, the rest had done him good. In the early light, inside the tent, it was hard to examine the cuts, but they seemed to have started scabbing. Don said the pain was less intense than before; in fact, he refused to take even an aspirin. We had debated whether or not to give him penicillin. Don's natural aversion to medicine made him reluctant; we thought the glacier should be pretty much germ-free and agreed that the chance of a reaction to the drugs was enough reason not to take them as long as he did not feel ill.

Don's powers of recuperation amazed me. As we packed up camp, he insisted on helping, although his swollen and blood-caked fingers made even the easiest of chores, like tying his boot laces, very difficult. As soon as I had my snowshoes on, I could tell that the snow was in much better shape; however, it had not actually frozen. I set off in the lead, full of apprehension. Don followed, ready to belay me on an instant's notice. I wove my way through a series of real crevasses and hundreds of imagined ones. We could see the bare, icy glacier in the sun half a mile below us; for all my caution, I was consumed with eagerness to get to it.

At last the snow began to thin, and at 7:30 A.M. we reached the bare ice. I stopped and pulled in rope to bring Don up to me. Our sense of relief was tangible. We took off our snowshoes for the last time, thoroughly glad to be done with the treacherous upper reaches of the glaciers. Fittingly, we had just emerged into the warm early morning sun. During a brief rest, I looked at Don's cuts. The pus had filled the hole in his lower cheek so that he could no longer breathe through it. His skin was a gruesome pastiche of black and red scab, gray pus, and white cotton; but it looked better

▲ 177

than the open wound of the day before, and Don felt little troubled by it so long as we kept moving. He still, however, had to speak slowly and laboriously, like a man with a speech defect.

There were small channels of water gushing over the hard ice all around us; we could drink our fill at any moment. Don had trouble drinking from a water bottle but managed to get about half what he poured out into his mouth. Our overboots, which we had worn almost steadily for the last five weeks, were soaked and tattered; we took them off now and spontaneously agreed to throw them away. The act gave us a moment of almost wild enthusiasm, not only because it lightened our packs by twenty pounds, but because it stood for all the restraints and fears we could throw off, now that we were in safe, low country.

Yet there were still obstacles to worry about: rivers, especially, but also the lower part of the glacier and the eventual swamp; perhaps even wild animals. All the same, we set off again with a kind of abandon. To avoid carrying the rope, we stayed tied together; but instead of being ready to belay, we let the rope drag across the ice between us. Don took the lead and set a terrific pace down the glacier. I was amazed; it was as fast as I could go, and I had not bruised a leg recently or hit my head or lost any blood. All around us were signs of warmth and wetness and life; it was as if we were walking into a land of spring after a hard and oblivious winter. The glacial brooks and trickles made soft, rich, rushing sounds, and an easy breeze carried a breath of willow bark with it. On a rocky slope beside the glacier grew patches of green grass, impossibly green: the sight was sweet enough to taste. The sun lit the hard glacier before us like fields of crystal.

At Don's fast pace, it took us only about an hour to cover the three miles down to the junction of our glacial branch with the main fork of the Susitna Glacier. We stopped for lunch on the first big moraine, a long ridge of boulders and gravel stretching like a highway down the glacier. We climbed to its highest point for our half-lunch. Behind us to the east we could see Mount Hayes again, now nine thousand feet above us. The whole upper part of the glacier was a jungle of crevasses and shattered icefalls. We picked out the branch that led to our airdrop basin: it looked at least as broken up as the rest. A single, slender peak thrust up before Mount Hayes, a peak we had known only as "10,910"; it was the one we had most cherished the chance to climb, by all odds the sharpest and most graceful, the only one that shared something of Deborah's perfection. Now it lay tantalizingly near, only seven miles from us; but it might as well have been a hundred.

Turning to look southwest down the glacier, we could see that the middle strip of ice seemed to reach the farthest. It would be our aim only to get off the glacier today: we would hope to cross the lowlands in three more days. The sun was just warm enough to ward off the chill in the air; but even as we anticipated the warmth of the lower country, we began to long again for the high, cold, and dangerous world behind us.

Don managed to cut his sausage and candy bars into

small pieces that he could chew. But he had no way of licking the candy-bar wrappers, a procedure we had come to practice with all the pleasure of dessert, since a thin smear of chocolate had melted onto them. He gave me his wrappers instead. I felt prodigally greedy to have his to lick as well as my own; but they would have gone to waste otherwise.

The easy travel on the glacier became monotonous. For several hours we stayed roped, but when we entered a region of little ice horns on which the rope often snagged, we unroped and coiled it up. For a while after that we walked side by side, a luxury we had never enjoyed on the mountain or the upper glaciers. We chatted happily as the high walls of the surrounding peaks slowly inched by. In the distance we could see the hazy blue of the tundra, but it was scarcely distinguishable from the pale sky.

At one point I noticed a sparkling object ahead of us that somehow looked different from the ice. I kept my eye on it as we neared. When we got to it, I picked it up; to my complete surprise, it was a strip of aluminum foil, about two inches long. I showed it to Don. We felt, instead of excitement, a surge of disappointment: we had thought we were the first ever to walk on this glacier. In fact, as we realized, the little strip was the first human object not our own that we had discovered on the whole expedition. Don suggested, after some thought, that it might have been dropped by an airplane, perhaps for radar purposes in a storm. His explanation made us feel better; perhaps we were the first, after all. Farther down the glacier, we found two or three more pieces of foil. We could think of no reason for a glacier traveler to leave them, so we accepted the airplane theory. The nostalgia a human object might have aroused in us was lacking; the foil even suggested a hostile, mechanized world to which there was no reason to return. But if we thought of food, the civilized world regained its appeal.

As we got lower on the glacier, the rock debris became more prevalent, and the little rivulets began to gather into solid streams. We crossed the smaller ones easily, but as we edged toward the south side of the glacier, in hopes of leaving it, we confronted a huge torrent, thick with spray, spewing furiously downwards. Wading it was out of the question because of its speed and icy bottom, but we could find no place narrow enough to jump across. I wanted to hike back up the glacier, in hopes the stream would get smaller. Don thought it was likely the stream would drop into a hole in the glacier farther down, so he wanted to go on. We were getting tired from the loads, and our argument began to provoke old irritations. At last Don offered to scout ahead, without a pack, while I waited. I accepted rather selfishly and enjoyed the rest while Don went ahead. Soon he was back, claiming he had seen a little cloud of spray where he thought the stream might dive into the glacier. I was dubious but agreed that it was worth going ahead to investigate it. We went on, feeling slightly hostile toward each other; but I actually hoped that Don was right.

When we reached the cloud of spray, we saw that it was exactly what Don had suspected. I congratulated him, without any rancor. We stood for a moment, trying to look inside the frightening hole into which the violent water plunged. Much as we enjoyed the sight and taste and novelty of water, it seemed the last sign, and the most treacherous, of the chaotic power of the mountains we were leaving. The next few days, when we should cross the drab and otherwise peaceful tundra, the turgid rivers, born in the frozen heights we had left, would be our last reminders of that world.

A few hundred yards beyond, we crossed the empty channel in the ice where the glacial river had once run. It was deeper than we were tall. In the bottom of it, I could not escape an uneasy feeling, as if at any moment a flood of water might sweep down upon us.

From there it was a short walk to the edge of the glacier. We saw a few withered purple flowers on the edge: they seemed fragrant and beautiful. Rounding a rocky corner of the last mountain shelf, we met a carpet of rich tundra grass sprinkled with willows. The thronging greenness swept like a fire across the valley before us. We waded two tiny streams, taking off our boots. On the far side of the first, we let our toes revel in the soft tufts of grass. Simply to stand there barefoot was an intense pleasure.

Beside the second stream we set up camp. We were on the edge of our map, at 3600 feet. The grass was dry, the stream as clear as the sky. We lounged sensuously in the spongy grass: we had forgotten what a joy easy camping could be. We bathed Don's wounds again but left the core of pus in the cuts. As we prepared our chicken stew for cooking, we forgot where we were for a moment and put a pot of stream water on the stove in order to melt it to water in which to soak the stew. Everything seemed so easy: the memory of stinging blizzards in a cramped tent, when it had been a considerable effort to open the door and scoop a potful of snow, seemed as remote now as an adventure in some book.

There were a few mosquitoes around camp, but we almost welcomed them. After dinner we were, as usual, still hungry, but the feeling could not intrude on our sense of ease and luxury. We gathered willow branches for a fire and soon were sitting around the sparkling flames, gazing hypnotically into them, as we had on the first evening of the expedition. The sun set in the northwest. Deborah was silhouetted in ghostly blue against the bright sky, beyond two glaciers, as sharp as in our best dreams.

The night looked so clear that we dispensed with the tent, pitching only the plastic fly between our packs. We lay talking, half in our sleeping bags, conscious of the unfamiliar softness, like infinite mattress, under our backs. We were tired; Don fell asleep in the middle of our conversation. I lay awake for a few minutes longer, but the gentle sound of the stream soon lulled me into a deep, peaceful sleep.

In the morning we got off by 9:30 A.M. The weather was still clear and pleasantly warm. At once we were off the map. I suggested following the glacier along a side-hill, but Don vaguely remembered a short cut he had seen on the more extensive maps in Cambridge, months before, a low pass to the south that seemed to cut through the foothills. I was unsure, but Don talked me into his decision again, and for the second time he was right, saving us at least several hours' work. We found easy going over dry, soft tundra, skirting a few lakes, up to the pass. Near the highest lake we saw a solitary caribou that panicked at the sight of us and ran far up the opposite hillside.

The greenness still seemed marvelous to us, and we could not take in enough of the scenery. The country was so different from the world of glaciers: in its peculiar way, it seemed freer and emptier, even lonelier. For several hours our enthusiasm stayed high. After crossing a little stream at the top of the pass, we stopped for lunch. Again Don offered me his candy wrappers. I noticed another virtue of the gift: it took him so long to eat, with his careful chewing, that I would surely have grown impatient had I not had something else to do, like lick all the wrappers. The pain of his cuts was minimal when we were moving, Don said; it only bothered him now, really, in the evenings; hence he would take Empirin tablets only before going to sleep.

We continued across the long plateau. Below us, we knew, even though it was partly off the map, we would face the East Fork of the Susitna River, a fairly large, and probably fast, glacial stream. We were worried about crossing it; it seemed the last obstacle of all.

At 2:00 P.M. we reached the edge of the plateau. As we walked to the edge, we caught our first sight of the river. It was still more than two miles distant, and this deceived us, for it looked like a thin, harmless ribbon of blue. Confidently, we started down the long slope.

At once the mosquitoes discovered us. We walked through thick, sporadic clouds of them, batting them off with our hands and even with our ice axes. We grew suddenly tired, and the annoyance of the mosquitoes added to our weariness. The going seemed interminable. Soon we were enmeshed in thickets of willows; through the denser parts of them, we beat our way clumsily, like bears. Finally, the tundra, which had been so wonderfully springy and dry, grew soggy and sloppy with mud.

As we neared it, the river began to look bigger and bigger. What was more, it was obviously swift. All at once we were not so sure. A little after three, we stopped at a lake just overlooking the river. We sat on our packs, since we could not find dry ground. The mosquitoes attacked us in hordes, biting even through clothing and the repellent we had carefully carried all through the expedition. We could not get clear water to drink; the lake water tasted slightly rancid, but we drank it anyway. We were very tired and covered with sweat; the rest of our lunch passed in depressed silence. Our ears were alert to a nearby, ominous sound: the heavy thunder of the river that lay blocking our path.

14 ▲

The mosquitoes drove us on. We wandered downward through the dense, scratchy thickets and the soggy swamp toward the unavoidable river, looking for moose trails through the worst of the brush. Evening was approaching; we could see the huge main stream of the Susitna River, wandering across the tundra in the hazy distance. We would have liked to stop and camp, but it would not be safe until we had crossed the river.

When we reached the bank, we stood staring unhappily at the churning water. Don shouted over the stream's roar, "Looks like a rocky bottom!" We knew this would mean treacherous wading. There was no question of going barefoot here; we would have to keep our boots on to have a chance of staying on our feet in the numbing torrent. We scrambled down to the edge and took our packs off on the weed-choked bank. Then we removed our pants; at least we could try to keep them dry.

The going looked so bad that we decided to rope up. Since Don was heavier, he stayed on the bank to belay while I carefully waded in. The mosquitoes swarmed to his bare legs and he could not swat fast enough to keep them off. The water hit me with a sudden, chilling shock. I stumbled but caught my balance. At once the stream got deeper, and the farther under my legs went, the greater was the surface the water had to attack. Moving one foot at a time was a tricky business, for the current seized them at every movement, and the round rocks on the bottom were slimy and irregular. I unhooked the waist loop of my pack so that I could get rid of it in an emergency. Keeping my eyes away from the dizzying water, I tried to concentrate on the opposite bank. But by the time I got only ten feet from shore, the current was surging around my thighs. I felt just barely in balance. I looked back at Don, who seemed to be holding his breath; our glances agreed, and I returned to the bank.

We coiled the soaked rope, put on our pants again, and headed downstream. It was not easy to follow the bank, for it was steep, thick with brush and weeds, and often cut by little ravines. We fought our way about half a mile downstream, then tried again.

This time the mosquitoes were even worse. The clusters of them on our legs, the unpreventable bites, several each second, put us in a kind of panic. The water was the only place to avoid them. This time the stream looked wider, and consequently shallower. We left the rope in my pack and edged into the current, facing upstream, our arms locked together. Don went first, counting on his greater stability. At first this seemed to work. We got about forty feet out and were entering the main channel. But again we seemed only precariously in balance, and it was hard to move together. We stopped for a moment. Both of us sensed that if we lost our footing we would never regain it. The water was so cold that we could not feel our feet, and our legs ached. I shouted, "It's no good! Let's go back!"

Very carefully, we made our way back to shore. We were getting extremely tired and hated the thought of going on downstream. But it was the only choice.

A little farther on, we made our third try. It was less successful than our second. Above all, the rocks on the bottom made us nervous: they were impossible to see and treacherous to feel.

As we sat on the bank, pulling on our pants again, I felt almost like crying. I swore at the mosquitoes, blaming them for our troubles. There was one remote, dependable solution: that was to hike up the stream, perhaps as far as whatever glacier it sprang from, and cross it where it was small enough. But that could take days and an agony of effort.

I had another hunch. The main branch of the Susitna, in the flat land below us, looked slower, broader, and, most important, muddier. Perhaps, if we kept on downstream, we would get out of the rocky-bottomed region and find smoother silt under the water. It was worth a try. We continued down the bank for another half mile. I had to keep telling myself to push a little farther, to keep going, and to resist the impulse to cut down to the river too soon.

At last the river seemed to slow and broaden; it even looked muddy. But it also looked very deep. We went down to the bank, picking a part of the river where a small grassy island cut it into two channels. I started into the current first. The floor, happily, was smooth silt, and it was much easier to slide through the slower water. But it rose above my knees, above my thighs, at last to my waist, and I had to go back. Don was trying upstream from me. I watched him go in to his waist, hesitate, then forge on. All at once the water dropped to his knees again, and he easily reached the island. Jubilantly, I followed him. It went a little deeper on me, but Don coached me to the shore. The second channel was trivial by comparison. Suddenly we had crossed the river; we threw our packs down gratefully on the sand of the far shore. We hurried our pants on, trapping mosquitoes inside them. Then we decided to eat a breakfast on the spot. After all, the sun was just setting, and we had been going since nine-thirty in the morning.

The river water was thick with silt. We had to let it settle before we could drink it. For that reason we decided to go on, only as far as the first usable water, rather than camp at the river bed. As the sun's rays left us, we quickly got chilled. We were soaked above our waists, and our boots were as soggy as they could get. Tired as we felt, we were anxious to get moving again so that we could warm up. We shouldered our packs and started uphill.

Now, paradoxically, we could not find water. We had hoped to go only a few hundred yards, but we found ourselves crossing half, three-quarters, then a whole mile, desperately looking for a stream. We gave up the search for running water and agreed to settle for a pool; even if it were rancid, we could boil it. But we could not find even a puddle. The logs and bushes were covered with a dusty, deathlike moss. The mosquitoes reached a peak density, the worst we had ever seen in our lives. As we talked, we could not keep them out of our ears, noses, and mouths; some of them even flew into our eyes. The darkness was growing fast, and the swarms of mosquitoes seemed to darken the sky even more. They surrounded us with a dull, droning sound that we kept mistaking for the sound of a stream. I found myself wondering whether it was the same group of mosquitoes following us, or a constantly changing segment of a universal horde through which we passed. Don had a nylon headnet, which he put on now: it was a good thing, for the insects were driven mad by the smell of blood and pus in his cuts. I had thrown away my headnet up on the glacier in a moment of weight-saving zeal. Now I relied on repellent, but the mosquitoes ignored it, and my sweat washed it off quickly anyway.

It was growing very dark. We were on the edge of

total exasperation and exhaustion. We had to have water; the more we searched for it, the thirstier we grew. At last I caught sight of a faint glimmer from something white in a ravine to our right. We hiked down to examine it and found not water, but a small patch of caked, dirty ice that had somehow stayed frozen in this dark hollow. It was good enough for us.

With the last of our energy we gathered logs and branches for a fire, the only remedy we could think of for the mosquitoes. But when we tried to light it, the wood only smoked and smothered the flames. It was all rotten and damp inside; it was as if the greedy wood had soaked into its foul core all the water we so desperately needed.

We contented ourselves with our stove. The ice was very hard and took a long while to melt. We could not filter all the dirt out of it either. In his tiredness, Don cooked the powdered eggs wrong, and they tasted like rubber; still, we eagerly ate every scrap. We could not keep the mosquitoes out of the food or out of our mouths as we ate.

Miserably, we went to bed, too tired to pitch the tent. We crawled into our sleeping bags and pulled the rain fly over us. Don kept his headnet on; once he had grown used to the whine in his ears, he could sleep. I pulled my bag all around me, except for a tiny breathing hole. But the mosquitoes found that out and landed constantly on my nose and upper lip. I was too tired to brush them off: most of the time I tried to blow them away. But the sluggish insects ignored my puffs and bit until I squashed them.

I slept only fitfully. It rained a little in the night, but we did not get very wet. On the other hand, neither did the rain discourage the mosquitoes.

In the morning, as we got up, I felt irritable and unrested. My upper lip was a swollen mass of bites, partly blocking my nose. Don felt only a little better. We ate breakfast hurriedly and set our watch at 8:30 A.M. as we started off.

We had a fairly good idea of where we were and a vague confidence that it should take two more days to get out, barring any obstacle. We had two days' food left. Don set a good pace, contouring across the side of the long hill we had been traversing since the river. I followed him for a while in silence, but I felt tired enough so that his pace began to wear on me. At last, in an irritated voice, I asked him to slow down.

The first two or three miles were the worst. Both of us were still weak from the strenuous effort of the day before; our pace seemed to get slower and slower, our rest stops more frequent and longer. We could see, from the part of the map we carried, that we would soon have to cross another stream, a fairly big one, but by no means the size of the East Fork. With that as a goal for lunch, we tried to forget our hunger and weariness. The mosquitoes, still thick, were not as bad as the night before. The sky looked as if it might rain, and for once we hoped for it, to drive the rest of the insects away.

The going became worse. The willow and alder thickets blocked our way more often; although we followed moose trails through some of them, in others we had to crawl, like natives in a jungle. Don was carrying some long stakes and the extra ice axe on the top of his pack; they kept catching on branches and holding him back. He complained loudly about it but was too proud to ask me to carry them; I was too stubborn to offer.

The slope was so soft and so constantly tilted in the same direction that our feet began to wear blisters on the downhill sides and our ankles grew sore from correcting the tilt. We could never see very far ahead; there was always a green patch of willows before us, blocking the view. Our rests became blessed, silent intervals: each time we stopped, we would throw off our packs, collapse on the soft, matted slope, and lie gazing lethargically at the storm clouds dancing above the flat plain to the west. Somewhere out there lay the ground we had crossed forty-one days before, full of hope and energy, on the hike in.

We reached the small canyon of the expected stream before noon. From the edge we could see white froth below as the river spilled down its rocky channel. It was swift and noisy but looked small. We plunged down the bank, which was a tropical tangle of weeds and bushes, and fought our way to the edge. We happened to hit the stream where it was broken into three currents by little islands. Soon we were wading in. The knee-deep water had surprising force, but we waded across without incident. The pounding of the stream on our legs and the spray in our faces was almost exhilarating; in the middle of crossing, we bent down to drink. On the far side we scrambled out of the ravine and stopped for a first lunch.

My feelings of irritation had gradually worn off, but we were too tired to feel very friendly. Nevertheless, I reflected that we had got along better the last four days than any before, at least since the hike in. Perhaps at last we were adjusted to each other—how absurd that would be, at the end of the trip! More likely, we had been too busy to quarrel, and too worried abut crevasses and river crossings to worry about each other.

After our lunch some of my energy seemed to return. We had decided not to push hard that day, but to camp early, eat in relaxation, and save the hard push for what we hoped would be the last day. After that, if necessary, we could go without food for a day or two. The only thing that could stop us was a river off the map. We were already nearing the lower corner of our map. From there, Don thought the road could not be more than fifteen miles distant.

We crossed three more little streams, scarcely getting our feet wet. On a game trail a little farther on, we saw our first moose: a cow and a calf. They looked us over calmly, and we carefully stayed out of their way.

The rain started falling, lightly at first. Then suddenly we were in a deluge. We put on raincoats and continued. The rain lent some variety to the going but it managed to get us wet everywhere except about the chest. We could not avoid brushing through the soaked grass and bushes.

After the rain stopped, we found the mosquitoes had almost totally disappeared. It was the happiest event since we had got across the big river. At the fourth of the little streams, the end of the terrain marked on our map, we stopped to camp. In a tiny clearing among the dwarf spruce trees we pitched the tent. This time we had a clear nearby stream, dry wood for a fire, and no mosquitoes. For the first time that day we did work that seemed a pleasure. By contrast with the grueling hiking, camping was pure delight: evenings were our favorite part of the day, and we tried to stretch them out as long as we could.

We cooked on the stove as we sat around the fire. The food seemed inadequate, as usual, but every mouthful was a tiny feast. As it grew dark, we built the fire higher; the flames held our eyes for hours, and we managed to dry all our clothes on the surrounding bushes. Don and I sat on the same side of the fire, away from the smoke. We talked aimlessly, neither about getting out nor about Deborah. I felt sad, in a way I scarcely had during the whole expedition. For once, Don and I felt close and congenial. I thought with admiration how little he had complained about the cuts, even though it looked as if they were starting to infect and still caused him enough pain to require pills at night. I thought, also, how little his injuries had slowed him down: if anything, in the last few days, I had been the one who had had trouble keeping up the pace. The night seemed suspended around us; for a few miraculous moments we talked about other mountains, about coming back next year, almost in the same spirit as we had before we even knew about Deborah.

Before getting into the tent, I walked down to the

stream for a last drink. It was the darkest night yet; the blackness gave me a feeling of malaise, and I was inordinately glad of the fire behind me, up on the little hill. There were a few stars visible among the clouds; in the north, a red bank of clouds hovered above the horizon. I saw a sharp, single mountain silhouetted in black under the clouds; caught by surprise, I realized it was Deborah. With the surprise came a burst of sadness, of longing to be back in the snow and wind. But that passed, and I walked back up to the fire, grateful again to be camped in comfort and safety.

Inside the tent it was almost pitch black. We fell asleep in the middle of a murmured conversation.

After a deep, healing sleep, we woke to the soft morning light. We felt much better and ate our last breakfast quickly, in order to get moving. The weather was clear again; we were off by 9:00 A.M.

Somewhere ahead of us we knew we should run into the gold-mining ghost town of Denali. From there it could not be more than ten miles to the road, and perhaps as few as five. But there was still no sign of man anywhere about us; for all we could tell, this dreary sidehill had never echoed to a human step or voice before that day. Three miles ahead of us we could glimpse the final corner of the long slope we had been three days in crossing; from there, perhaps, we would see Denali, or see that we still had far to go. We resolved to resist the first half of lunch until we got to the corner.

The willows were thicker than ever. Sometimes, to

get through them, we were reduced to crawling on our hands and knees, like animals through a cane brake. We saw dozens of moose and discovered that, for all their size, they found it much easier than we did to get through the thickets. On the other hand, the moose didn't have to carry seventy-pound packs.

At one point Don looked down to the broad, silver Susitna River below us and caught sight of a bull moose swimming easily across it. Although we were getting tired and irritable again, we stood watching for a long moment, awed by the beast's power and grace.

Don's boots, saturated with water, were beginning to lose their shape. The right boot especially was failing to give him support. Walking on the continual slope, he was slowly spraining his right ankle. It began to grow very painful, but there was nothing we could do about it.

A mile before the corner, we stopped to rest. As we were sitting, looking down again at the river, I suddenly noticed a half-collapsed cabin on its bank. We were tempted to hike down to it, on the chance that an old trail might lead away from it. But there was too great a likelihood that it had been approached only by boat, from the river. Still, the sight encouraged us about the possible nearness of Denali.

At noon we reached the corner. I hurried ahead to look around the edge. At first I could see nothing but grass and brush, the same as we had crossed for the previous two days. Then suddenly, about a mile off, I spotted a shiny object, apparently the metal roof of a cabin. I yelled to Don, who brought the binoculars. Through them we could see the building itself, and several others clustered around it. It must be Denali!

After our half-lunch, the mile passed quickly. In my enthusiasm I almost doubled my pace, but Don's ankle was seriously sore, and I had to keep waiting for him. At 1:00 P.M. we reached the first of the buildings, a wreck of a shaft with the dim legend "Ladybird Mining Co." still visible on it. We ate the rest of our last lunch on the spot. Almost symbolically, Don's watch stopped as we sat there and would not start again.

A little shower urged us on. We followed an old rut of a road into the main part of the ghost town; but it took most of an hour to get there, for we had to wind deviously down, almost to the Susitna River itself, then back up a hill, crossing a medium-sized stream on the way. Though we had to wade above our knees, we didn't even bother taking off our pants or boots.

We rested for a long while on the porch of the main cabin, which looked recently rebuilt. It was also apparent that a tractor trail led off through the woods toward the road. There could be no more obstacles, then: we had made it. As the sun set, we tried to dry off in its last, warm rays. We cooked our final meal and ate in leisurely silence, trying to make the food last as long as we could.

There was nothing left to do but to hike down the tractor trail to the road. We should be able to make good time; even if it were ten miles long, we might cover it that night. It seemed to me that we should have felt more excited than we did. There was a tinge of excitement, to be sure, but it was absorbed in a dull sense of loss. And there was something else—a hint of foreboding connected with all the thoughts we had nourished in the last weeks, the thoughts of food, of ease, of company and conversation.

As the twilight deepened toward night, we started off. The trail was easy to follow and consequently monotonous. For about a mile we kept up a good pace, without a rest. But in the absence of suspense about our goal, a dozen physical irritations began to show up: the beginnings of new blisters on our feet, our aching shoulders, sores around the hips from the waist loop, the scratch of wet flannel on the crotch. Soon it was genuinely dark: we could barely make out the trail and the enclosing columns of trees. We crossed half a dozen little streams, wading them without caring about getting wet.

We had been going more than twelve hours; all at once both of us felt very tired. We rested several times each mile. After every rest we would slowly get to our feet, jerk our packs up, and set off again.

Three hours later there was no sign of the main road. It was too dark to guess where we were. We were so tired that we seemed to be stumbling along in a dream. We took another rest; I suggested to Don that we stop to camp. It would mean going longer without food, but we agreed we could make the last few miles more easily in the morning, after a sleep.

We went ahead a little way to look for dry ground

on which to pitch the tent. All the tundra around us was soaked. A dim, light-colored shelf ahead of us looked better, so we aimed for that. As we got near, the shelf seemed to stretch in either direction. Then we saw that it was the road.

We took one more, giddy rest, then hiked up the road. It was only a mile to the Susitna Lodge. We came over a rise near it and saw its light ahead. Within minutes we were turning in the driveway. The place seemed deserted. It was the darkest part of the night, probably after midnight. We remembered the lodge from the first day, when its owner had driven us out to our starting point. Now we had come full circle.

We climbed the steps and tried the front door; it was open. In the kitchen, a light was on. We looked in; a girl saw us and gave a frightened gasp. We calmed her, told her she was the first person we had seen in forty-two days, and asked if she could give us something to eat.

Nervously, she cooked us cheeseburgers and served us blueberry pie. As we devoured the food, the girl looked at us in silent fright. She seemed most upset by the sight of the lower part of Don's face. We asked if the owner was up; no, she said, everyone else was asleep. We were still hungry after the food, but the girl obviously wanted to go to bed. We could wait till morning.

In the parking lot we set up our rain fly again, as we had on the first day of the trip, and crawled into our sleeping bags beneath it. An electric light glared over us like a watchman, and a generator roared noisily from a power shed beside the driveway. It looked as if it might rain again. I asked Don how his feet were. He said that they felt all right. In his single, short answer I heard all the vague sorrow that was also building in me. Don fell asleep just as it began to rain lightly. I lay there, on the verge of sleep, thinking of ice-cream cones and baseball games and the wonderful ease, the ease of walking on sidewalks and of driving cars, the luxury of soft chairs and indoor fires, and especially the ease of unanxious sleep. But sixty miles north of us, already touched with winter snows, Deborah lay fathomless in the darkness, and nothing would ever be easy again.

Looking sideways (south) from the east ridge of Deborah across the 6000-foot-high east face.

Interlude ▲

Don and I had resolved to make a temperate transition back into civilization, but the sudden availability of food in limitless quantities did us in. In Fairbanks we gorged on gallons of ice cream; then a friend invited us over for a wild game feast. We ate moose and bear and caribou and homemade cranberry sauce until we could hardly walk. By the time we flew to Seattle a few days later, we were both ill.

I have a vivid memory of Don and myself somewhere near the bus station in Seattle. We were both feverish, we had the trots so bad we had to stop in every café we passed to use the bathroom, somehow we had developed blisters, and a miasma of enervation hung over us. As we lugged our packs, the bus depot seemed a distant goal; we counted on public benches for rest stops. It was a warm, cloudless day. All at once, as we sat on our third bench gathering our feeble energies, we saw Mount Rainier in the distance. We burst out laughing, the joke unspoken. Before Deborah, we would have regarded Rainier as a walk-up, a picnic outing on the way to a real climb. Now the mountain, hovering far above a grassy park in downtown Seattle, seemed as unattainable for us, in our dilapidated condition, as the upper reaches of Deborah's east ridge. What had we come to, staggering like winos from bench to bench?

What Don and I needed above all else was to get away from each other. Foolishly, however, we had agreed to spend a week together at his parents' house in Walnut Creek, California. I had not met them before, nor Don's older brother, who was there with his new wife, who was seven months pregnant. I liked them all, especially Don's warm-hearted, unpretentious father and mother. We toured a Napa Valley winery, and Don and I managed a short hike on suburban Mount Diablo.

The gouges in Don's lip, which he suffered in the last crevasse fall, had become badly infected. I remember the doctor's groan of disgust at the sight of the congealed pus and blood. Eventually Don developed cysts in his mouth and had to have several operations to remove them. By the time we reached California, he was on antibiotics, and just as he feared, he suffered a reaction to them, which took the form of a strange, arthritic stiffening in his joints—especially the fingers, and especially first thing in the morning.

We had no obligations, nothing to do but lie back and take it easy while we downed Don's mother's generous meals. And of course, this was the worst possible regimen. Everything each of us did or said drove the other off the deep end of vexation. As Don jerkily climbed out of bed in the morning, like some robot in a bad science-fiction movie, it was all I could do to keep from laughing. I had learned that Don had a deeply psychosomatic makeup, and I was tired of being sympathetic. We worked in Don's closet darkroom to develop his black-and-white pictures from Deborah. His fingers were so bad he spilled fixer and fumbled negatives, but when I tried to take over he screamed at my incompetence.

The tension was there every waking moment. If I prattled on glibly to Don's parents, I could feel him sitting there in silent disapproval, red-penciling my blithe assertions in his mind.

Our pathetic comedy reached a climax on my last night in Walnut Creek. Just to annoy Don, perhaps, I started flirting with his pregnant sister-in-law. She didn't seem to mind, nor did Don's laid-back brother, but my cavalier (and, I thought, innocent) play drove Don into a rage. After midnight, with everyone else asleep, we confronted each other on the patio. I cannot recall the harsh words we exchanged, but soon we were in the midst of a physical fight. We didn't throw punches; instead, Don tackled me as he had opposing fullbacks in high school, and drove me from one wall to another, slamming me against the patio furniture, some of which broke.

In the early morning he drove me to the bus station. I don't think we spoke a word, except to say goodbye. As the Greyhound rolled east toward Colorado, I did not expect to see Don again, perhaps not even to hear from him in writing. For years afterwards, our fight on the patio seemed one of my most shameful secrets. In the bus I felt a heavy sadness, too: Deborah had been bad enough, but at least we had climbed bravely and got ourselves out alive. The tawdry scene in Walnut Creek was an ending nobody should have written.

In the fall, Don was in California, while I was beginning my senior year at Harvard. A thaw of silence began to melt our frozen hostility. We wrote to each other, at first mere briefs tidying up logistical odds and ends, then real letters in which we dared to let reminiscences about the best moments on Deborah creep in. Sometime in the winter, we actually began to think about doing a climb together again. Maybe even a climb that would make up for Deborah.

▲

THE
MOUNTAIN
OF MY FEAR

▲

▲ Contents

The Mountain ▲ 215

The Plan ▲ 228

The Long Road ▲ 239

The Unknown Glacier ▲ 250

Twenty Days' Despair ▲ 271

Blue Sky and Hope ▲ 304

The Summit ▲ 320

The Accident ▲ 337

Remnants ▲ 348

1 ▲ The Mountain

The mountain had been there a long time.

If we could define its beginning, perhaps we would place it in the Jurassic age, when several cataclysmic faults thrust the granite core of the Alaska Range into the sky. After that time the mountain may have looked much as it does now. But we must imagine as legacy to the violence of those faults only voiceless eons spent in the silent wear of ice and wind; for the mountain stood one hundred and thirty million years before man would walk upright on some tropical plain. We must imagine an emptiness of time that can be matched only by the emptiness of space: ages explored only by the dark wind that must always have been there, silence broken only by the occasional clatter of a rock set loose in the brief summer thaw, or the wet hiss of an afternoon avalanche.

But a similar history belongs to any mountain, and the rounded Appalachian hills are far more ancient than Alaska's giants. Mount Huntington is remarkable not for its past, but for its present. For the sixty years men have known about it (not many men either), it has possessed a quality common to only a few mountains in the world. A sense of arrested grace, perhaps; a sculptured frailty too savage for any sculptor's hand; a kinship with the air around it that makes it seem always in motion—but these are only metaphors, unable to capture the essence of the mountain. And though we might presume it has no essence, knowing that time will wear it beyond the bone to a heap of detritus, knowing that it cannot outlive the sun, still we are sure that any man's lifetime can span but one flaking of its skin, and that the mountain, doomed as surely as the earth, still possesses something like the earth's persistence, something alien enough from man to partake of a universe he wished he could own.

It is impossible to determine which man first saw Huntington. The Indians, who gave a worshipful name to McKinley (they called it Denali, "the Great One"), made little distinction among the masses that surround it. Since they never got into the heart of the range, none of them may have ever seen Mount Huntington.

But they named the river that comes from the glacier that Huntington heads; and the name, Tokositna ("the river that comes from the land where there are no trees"), suggests that they were familiar with the river's origins, if not the glacier's. Perhaps some hunter, chasing a caribou herd toward the highlands, crossed the tundra hills one day in late summer to see the dirty tongue of the glacier stretch back before him into the bewildering chaos of rock and ice that fringed Denali; perhaps he glimpsed in that chaos a peak or a ridge of what would come to be called Mount Huntington. It couldn't have been more than a glimpse. On a clear day, it is true, one can see Huntington from points in the southern lowlands more than a hundred miles away; but it takes a sharp eye to discriminate its slender peak from the hulking mass of McKinley behind it. No one unaware of the intricate wanderings of the glaciers in the heart of the range could tell that what he saw was a separate mountain, much less a beautiful, virtually unique one.

It remained for the first mountaineers, whose goal was McKinley itself, to approach Huntington. Dr. Frederick Cook, the sadly infamous explorer whose fraudulent claims not only to have stood on the summit of McKinley in 1906, but to have reached the North Pole two years later, obscured his genuine accomplishments, led the first party to explore the Ruth Glacier. At the end of his trek, perhaps only a day or two before he photographed his friend Edward Barrille on the top of a minor peak he would pass off as the highest point in North America, he may have glimpsed Huntington's ice-ribbed northern wall across the glacier's great amphitheater. Four years later Belmore Browne explored the northwest branch of the Ruth to its headwall, passing directly beneath that fluted face in a hopeless effort to climb McKinley from the south (something that was not done until 1954). On July 24 he named the graceful mass of ice and rock that loomed over his tracks after the president of the American Geographical Society, Archer Milton Huntington, who had helped sponsor their trip.

Later that year a group of unsystematic sourdoughs discovered that the key to McKinley was in its northeast flank, and in 1913 the summit was finally reached from that side. For twenty years afterward there seemed to be little point in repeating the exploit; the interests of mountaineers had not yet turned to the lower but beautiful and difficult mountains and routes. Height was the only criterion, and the highest thirty or forty mountains in the world, all in the Himalayas, had still not been climbed. When interest in Alaska returned, it concentrated on McKinley; the northeast route, moreover, seemed the only one possible. Men began to fly near the mountains, but their wary approaches left the smaller mountains too distant to reveal their splendors. Eyes riveted on the hulk of McKinley (a mountain bigger than Everest or Aconcagua or Mont Blanc) scarcely had time to examine the mere 12,240-foot tower of Huntington.

Until 1951, indeed, all that had been accomplished in

the range were six ascents of McKinley (all by the original Muldrow route) and the first ascent of Mount Foraker, the second highest mountain in the region. But one man had, since his undergraduate days at Harvard in the early thirties, climbed and photographed these mountains with a quenchless interest. Bradford Washburn had managed to talk some of the best Alaskan bush pilots into flying right next to the gigantic walls of the McKinley Range. Using the photos from these flights at first only for the sake of planning climbs, he amassed over the years probably the finest collection of mountain pictures in the world. Washburn, born too late to have invented Alaskan mountaineering, should be called its greatest figure. His brilliant schemes seem so sensible today that it is difficult to imagine what boldness they took twenty years ago, his planning so thorough and careful that among some twenty different Alaskan expeditions he seems never to have led a failure. For two decades Washburn made one first ascent after another, not only in the McKinley area, but in the Chugach, St. Elias, Hayes, and Fairweather ranges. He was the first man to climb McKinley three times. He was the first, in 1951, to succeed on it by any route other than the Muldrow, when he led the now-classic first ascent of the West Buttress. Once, in the St. Elias Range, he and Bob Bates had to make a forced march more than a hundred miles out to civilization, low on food; but they traversed 17,000-foot Mount Lucania (making its first ascent) simply because it was in their way. Now director of the Museum of Science in Boston, Washburn still has the ageless, hawk-faced look that glares out of the summit photos of his youth. With an impatient dynamism if anything enhanced by age, he urges mountaineers all over the world to climb in Alaska, knowing they will supersede his own accomplishments. But Washburn, strong-willed, dogmatic, has no time for nostalgia: "Now that route on Foraker's simply *begging* to be done—no question about it, the best thing left in the range." Every expedition that goes to Alaska owes something to his experience. His generosity with advice, praise, and access to his photos has, more than any other factor, encouraged Alaskan mountaineering in the post-Washburn generation. But he cannot rest content to know this. Through his clear, proud eyes speaks the urge for just one more try, the sad knowledge that climbing, like life, is one of those things you can never get enough of.

It was Washburn's pictures, far more than the one that had appeared in Browne's *The Conquest of Mount McKinley,* that made climbers first pay attention to Huntington. Flying by its northwest ridge, which seemed to offer the only hope for Huntington's ascent, Washburn in the late fifties took a series of pictures that captured the mountain's incredible sharpness, its slender symmetry, projected not against the flattening backdrop of McKinley but against the limitless vista of lower peaks, glaciers, and tundra to the south. Primarily through these photographs, Huntington became known as Alaska's hidden prize. A limited attempt in 1957 by several Americans on the northwest ridge convinced them of the difficulty of the huge snow towers that studded this knife-edged route, problems which, because of time and supplies, they could not even begin to attack. In the 1962 *American Alpine Journal,* Washburn indicated briefly what sort of attack he felt would have the best chance of subduing the mountain. But not until 1964 did a full-scale effort assault Huntington.

The idea, one he had long cherished, was Lionel Terray's. Washburn had sent photos of the mountain to Terray, the most famous French climber of his time and perhaps the greatest expedition mountaineer who ever lived. In the spring of 1964, with the support of the French Alpine Club, Terray and seven of his countrymen, all outstanding alpinists, flew to Alaska with the ambitious plan of climbing Huntington, a new and extremely difficult route on McKinley, and a new route on Foraker, all in one summer. That they had underestimated Huntington quickly became apparent to them. In addition, they ran into an extraordinarily cold and stormy May. After two weeks of determined effort on the northwest ridge, they were still far from the summit, cold and demoralized. In addition, Terray had seriously injured his shoulder in a near-fatal accident and was forced to direct the attack from a low snow cave. But with fine tenacity, the expedition kept at it. At last, on May 25, two of them stood in a biting wind on Huntington's summit, the first men ever to reach it. The next day the other six, including Terray, who could use only one arm but had gamely insisted on continuing, were also able to get to the top, following the ropes left by their friends. The victory was a sweet one, but its arduous severity left the men in no mood to attempt their other objectives. They flew out from the Ruth Glacier a few days later. For Terray, it was to be the last great mountain he would ever climb, the last achievement in a career that stretched back beyond the already legendary Annapurna ascent in 1950. He was killed on an unimportant cliff in southern France, with Marc Martinetti, also a Huntington veteran, on a sunny day in September 1965 when, for some unknown reason, the two of them fell, still roped together, 1,200 feet to their death.

Usually after its first ascent a mountain passes into a period of disregard. Perhaps fifty Americans had had their eyes on Huntington before the French succeeded in climbing it; none of them felt much desire now simply to repeat their route, especially since there were so many other good climbs left in Alaska.

One of the people who had wanted to do Huntington was Don Jensen. Don had grown up near San Francisco, where he had learned to love the outdoors. As early as he could remember, his parents had taken his older brother and him on long hiking and camping trips in the Sierra Nevada Mountains. The summer peacefulness of those mountains had stayed with him. During high school, while he had enthusiastically thrown himself into football, debating, and half a dozen other activities, he had always longed to get away from the city and back into the mountains. When Don had gone to Harvard as a freshman in 1961, one of the first things he had done was to join the mountaineering club. It was through the club, the following year, that I met Don. We liked each other from the start, and soon became best friends. On weekend trips we climbed rock cliffs in New York or ice gullies in New Hampshire. Over Christmas, we spent a week climbing together in Colorado. But while I liked Harvard, Don felt oppressed by the school and decided to drop out the next spring. In March, we regretfully said goodbye to each other at the Boston bus depot. We got together that summer on a Harvard Mountaineering Club expedition to Mount McKinley, when with five others, we made the first direct ascent of its north face.

The next year, Don was back in school. We both lived in Dunster House, and got together to talk mountaineering nearly every day. We climbed again in Colorado during Christmas vacation, this time for eleven days. Meanwhile we planned an expedition to Mount Deborah, in Alaska's Hayes Range, a mountain almost the same height as Huntington and remarkable in many of the same ways. Toward the end of our planning, we decided, perhaps as proof of our friendship, to limit our party to the two of us.

The trip was a failure. We failed to climb Mount Deborah, and ran into a dozen dangerous situations during our forty-two days there. The mountain was made of a crumbly, ugly gray-blue schist, often little solider than the snow plastered to it. The climbing we found on it was spectacular and frightening. Toward the end of the trip, Don fell sixty feet into a crevasse from which it took a whole day to extricate him. On our hike out, we ran out of food. Because of the intensity of being forced together for so long (for more than a month, we never got farther than a rope-length apart), we began to antagonize each other. We spent much of the trip in silent anger and parted at the end of the summer with harsh words. Don had dropped out of Harvard for good, so we saw each other during the next school year not at all. Gradually, though, our feelings of hostility wore off and nostalgia wore on. We wrote each other letters, business-like at first; but we softened, and awkwardly apologized. After that, it didn't take long to decide to give it another try. Don was working in California. The difficulty of arranging another expedition was thus compounded by the difficulty of communication. We independently ran through the possibilities: Foraker, Deborah again, the new south face route on McKinley, Mount Dall, and eventually Huntington. Don and I had glimpsed Huntington among the clouds for a moment in July 1963, as we stood on the top of McKinley. And we had spent long winter afternoons in Washburn's office, before Deborah, going over pictures, some of which had revealed to us the beauty of Huntington. We knew the mountain was likely to be made of the good granite climbers had found nearby, though the French had run into so little rock that they couldn't vouch for its general quality. I went to Washburn's office again, but the verdict we had drawn from the pictures the year before seemed inflexible: the northwest ridge, to which the French had beat us, was the only reasonable route. Huntington is shaped like a triangular pyramid, and on such a steep mountain only the ridges seem feasible. But the east ridge, though perhaps not much more difficult than the French route, was bound to be more hazardous: huge hanging glaciers, the most dangerous formation imaginable, sprawled obscenely down the ridge. This route, it was clear, would be the kind that would put a party in a state of perpetual nervousness. When the risks depend solely on chance, not skill, the mountaineer enjoys them as little as anyone. On the other hand, the south ridge looked incredibly difficult; it was not so much a ridge as five separate, serrated peaks, each increasingly higher. To traverse them all would involve gaining perhaps three times as much altitude as the east ridge would require, and the necessity of cutting oneself off from the base camp might be unavoidable.

We thus began to forget about Huntington, not without a sense of wistful regret—after all, this was the mountain that had been described as "the most beautiful in Alaska"; surely it was one of the most striking in the world. I sat in Washburn's office one day in January 1965, frustrated by what his pictures made clear as I flipped through the last of a batch he had taken only four months before. There were a few of the west face, a magnificent wall of sheer rock that Washburn hadn't photographed before, but obviously impossible . . . unless that barely protruding rib might divide the avalanches and falling rock . . . but no, it was ridiculous. A pair of pictures, though, made a stereoscopic pair, and by crossing my eyes I could suddenly see the wall in three dimensions. Astonishingly, the rib actually did protrude—what a beautiful, natural line it seemed, then, arrowing straight toward the summit. Full of excitement, I wrote Don that night. Yet as I began to think about it, the hunch seemed more and more impractical. No one had ever climbed a real face in Alaska; nearly all of them are too dangerous. Furthermore, the route looked more difficult than the one we had tried on Deborah, and if we hadn't been able to climb that, how could we hope for Huntington? But I sent copies of the pictures to Don. He quickly wrote back telling me what nonsense the idea was, scolding me and enumerating the problems and disadvantages. Sobered, I agreed and started thinking about Foraker again. But Don's next letter admitted that the Huntington idea had, of course, intrigued him even though it was unthinkable. I wrote back wondering if we could make a reconnaissance over to Huntington at the end of a Foraker expedition. But the fever had traveled 3,000 miles across the antiseptic table of America, and Don's next letter was ungovernably enthusiastic about Huntington. "We've *got* to do it," he almost said. It wasn't hard for me to cast off my newborn doubts and enter with him a pledge to a challenge in which, we admitted to each other, there was certainly less than an even chance of success. Yet a gallant failure, a failure on the sort of route that had never been done in Alaska, seemed more valuable to us than another "good route" in the style of our McKinley climb, one generally admired, but which added little to the possibilities of mountaineering.

2 ▲ The Plan

Don and I agreed that a four-man expedition would
be best. Our third, Matt Hale, was a certainty from
the beginning. Matt, a year younger than Don and I,
had grown up in Virginia, where there was little to
stimulate his interest in the mountains. But during sum-
mers spent in the Adirondacks of New York, he had
discovered the excitement of woods and cliffs, of
getting above the trees where there was only sky and
rock. Yet he had never been in big mountains, nor
hiked any trails west of the Mississippi, before college.

Matt came to Harvard from St. Paul's School in

New Hampshire, where he had done very well academically. But, like Don, Matt probably felt more of an inclination toward the athletic than toward the scholarly life. He joined the mountaineering club at the beginning of his freshman year. Matt's father had also been a member of the HMC, during the years that Washburn and Bates had been there. Perhaps Matt was conscious of family tradition; in any case, he soon discovered that mountaineering would be his primary interest in school.

I first met Matt on a beginners' trip to the Shawangunk Cliffs in New York, in the fall of 1962. While all the other beginners were sweating and trembling on the easiest routes (as a beginner should, we presumed, if he had a safe respect for the mountains), Matt was having astonishingly little trouble. He surprised me at first. He looked thin and frail, and he was almost painfully shy, speaking politely and only when someone asked him a question. He was climbing so well, however, that he was attracting a lot of attention among the older members of the club. Matt seemed almost oblivious to the attention. Obviously, he was not showing off. I liked this quality in him immediately.

However, prodigies often appear in a sport like climbing, especially in rock climbing. Balance, strength, and smoothness may be as much innate as learned; hence a beginner often can climb a very difficult cliff, with a rope from above. It is the subtle matter of judgment that makes a good mountaineer, that requires season after season in the mountains; the HMC's (or any other club's) function, far more than to teach skills, is to teach judgment. Often, the rock-climbing prodigy loses interest as the novelty wears off, and as he sees how much there is yet to learn, even for him. Matt seemed to be the opposite sort. He wanted to know everything about climbing, and he was clearly aware of the gaps in his experience. He seemed as much embarrassed by the attention he was arousing as eager for it. His shyness, of course, could have camouflaged a strong private ambition, but so could the enthusiasm of any of us.

Matt climbed with Don and me in Colorado over Christmas, 1963. During the school year, he quickly became an accomplished climber in all respects. After Deborah, I climbed with Matt in Colorado in August, where we first tackled a high mountain together. We began to sense a technical co-operation that is rare even between long-standing partners. With Don gone from Harvard my senior year, Matt became my best friend.

We had talked about the expedition as early as December 1964. Matt was attracted to Huntington, but admitted he had little basis on which to judge our chances. He seemed wary of our wild enthusiasm, especially in the face of a doubtful success. It took longer to infect him with the excitement of the plan, with what Don and I called "commitment."

We needed a fourth. Matt and I climbed together often during the school year, discussing possibilities, keeping our eyes open for the "right" man. I enjoyed climbing with Matt then more than with anyone else. We had developed the camaraderie and communicative precision that makes a good "rope." We were roughly equal in ability, and got increasingly better at much the same rate, so that our climbing partnership never grew one-sided. I tried to share with Matt some of the anticipatory pleasure I felt for Alaska, an exultation blended of nostalgia and the appeal of a "perfect" route, untempered by fear or reluctance. But he couldn't help but feel divided, as I had felt before my first expedition, between irrational fear and rational conservatism, between the dregs of dread and the appeal of the plan. His imagination dwelt on reports he had heard of post-expedition exhaustion and satiation, projecting over two months the little discomforts he had known camping and climbing on weekends. (How long could he stand eating the same dehydrated foods, drinking melted snow, never having his hands warm outside a sleeping bag, never being able to relax in front of a warm fire?) He had no nostalgia to feed his excitement, no experience to cement his expectations. He knew that big mountains are always dangerous.

This is to say that Matt, as yet, lacked the feeling of total commitment that Don and I not only had but demanded. Yet one might well wonder why we should ask that kind of involvement—indeed, how was it possible for us to feel it? Without being necessarily "antisocial," climbing of the sort we were preparing for, a four-man party alone for two months in the most rugged mountains in North America, requires if not a

fundamental loneliness of soul, at least a temporary
ability to do without most of the other people in the
world. Don and I had found we could enjoy long
periods of self-sufficiency in the mountains. If we grew
to miss many of civilization's comforts, their appeal
never equaled the taut excitement of the way of life we
could lead on expeditions. Although I could rational-
ize it, I never understood the intensity of my feeling
for Alaska. To chalk it up to nostalgia would have
avoided the question. To observe that once life has
become momentarily precious it can never again fail to
dissatisfy when it is merely routine still barely gets
beneath the skin of the problem. The sense of commitment was, for us, not primarily a personal loyalty we
felt toward each other. The expedition's personnel
were interchangeable in a way its ambition was not;
that is, for me not to have climbed with Don would
have been disappointing, but not to have climbed at all
would have been much more so. Hence the mountains,
in a sense, could mean more to me than people could.
But what sort of relationship is possible between a
man and a mountain? If any, an obviously one-sided
one; and if the mountain only mirrors the man, if the
route he chooses is not made out of rock, snow, and ice
so much as out of some tortured translation of his ego,
then that clean love he can feel toward his objective
would become a barren narcissism. "Have we vanquished an enemy?" Mallory said. "None but ourselves." Put that way, it sounds noble, it rings with
aphoristic authority. But what would happen, I wonder,

if the self could be vanquished? What would be left of life but to live it out in smug lethargy? Could any man who had vanquished himself ever want to climb another mountain? I would like to believe that Mallory himself could never have relaxed into complacency; that when he climbed into the clouds on Everest never to be seen again, he died, like Terray, still full of dreams of other summits. I need to believe, if only to explain climbing, that the dissatisfactions of life ultimately become its joys, that to resolve may be only to die, not to answer. Therefore for me the mountain must be there, real; it must, as much as anything I will ever have contact or combat with, exist outside myself. The mind may be wonderful, and even self-sufficient, but for the mountaineer it is not large enough by itself. It and the heart and the body, all that make up man, require response, not only love and co-operation but hindrance and hate, not only friends but enemies. If a mountain, Huntington for instance, was not an enemy we could impute any malice to, did that make it a less formidable one? What can be more appalling than the sovereign power of nature directed by no mind, spirited by no will, indifferent, dwarfing? What vision of malignity can equal the darkness of that of a universe that is running down, of a cosmos that neither orders nor obeys man's yearnings, but blindly collapses toward a final motionlessness? Death, our only glimpse of that entropic end, has its seductive fascination. Hence, the risks of climbing stir and motivate us, just as other risks may someday stir some cosmic voyager.

But I suppose this does not really explain. At best it can hint at what the mountain meant to me; yet if I understood that at all well I would explain it better. If I understood it, though, perhaps I wouldn't care enough about it to want to explain it. Nor does all this explain how Don felt, or how Matt eventually would. The mountain was beautiful; perhaps that is all that need be said. That, and that it would be very hard to climb.

But as the months flew past, and Matt and I in Cambridge and Don in San Francisco went through the welcome frenzy of figuring out every detail of food, time, and equipment, we still lacked a fourth. At last we agreed to ask an Alaskan mountaineer whom Don and I had met on McKinley. He wrote, regretting that he'd be unavailable for the summer. The same obstacle snagged our second choice, a Washington native who had made Mount Foraker's second ascent.

Lurking in the back of my mind had been another possibility: a close friend of ours at Harvard, a climber whose only drawback seemed to be inexperience. But Ed Bernd had learned climbing more quickly in his two years with the HMC than anyone I'd ever known. In addition, that spring he seemed to get even better, as if he had skipped several grades to emerge as a good technical climber. That kind of progress always makes one wary, but Matt and I agreed that Ed showed uncommon judgment as well. Personally, he would be very good. His outstanding characteristic was a cheerful easygoingness that Matt, Don, and I were incapable of.

In the middle of April Matt and I went up to talk to Ed. When we asked him to go with us, he didn't know at first what to say. He was too flattered to conceal it, but we insisted that he not let that influence his decision. Whether or not it did, only he could have said. Yet there never seemed, after the first moment, to be any hesitation in his mind. Even though it would be hard for him to finance, he assured us he would make it work. Ed was like that. If he wanted things to work, they usually did. He immediately joined us for the final planning period, a last six weeks of school that passed beyond the hectic into the frantic. Not only did Ed's buoyancy through it all surprise and please us, but it added to our confidence. Don noticed in our letters how perfectly the expedition had congealed. Now that Ed was with us it seemed ridiculous that we should ever have had doubts about him.

So despite finals, despite running the HMC, putting out its biennial journal, and helping to arrange another expedition, Matt, Ed, and I spent three or four hours a day preparing for Huntington. We would get together at dinner in Quincy House, so as not to waste the time merely eating that we could use for talking. The discussions would start rigorously: how many angle pitons we were going to take *had* to be decided today; could we talk that guy out of his microbus for less than $800? What was Ed going to do for a down jacket? By the third dessert we were always lost in aimless speculation: Ed's "What if" trailed into Matt's "The chances are"—both drowned out by my "Last year

▲ 235

on Deborah"—. Don's letters grew more and more excited and less and less coherent. It was becoming obvious that the time it took for him to write them (since our poverty precluded cross-country phone calls) was actually beginning to interfere with more important things. There just didn't seem to be any time left. Yet had it taken any longer for summer to come we couldn't have waited.

Everything around me, the color of the sunset over the Charles, the shape of Leverett Towers, took on the aura of an invisible world of pure rock, ice, and air 5,000 miles away. When I descended the steps in Harvard Square to the MTA train I half expected to find in the dark the cold blue inside of a crevasse. When I scanned clusters of symbols in a detested math book, I saw a joyous jumble of rock towers strung along some windswept ridge.

Whether or not Ed and Matt suffered the same hallucinations, the obstacles and hours proved finite. One afternoon in early June, after a ritual beer at Cronin's (the precedent having been set by Don and me the year before), we lumbered west in the overloaded microbus we had bought for $800 anyway, intending to meet Don at my home in Boulder, Colorado, for a last fit of packing before we could head for Alaska.

We made only one stop so Ed could drop some things off at his home near Philadelphia. Ed had lived there all his life. He had grown up in typically urban surroundings. Family vacations had ranged as far as Jones Beach, but there was nothing in his childhood to spur an interest in mountains. He had read about mountains, seen hills, but the high, white cold of Alaska might have seemed remote and uninteresting to him then. Yet Ed seemed to succeed at everything he tried. He was a school hero: tall, and ruggedly handsome, he became a football star, president of his high-school class three years in a row, the most popular student, and the first from his school ever to go to Harvard: at eighteen, almost something of a civic monument. At Harvard, the HMC had been for Ed just another activity at first, something new to try. But as he discovered the fear and fascination of climbing, he must have realized that this was an entirely different sort of thing. Mountains might end in summits, but there was no limit to the mountaineer's urge. In the summer after his freshman year, he hitch-hiked to Canada. There, for the first time, he saw the Rockies. They looked huge and mysterious. Sadly enough, Ed couldn't find anybody to go climbing with him, so he had to content himself with a few hikes among their lower reaches. By the time he got back, the mountains had infected him. The bigger, the better; if he could have gone to Alaska alone, he probably would have, much as his parents might have opposed it.

We arrived at his house at 3:00 A.M., waking up Ed's parents, whom Matt and I met then for the first time. They were glad we had stopped, even at that hour. Ed's mother made us sandwiches while we talked. We sensed the edge of an awkward feeling, because none of us really wanted to talk about Huntington, yet that was clearly all any of us could think about. Then we got ready to leave; they told us to be careful. We said goodbye, stepping out the door into the cool, wet scent of azaleas that saturated the predawn air.

3 ▲ The Long Road

Don met us in Boulder. It had been nearly a year since I'd seen him, and I scarcely recognized him now. He had a magnificent tan, a mustache, and was thirty pounds lighter than I'd ever known him, in the best shape of his life. Ed, who hadn't got to know Don very well in their one year together at Harvard, quickly grew to like him now. The pace of preparation, decelerated briefly during our drive to Colorado, picked up again. To divide and pack the food we usurped most of two houses for a week. A further complication was our having to buy all our supplies in Denver, and on our second day there, the worst flood in the city's history hit it. We bought our canned food the afternoon before the warehouse they came from burned down in the night; we had to outwit National Guardsmen to get across town, and by the time we were ready to leave, the only roads open led, fortunately, to the north.

Everything we would need on the mountain somehow managed to fit into the microbus, even leaving room for us to be comfortable. The back of the bus became our bedroom where two people could lie full-length in sleeping bags. We were determined to drive straight through to Alaska, a feat that didn't seem difficult with four drivers. The year before, Don and I had driven nonstop from Boston, six days and six nights that passed in a delirium of No-Doz numbness, oncoming headlights, and trees that suddenly jumped into the road. But this year the road was shorter, because of our Colorado headstart, and the driver, far from ever having to feel ill-rested, could be reasonably sure of someone to talk to during his spell at the wheel. Near the Wyoming border we stretched the expedition budget to include the latest *Playboy* and a bagful of firecrackers, the latter of which somehow showed up in Ed's pockets on the Tokositna Glacier on July 4.

The driving, for a while, was easy. As we got farther and farther north, the land grew rockier and less populated, the air cleaner and colder, the nights shorter. At stops for gas or picnic supplies, we played football on the highway, or, if a building looked challenging enough, worked out first ascent routes on its walls. After a few moments of frantic exercise, we would pile back into the bus, to lie catching our breath as the driver headed north again. We had planned to stop to eat, but we found it easy to spread our picnics in the back of the bus.

Ed especially enjoyed the driving. He waited eagerly for his turn, and never seemed to have any trouble staying alert, even in the small hours of the night. In fact, when someone else was driving, Ed would stay awake as long as he could, staring out the window at everything that flew past, even during the long stretches that were monotonously similar. Ed had been through some of this country the year before, hitch-hiking, but he could never see enough of it. Don and I were familiar with it, too, but less curious. Don, who probably had been working at a more feverish pitch than any of us during the last month, used the trip to relax, sleeping as often as he could. But he had trouble getting a good sleep in the moving bus, as did Matt. Sometimes one or the other of them would dream the bus was going off the road, and wake with a lurch to grab the wheel. Ed, who always seemed to be driving during the night, had no trouble fighting them off.

All in all, though, it was a relaxed and relaxing trip. Wyoming meandered by, and a long night's drive into Montana got us to Billings just as we ran out of gas. During these days, the first all four of us had shared, we began to feel a cohesive spirit, to believe that we were an expedition. Just as we would later on a high glacier and a precipitous wall of rock, we carried with us everything we needed, and cared about little except getting to our goal.

We had decided to cross Glacier National Park, not only to whet our mountain appetites, but because its border station stayed open most of the night. As it was, we got there in broad daylight. Poverty-stricken as we were becoming, we could scarcely justify to ourselves spending the half-dollar-a-head entrance fee; so Matt and I hid under the sleeping bags, several boxes of food, and the distractingly opened *Playboy* a few miles before the entrance. It was terriby hot under all that stuff. When the bus came to a stop we held our breath. We could hear Don's end of a conversation; then we were moving again. I started to fight my way out, but Ed put his hand on top of the bag and whispered tensely, "Stay under there! There's a detour and the gate's only three miles ahead."

There was no choice but to suffocate a little longer. Enough time seemed to go by for anything but a donkey to travel three miles, but still no gate. Ed whispered, "Don't move now."

We held our breath again. The bus stopped. We heard the jingle of change as Don paid the attendant.

"Yeah. Just two of us."

A deadly pause. Then Ed's nervous voice:

"No, that's nothing but boxes and sleeping bags and stuff."

I tried to make my heart beat a little more gently so it wouldn't shake the bus. Then Ed yelled, "Move out of here, Don!"

The bus shot off with a squeal of rubber. Matt and I were flung back and forth among the boxes as the bus negotiated some sharp turns.

"Oh God," screamed Ed, "they're coming after us!"

I tried to burrow deeper in with the food. Would they shoot first and ask questions later? Would we have to run a roadblock at the exit?

Suddenly Ed started laughing hysterically. He'd gone berserk. Then Don started laughing, too, and the bus slowed to a stop. Matt and I peeked out from our sarcophagus. We were parked beside a peaceful lake, obviously far inside the park. And Don and Ed couldn't stop laughing.

It took Matt and me a while to regain enough composure to compliment their performance. Then we had lunch, congratulating ourselves on saving a dollar.

But crime does not pay. A few hundred yards beyond our lunch spot, the engine suddenly howled like a cat caught in a garbage disposal; we limped to a pull-out, where it died. The nearest Volkswagen dealer, the park ranger informed us, was in Kalispell, forty miles back, and there was a man who, for a dollar a mile, would be more than glad to tow us there. Necessity is the daughter of disaster, so we accepted the offer.

When we got to Kalispell, it seemed to be Sunday. The tow truck left our bus in the parking lot of the VW place, where we would have to wait for morning.

At the time Mount Huntington might as well have been on the dark side of the moon. We felt miserable. Even football offered us little solace. With nothing to do we walked down the long, dusty road into the main part of town. Outside an open supermarket we held a colloquium to determine whether a hunk of cheese or a loaf of bread would offer the better combination of fillingness and nutrition for the money. Finally we skipped both. After this demonstration of our will to economize, we walked a little farther and decided to waste a dollar each on a movie.

Gradually our spirits improved. We held a conference to decide whose parents we dared call for money, and scraped together all we could of our own. Out of Don's and my pockets came traveler's checks; Matt dug for some loose bills; and Ed dipped into the emergency cache he had sewn into his underpants. The very sacrifices we made healed our feelings; soon we were joking again, and we slept well that night on the parking lot. The next morning, a man put a new engine in our bus for a hundred dollars less than we had anticipated. Joyously we set out again around noon. Though disclaiming any superstitiousness, all four of us paid for readmittance to the park. Without even crossing our fingers, we passed the spot of our earlier demise. But a few miles farther, Don swerved to avoid a tourist troupe blundering down the middle of the road, and hit some rocks that inflicted simultaneous blowouts on our right front and rear tires.

This time only Matt and Don had to leave the park, and they courageously found service stations before Kalispell. They returned, the bus rolled again, and at last we crossed the mountains into Canada determined to push or carry the bus the rest of the way if it quit on us again.

We got through Calgary with comparative ease and stopped for final purchases in Edmonton, the last big city on our route and the farthest outpost of the land of reasonable prices. At last, about two weeks behind schedule, we began the 1,200-mile trek of the Alaska Highway, nearly all of it dirt road. Every gas station along the way pumped nostalgia into Don and me for the two previous years we had traveled the road. We stopped at Liard Hot Springs near the Yukon border and bathed in the steaming pools in the rain. We talked to a man who had driven alone from South Carolina and had just decided to go back because it was getting too cold. But to us, the cold spoke only of the nearness of our mountain, as did the suddenly lengthening days. Driving became a pleasure now; the thirty miles an hour the road demanded permitted us to see what we were passing.

Yet it was all the same, a wall of scraggly trees that reached from one end of the Yukon to the other. Their monotony echoed a loneliness not so much primeval as insidious, empty. I was physically aware that back of the first trees on the right-hand side stretched a dull gloom unbroken to the Arctic coast, far beyond the distant MacKenzie River; that, on the other side, the forests subtly inclined until, abruptly, the trees confronted the frozen edge of the St. Elias Range. I was dimly aware that nothing touched that gloom but three months of rain and nine of snow; that rivers raged somewhere in that wilderness where only bears and birds had ever heard them. The road is not beautiful. Its scenery oppresses rather than enthralls. Wordsworth could not have written there. One senses in that country only a self-sufficient, ragged evenness, broken occasionally by the whelming power of a river in flood.

In the afternoon we approached the St. Elias Range, and glimpsed through the foothills one of the high peaks far within it, perhaps Mount Kennedy. The wind blew us around Kluane Lake; soon we were driving in a furious storm. The gusts lashed our bus with a staccato of rain through an unnatural, foreboding darkness as we crossed the swollen Donjek, the river along which Washburn and Bates had had to backtrack twenty miles to find a crossing in 1937, during their escape from Lucania. But overnight the storm blew itself out. I woke around 4:00 A.M. to find the bus stopped in the road in a heavy drizzle several miles short of Alaska. Our vehicle seemed to respect national boundaries too highly. We couldn't figure out what was wrong, and it was no fun lying under the bus in the cold mud guessing. At last two natural mechanics who happened by unplugged our fuel line with a coat-hanger.

Suddenly we were in Alaska. Matt didn't acknowledge my boisterous claim that things immediately looked bigger and better. Instead he replied that all he noticed were more trees and more holes in the road, now that it was paved. We stopped for a picnic and shave near the Delta River, then started down the highway to Anchorage. Along the road we could see a different

246 ▲

South-Central Alaska

kind of mountain, almost Colorado-like; but, as if to assure us we hadn't driven in a circle, the huge, clean Matanuska Glacier sprawled out of the Chugach Range almost down to the road. We spent a day in Anchorage gathering the last of our equipment, a few impulsively chosen delicacies for our candlelight dinners in August, and the indispensable pint of victory brandy. Then we gassed up the bus, prayed over it, and started our last drive through the night to the tiny town of Talkeetna.

I was driving at 3:00 A.M., the others asleep, as the bus topped a little ridge suddenly to reveal the Alaska Range filling the horizon. There was a cloud layer at about 12,000 feet, so the summits of McKinley and Foraker and a few others seemed cut off; but the recognizable bulks beneath, eighty miles away, through the occasional gap in which rays of the northern sun flashed, seemed to draw the bus onward the last few miles to Talkeetna. We arrived, threw our sleeping bags down on Don Sheldon's airstrip, and waited for morning, when we would accost Alaska's most famous bush pilot.

4 ▲ The Unknown Glacier

Sheldon was glad to see us, but the clouds had lowered around McKinley by morning, so that he couldn't fly us in right away. We unloaded the bus in his hangar while he showed us relics from other expeditions stored there. There was an especially large pile from the French Huntington expedition to which Sheldon urged us to help ourselves. Within a few hours we were ready to go, but the weather was getting worse. There was nothing to do but wait. We managed a few patchy conversations with Sheldon, who literally never stood still. We wanted to make sure he could land in the narrow basin of the upper Tokositna Glacier; he impatiently said, "Yep, we'll get her fixed up," and forged back into the middle of whatever anecdote he had been telling. His wife, Roberta, smiled at us knowingly, then tried to interpret her husband's cryptic assurances to us when he was gone.

We wasted as much time as we could writing letters, walking around Talkeetna, or greeting the twice-daily train. Matt and I, tired of football, found an old softball and bat in the schoolhouse, repaired the backstop behind it, and invented an elaborate two-man game. A couple of eight-year-old girls fell in love with the newly arrived diamond heroes; in despair we converted them to outfielders. With them they brought a retinue of more fearless, younger natives, who insisted on digging holes and tunnels in the sand between the pitcher's mound and first base. Most of the time our game was reduced to a bunting contest.

Don, who was at last in his element, spent the hours fiddling with equipment, studying the maps, or climbing on top of Sheldon's hangar to look at the weather. Ed, on the other hand, seemed gloomier than usual. He sat in the bus, writing long letters, and declined our invitations to softball or football. He seemed apprehensive. Perhaps it was a combination of excitement and awe. We walked a few blocks down the small lane that was Talkeetna's main street, to the edge of the Susitna River. The churning current, nearly a mile wide, was carrying dead trees and branches swiftly past us. Fascinated, we stared for most of an hour at the

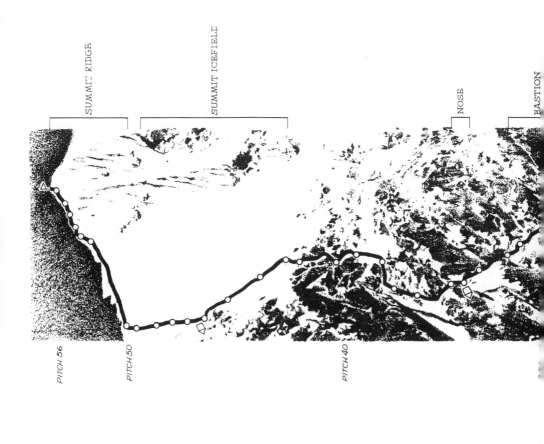

SUMMIT RIDGE

SUMMIT ICEFIELD

NOSE

BASTION

PITCH 56

PITCH 50

PITCH 40

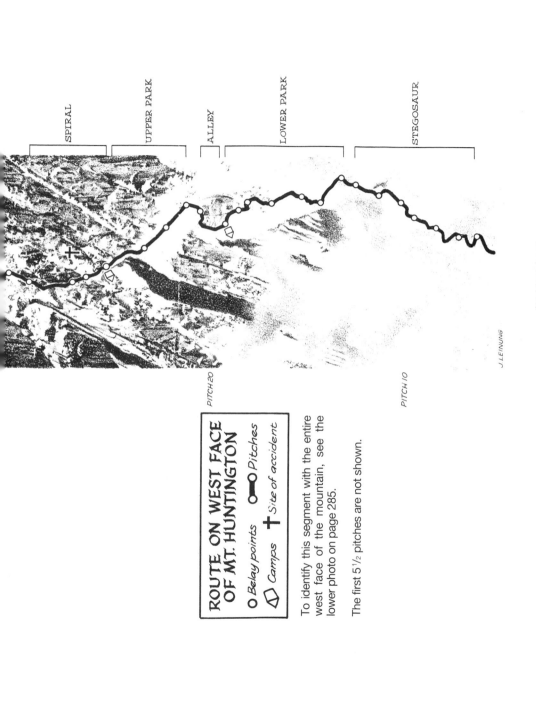

ROUTE ON WEST FACE
OF MT. HUNTINGTON

o Belay points   o━●o Pitches
◇ Camps   ✝ Site of accident

To identify this segment with the entire west face of the mountain, see the lower photo on page 285.

The first 5½ pitches are not shown.

SPIRAL

UPPER PARK

ALLEY

LOWER PARK

STEGOSAUR

PITCH 20

PITCH 10

J. LEINING

intricate weavings of the river. For me, it was like a glimpse of the mountains themselves: the mountains which, however motionless, had the same kind of chaotic power.

By evening of the second day, the clouds lifted from the range. Sheldon told us to be ready at four the next morning, so that he could fly us in with the best possible snow conditions for landing. As we went to sleep, I still pessimistically expected it to be raining in the morning. But Sheldon woke us with, "Let's get a move on, she's a fine one." Matt and I quickly dressed, dumped our gear in Sheldon's Cessna, and put on our down jackets, despite the 70-degree warmth of Talkeetna, for we would step out of the plane in a cold glacial corridor at 9,000 feet. Just before taking off, Sheldon seemed to remember something. He got out his jackknife and started to prune one of the trees in his yard. Matt and I were impatient to go. I started to ask Sheldon if that couldn't wait till after he'd flown us in. Then I realized that he wanted some boughs to throw out of the plane while he was over the glacier, in order to judge the shape of its slope, which would be otherwise unreadable in the flat light of mid-morning. Matt piled the boughs on his lap, Sheldon started the engine, and we sputtered down the rocky runway.

Just before it seemed we would plunge into the Susitna River, at about forty-five miles an hour, we floundered into the air. The plane was probably overloaded, but once in the air it seemed content. So were Matt and I. Eighty miles away, the Alaska Range stuck into the faultless sky, differentiable only as three white masses: McKinley, Hunter, and Foraker. There was nothing else on which to fix our attention for the first fifteen minutes except the trackless tundra beneath us, threaded by silver rivers that wound their ways outward, like snakes escaping the mountains that spawned them. After a while we could pick out Huntington, its summit visible above a thin cloud layer. Its separation from the mountains near it seemed to increase. Then, as we passed over the snout of the glacier, Huntington was suddenly silhouetted against the sky rather than against McKinley. Its astonishing sharpness struck us, even though we were prepared for it. Suddenly the clouds broke; we were right in the gorge of the Tokositna. In a matter of seconds we flashed past the west face. Both of us had just run out of film. But we stared at the wall, so close I was half afraid the plane would crash. Sheldon banked sharply left, heading us up the basin toward Hunter. I looked at our pilot's face. He didn't seem perturbed, yet these incredible walls were just outside the plane's window. We were obviously too high to land, but too low to clear the pass ahead. The plane banked suddenly and as I gave up hope, Sheldon made a complete circle within the basin, lowering as he turned. Then he instructed us to throw the boughs out, carefully, one at a time. As they whipped out of my grasp, Sheldon kept circling, watching each one fall. The light on the glacier was so flat that the boughs never seemed to hit it, but simply to stop falling. We spiraled lower and lower. Then Sheldon said, "OK.

We're taking her in." He made a last turn and straightened out. I still couldn't tell where the snow was, whether it was fifty feet below or five hundred. Suddenly a wall of whiteness seemed to leap in front of the plane. Sheldon pulled back on the stick; the stall warning screamed; we topped the rise and landed in one motion. I kept saying "beautiful, beautiful" but Sheldon told us to hurry up and get the stuff out of the plane. I opened the door and jumped out; the snow was crisp and solid. Matt threw our stuff out; then we stood clear, and Sheldon took off down the glacier to get Ed and Don. We saw him round the bend, a dot now against the surrounding walls. Then even the sound of the engine was gone, and we stood there alone.

All there was for us to do was to place the boughs in a row to indicate a runway for Sheldon's next landing. We put on our snowshoes, roped up, and got this done quickly. Then we sat on our packs and waited. It wasn't nearly as cold as I had anticipated; in fact the fierce sun made the glacier seem like a summer beach. We were far up its northwest branch, much closer to Hunter than to Huntington. Steep avalanche slopes walled this precipitous basin. At the other end of it, five miles away, was our west face. It was too bad Sheldon hadn't been able to land closer, for it would probably take us most of a week to get our supplies over to a base camp; but that he had been able to land at all seemed remarkable.

In 1906 Belmore Browne's party had crossed the mouth of the Tokositna, putting a camp near a huge boulder that marked the middle of it. But for them, no one had ever stood on the glacier until this day, June 29, 1965. No one had ever explored any of its nine branches, which wind back into mazes of unclimbed, unnamed peaks, even though several parties have walked the full lengths of the neighboring glaciers, the Ruth and the Kahiltna. Our original plan had been to hike in; but the delays that had put us two weeks behind schedule demanded the quickest possible approach. Still, as I sat on this new glacier, enjoying all the sensual novelty of the air, the stillness, and the sun, I had a feeling that we had cheated, or at least a regret that we had forfeited the experiences of hiking seventy miles across the tundra and up the glacier. After two expeditions on which we had walked both in and out, flying, for Don and me, had to be a mixed pleasure.

Of course Matt's thoughts at the moment were different. He seemed, understandably, subdued; to suddenly find oneself in a place like this for the first time was bound to be chastening. Matt probably felt neither the sense of having cheated nor the sense of having missed anything. But I couldn't really know what he was thinking; and I wanted to, then. I could remember my first sight of McKinley, but that was from a road. I could try to empathize with him, but he was difficult to interpret. He couldn't explain the strange mixture of sensations he must have felt then, even if he had wanted to; and perhaps he didn't.

But what I write now must in some way stand for all four of us. Climbing together, which forces men

close to each other physically and sometimes spiritu-
ally, still can't overcome the irreducible barriers of
their separate selves. Nor can writing ultimately trans-
late the experience. So in words, all that may ultimately
get through is some third-hand filtration of life that
was once lived. A man's best moments seem to go by
before he notices them; and he spends a large part of
his life reaching back for them, like a runner for a
baton that will never come. In disappointment, he
grows nostalgic; and nostalgia inevitably blurs the
memory of the immediate thrill, which, simply because
it had to be instantaneous, could not have lasted. Now
that our whole expedition has passed, now that I sit in
a warm room with a pencil and blank paper before me,
instead of rock and snow, I feel our vanished moments
forever lost. I want to wreathe their remnants with
feelings I never felt before, especially not while the
moments lived. The frustration of it reminds me, too,
how I felt sitting on my pack on June 29 waiting for
the plane, wanting to know what Matt was thinking.
People placed in any isolation, even together, lose
something of their humanity; and a style of isolation
so complete as mountaineering begs for someone to
understand it, to convey it as it is, not as the melo-
drama of death and blind courage it seems to resemble.
Courage plays a smaller part than the tension and
dependence that being alone together in a dangerous
place forces on men. The drama is a largely internal
one, whose conflict stems from the stress between private desire and co-operative skill that climbing im-

poses. Perhaps this is why mountaineers are usually inarticulate; everything having to do with climbing seems to stifle the soul's urge to communicate. Part of the strange sorrow I felt then, on the glacier, must have arisen from the dilemma no more peculiar to me than to anyone, of being born alone with the desire not to be. If the mind can escape itself little better than the body can, still, something goes on between men, even in mountains, something lost in the static rigor of reporting it. The men who have gone through the tension of an expedition have not written about it well. No one has explained the basic truths of climbing, the interplay beneath its alternating fear and hope. What goes on in those lonely places is so much more than pitons hammered, camps moved; what goes on, not only within men, but between them, is sometimes profound. Yet I feel that I cannot get at the heart of it either. Perhaps I care too much; perhaps so long as I care, I can never explain; perhaps if I stop caring, I will forget.

Nor did these thoughts go through my head then. There was too much to see; it was only a slight pang, a feeling rather than a thought. There were little things to do, like putting glacier cream on our faces, or reading the temperature. Then suddenly we heard the plane's buzz, and Sheldon flew into sight around the bend in the glacier. He landed perfectly. Ed stepped out of the plane with a raucous whoop and pulled a remarkable pile of rope and food boxes out of the plane. In a few moments, Sheldon was off again. With

Ed, we moved our supplies nearer the center of the glacier, in case the avalanches had unusually long runouts. Before we expected it, Sheldon was back with Don and the last of our equipment. It was starting to cloud up, so Sheldon was anxious to get on his way. He snapped a few pictures of the four of us beside the plane, with our cameras, and took off.

We tried to think what we might possibly have forgotten. We had enough salt, plenty of matches; I'd even brought the football. Then someone remembered the radio. It was still in Sheldon's hangar. Matt and Ed were a little disturbed but Don and I tried to cajole them out of worrying. We hadn't had a radio on McKinley; the one we took to Deborah had quit working after a week, and we had to carry its six useless pounds all the rest of the trip. At best, a radio is a big help in an emergency; at worst, a false source of confidence. We could do without it. I think Don and I even partly welcomed the further isolation imposed by its absence.

After pitching our tents, we basked in the sun the rest of the day, not out of laziness, but because one travels on Alaskan glaciers at night. Until late July, it is light enough even at midnight for comfortable travel. Until then one never needs a flashlight or a candle, even for reading inside the tent. We fell asleep in the afternoon, then set out at 2:00 A.M. with heavy loads. The four of us were roped together at 150-foot intervals so that we would always be stretched as far apart as possible in case of a crevasse fall. I led; Matt came second, Ed third, and Don brought up the rear.

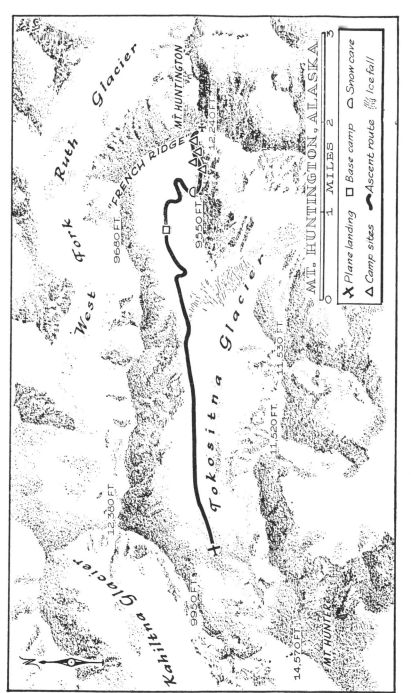

Mt. Huntington and the Tokositna Glacier

The Tokositna was, for Matt and Ed, their first glacier; for Don and me, our first since the day a year before when Don had plunged into a crevasse on the Susitna Glacier, badly cutting his face in the second of two serious crevasse falls in as many days. Now the glacial surface seemed utterly featureless under a gloomy, overcast sky. I felt nervous leading, especially since the temperature was a warm 35° F., but the snow's crust stayed firm all night.

Crevasses, just as they are popularly imagined, are long gaping seams in the surface of the ice, formed by the terrible strain of a glacier's flow. The deepest of them drop several hundred feet. But the open holes are no threat, except to the mountaineer's patience in skirting those that are too wide to step or jump across. What the climber fears, with the brutish terror reserved for only a few phenomena, like avalanches and falling rocks, are the hidden crevasses, the ones that form delicate skins of snow-bridge only a foot or two thick and which blend treacherously into the general contours of the glacier. Traveling on the Gillam Glacier in 1964, Don had fallen sixty feet into one of these hidden crevasses, with a 70-pound pack on his back. It was a miracle that he hadn't been seriously hurt. Even so, it took a full, lonely day for the two of us, barely able to hear each other's shouts at the tops of our voices, to improvise a way to get him out. Then, the very next day, when our problems at last seemed to be over, he had fallen thirty feet into another crevasse, sustaining cuts that had infected badly by the time we were able to get out to civilization five days later. The mountaineer never walks easily on a big, unknown glacier. Although he can read all sorts of subtle signs to try to outguess them, crevasses remain one of the least predictable of mountain hazards. And they are often extremely difficult to get out of, even for the uninjured climber, because they characteristically bulge halfway down, leaving overhanging walls of ice above, ready to collapse inward at the slightest pressure. Had I not been safely outside with a rope, Don could never have escaped the first crevasse he fell into the year before. Those icy sepulchers are dark, wet places; corridors shoot in all directions, hideously honeycombing the glacier; and shelves of ice that seem to bottom the crevasses often thinly mask even deeper chambers. In the early days of climbing in the Alps, when ladies in full-length dresses and petticoats strolled the ice, accompanied by well-dressed men who carried shepherd's crooks instead of ice axes, far more deaths were caused by crevasse falls than by any other kind of accident. The gothic imagination, moreover, was stirred to a morbid spasm by the occasional appearance, years later, of well-preserved parts of recognizable bodies, disgorged from the mouths of the ever flowing glaciers. No wonder, then, that contemporary artists painted these crevasses not as holes in the surrounding glacier so much as bottomless gulfs which, themselves, surrounded icy islands of safety.

But the Tokositna seemed pretty safe, at least with the snow as firm as we found it. We went slowly and carefully, and I never stuck so much as a foot in a crevasse. The first three miles of our hike were downhill; then we negotiated a level stretch, the worst-crevassed area yet, before climbing a mile up the other branch of the basin, the one that lay beneath Huntington. Along this route we passed under the uniformly impressive walls of a number of unnamed peaks. For diversion we picked out "impossible" routes that climbers fifty years from now might try, impossible not because of steepness or length or innate difficulty, but because they were swept by avalanches, or because great ice blocks broke off and hurtled down them.

In five and a half hours we had reached the spot beneath our face that we decided to call base camp. Wearily we dumped our loads—it seemed such a pitiful pile for all that work—and contemplated the face as we ate lunch. The temperature was rising and a drizzly snow-rain began to fall. We turned around and hiked back to camp, the long, final uphill stretch particularly tiring us. Our new base camp was actually at a lower altitude than where the plane had landed.

We got a late start the next night, because our tired backs encouraged us to improvise a sled. We taped together sixteen food boxes, about twice what we could have carried, then set up a complicated harness for pulling the thing. But we had to plow away a layer of fresh snow, and the hauling was more work than it was worth. The sled fell apart after two miles, so we simply carried half our load the rest of the way over. Especially tired that night, we slept until 5:30 A.M., and the next day would have been wasted if the snow conditions hadn't stayed so remarkably good. By 9:30 A.M. the temperature was 42° F., yet the snow surface remained hard and safe. In two more days, we had everything we needed at base camp. Already we were making better time on the glacier as we started to get in good shape. We finished the drudgery of hauling on July 4, a beautiful day; Ed appropriately set off a bunch of his loudest firecrackers to celebrate. The echoes rang all over the basin. Since it was so warm anyway, the rest of us refused to attribute any of the countless avalanches on the surrounding walls to Ed's noises.

For several days in a row, Ed and Matt occupied one of our two-man tents, while Don and I slept in the other. We pitched them so that we could roll the sleeve doors together, making a nice "hotel" arrangement, especially handy not only for cooking, but also for conversation. Both Matt and Ed had seemed a bit depressed during the first days; certainly Ed was less buoyant than usual, and Matt acted unenthusiastic. Neither Don nor I worried about this. It was an inevitable reaction to the sudden transition from the outside world; to five days spent in the dwarfing presence of bigger mountains than they had ever seen, the most awesome of which they would soon try to climb; to five days of nocturnal trudging across a glacier featureless enough to lull the mind into boredom, yet always dangerous; to five days filled with the nameless anxieties awakened by a route we could see but not yet attack. But Matt and Ed did their share of the work; if they left most of the decision-making to us, they were cheerful enough about going along with them. And Ed's firecracker outburst suggested that presence would make his heart grow fonder, as it would also for Matt and Don and me.

What I appreciated most was the absence of the tension Don and I had felt last year from the very beginning. On Deborah, because there were only two of us, we went through hours of waiting out storms in the tent, refusing to speak to each other, wishing we could see someone else, anyone else, yet unable to get away from each other. If those worst moments had been balanced by periods of intense companionship, there still had never been a time after the first few days when we could totally relax. We got to know each other, in superficial ways, better than people should; in some important ways, not well enough.

There were recesses in Don, whole areas masked by his outward calm, his self-sufficiency in the mountains, that I couldn't explore. I suppose he felt the same way about me. Once or twice he had said he couldn't understand how I could get so suddenly angry for no apparent reason. On Deborah we had had to hold some part of ourselves apart if for no other reason than sanity. I noticed then an actual tendency, when I felt antagonistic toward Don, unconsciously to identify him with the dangers and hardships of the mountain; both opposed me, both were a kind of enemy. Only a tendency, of course, but a frightening one, when I realized what I was doing. We lacked the balance that the presence of others could lend to the human situations, so that we could distinguish them from the factors over which we had no control. The mere fact that there were four of us this year tripled the possible relationships and added an inconceivable richness of communication, which made it possible for us to relax.

So I greatly enjoyed the first days camping with Don. It was a pleasure, if a frustrating one, to watch his fine mechanical mind at work, building or fixing something. He had a way of planning that overlooked no detail, a sense of orientation that once, on Deborah, had come in especially handy. We had been forced by the crevasse accidents to hike out via the Susitna Glacier, a route we had never anticipated, and one that lay off our maps. We had been going slowly along the side of the glacier, approaching a particularly bad slope we would have to traverse. Don pointed out a pass above us that, as far as I could tell, led aimlessly off into the foothills. He seemed to remember, from having glanced at a map in Cambridge five months earlier, that the pass would lead us out, short-cutting the bad slope along the glacier that we at least knew would eventually lead where we wanted to get. I was skeptical, but Don talked me into it. The pass was easy; it took us in a straight line in the right direction, and saved us a day which, since we eventually ran out of food, might have been crucial.

Don was tremendously strong, and could summon reserves, when he had to, as on that forced hike out, that one could expect from few men. That strength, combined with his carefulness, gave me a confidence climbing with him that was extremely valuable in crisis. And the loyalty to him that I felt after Deborah, once the antagonism had worn off, fed those quenchless fires of nostalgia that will for a long time raise up visions of all the stretches of the Hayes Range which, till now, he and I are the only men ever to have seen. I will never be able to picture those places empty, as they are now and have been since we left them. I have always seen Don there, his strong arms chopping a step on precipitous ice, his calm eyes looking into a storm-choked sunset, squinting against the wind flung from the turbulent north.

On July 4, the same day we finished the hauling, Matt, Don, and I started to explore the steep, crevassed section of icefall above base camp that lay between us and the face. To begin the real climbing, we had to reach a pass, which we called simply "the col," between Huntington and a small peak to the west. The connecting ridge joined the face two-fifths of the way up, where it merged completely into it. But we would have to climb that lower, jagged ridge to get to the face itself. The ridge was a blessing, however. It was what divided the avalanches from above and made the route less than suicidal. Moreover, it divided the upper branch of the glacier from a much lower one, and we knew that the col, so gently approachable (through the icefall) from this side, overlooked a frightful drop on the other. Now, as the three of us reconnoitered, Ed stayed at base camp nursing a bad blister. The icefall, though easy, was far from trivial. We managed to get all the way through it on snowshoes, but had to make some ingenious, steep traverses beside some of the bigger crevasses. Halfway through the icefall, I happened to turn around, and found McKinley staring over my shoulder, incredibly high above us. It was our first view of it since landing.

Don took over the lead for the last bit to the col. He was able to make three tricky snowshoe steps right up to the very top of it. Before Matt or I could get there, he let out an involuntary "Wow!" When we got to the col we saw why; we looked over a 3,000-foot gulf. We couldn't even see the bottom; mist was whipping by as the wind reached us, and all we could sense was an uncontainable space beneath our feet. The feeling was sudden and vivid enough so that I didn't really feel comfortable standing up, especially on snowshoes. The col was scarcely big enough for the three of us.

We started down to tell Ed about our progress. There, on the col, the serious climbing would begin. At last we would be getting somewhere. The sudden exposure had both excited and sobered us. None of us had ever come upon a cliff quite so unwarned. It was as if one got up in the morning, had a cup of coffee, and opened the front door to go to work to find his house was an airplane in flight.

5 ▲ Twenty Days' Despair

The jagged ridge had been the unknown factor on our route, since none of Washburn's photos showed it well. We had anticipated little trouble on it, though, because it was less steep than the face above. Now we weren't so sure. In the first place, large cornices studded every foot of the ridge, overhanging lips of snow that the wind had spent all winter building up and that were destined to collapse within a month. Moreover, all the cornices hung over the near side, so that the moment we began climbing on the ridge we would have to stay slightly below its crest on the other side, with that awful 3,000-foot gulf, in which the darkness seemed to gather and linger, constantly beneath our feet.

We divided the ridge with three names. The first, long, jagged section of it became the "Stegosaur," for its resemblance to the spiny monster that had flourished while the ridge was being formed. Above that we distinguished two steep snowfields, set sideways to the ridge, as the "Lower" and "Upper Parks." Connecting them was a 100-foot ice gully, the "Alley." We hoped in two or three days to reach the Alley, and from there to spend a day crossing the Upper Park, above which rose the face, monolithic, ominous.

But the first problem was simply to get started. On July 5, we carried a light load through the icefall and split into two pairs at the col to try different approaches. Matt and Ed went a quarter-mile closer to the face, beneath the ridge, to try to climb a steep ice wall, tunnel straight through a cornice, and thereby short-cut some of the Stegosaur. Don and I started right at the col. He belayed from the safe side while I led. For thirty feet I could simply walk to the top of a little snow plume. But to continue I had to climb down the back side of it, which was vertical for ten feet. One of the rough maxims of climbing says that snow cannot adhere at more than a 55-degree angle; but snow that undergoes the torture of the wind and cold of big mountains finds that it must disobey the maxim to survive. The little plume I now stood on was the first of many incredible snow and ice features we were to meet on Huntington. I started down the back side of it, trying to kick steps into the crumbly snow with my crampons. Suddenly, a few feet below me, a huge section of cornice broke. Watching it, I had the impression I was riding on top of it. Since it fell on the gentle side of the ridge, it went only a hundred feet; but the pulverizing power of that short fall, of tons of rotten ice sloughing to a halt, was frightening, especially since we had thought the cornices were more stable than that and had been considering pitching a camp under one. I quickly retreated to Don. We were both thinking of Matt and Ed, getting ready to tunnel through just such a cornice. Quickly we circled beneath the ridge, following their steps; we met them just as they were starting up the ice wall below the cornice. Not wishing to alarm them, Don said, "It looks a bit too warm today, guys. We had a little cornice break off near us, so maybe we should wait for better conditions."

Matt looked disappointed; Ed looked as if he were saying to himself, "What are they trying to tell us?" But they gave up the effort and returned with us to the col. When they saw the debris of the broken cornice, they were alarmed. Cornices look so graceful in position that it is easy to forget their tremendous weight and the ugly force with which they can collapse.

Convincing ourselves that the problem was only a matter of temperatures, we decided to spend the rest of the day digging a snow cave just below the col. With our two shovels we started into a 15-degree slope. Just below the surface the snow became the hard, chunky sort that makes a good cave. To me the digging was simply hard work, but Ed loved it, and insisteu on doing all the shoveling himself. That was all right with the rest of us; we leaned on our axes and looked at the route.

Despite our bravado, it was a terrible beginning. If we had to abandon a day's effort after thirty feet, how long would it take us to climb the thousands of feet that lay above us? The collapsing cornice seemed like a stern rebuke. The mountain might have been saying, "What do you foolish boys think you're doing here? Go home before you get hurt."

Mountaineers can't afford to be superstitious, though they often are. Perhaps a superstitious kind of feeling made Don and me begin to think, as we looked at the route, that perhaps the best way to start the climbing would be to go directly through the debris of the recent collapse. Of course there were logical reasons for it as well. That was the spot where the least overhanging snow remained, and cornices, more exhaustible than lightning, seldom strike twice in the same place. Since Ed was taking care of the cave, Don decided to try it. The short wall of recently fractured ice gave him problems; it was almost vertical, and parts of it were very loose. Don came down to let Matt, who was carrying some ice screws, have a try. Putting one of the screws in for protection near the top of the cliff, Matt felt safe enough to start tunneling through the snow. Soon we saw his head appear on the other side of the ridge. Ed and I cheered. Matt continued forty feet to a pillar of rock. As he reached it, the three of us apprehensively watched. It would be the first time we had been able to examine the rock anywhere in the basin; on its solidity probably depended all our chances of success. Matt touched the pillar and looked it over, not saying anything. Then he took a piton and began to hammer it into a crack. As the pitch of the pounded metal rose and began to ring like a bell, we cheered again. Matt returned, confirming our guess: the rock was a superb, sharp-edged granite. We went back down to base camp in much better spirits. Not only had the rock lived up to our highest expectations, but we had turned the first battle, which had looked like a rout, into a fair contest. From far down the icefall we could look back and see the beautiful tunnel Matt had dug, the most visible sign of climbing progress we could dent the mountain with.

The next day Don and I got an early start; by 4:30 A.M. we were advancing the route. The going was consistently difficult, but in half an hour Don had climbed a pitch of steep ice, and reached a spot from which he could belay me up. We were always able to get solid pitons in the rock for belays, so that we felt a certain sense of security despite the drop below us. The day was cold and perfect. In the sun on the South Buttress of McKinley, every speck of snow stood out; though it was seven miles away, we fancied that we could have seen a person standing on it. However, as I followed Don's steps in the steep ice, my head brushed the slope, knocking my glasses off. They went the way of every snowslide, probably to the very floor of the glacier. Fortunately I had another pair at base camp, but for the rest of the day I couldn't see very well. I led another pitch, then brought Don up to try what looked like the hardest bit yet. For twenty minutes he made no headway, having to clear masses of crusty snow out of the way to get to the ice-covered rock below. Then he was able to progress at a very slow rate, hanging on to pitons, inching up the slippery rock. So far, we had climbed only at night since the snow got too unstable during the day. Now, as I stood in shadow belaying Don only a few feet away, I got miserably cold. Climbing often involves that kind of inequality; since only one man can move at a given time, the belayer may nearly freeze while the climber gets overheated. Cold has a capacity to heighten loneliness, too. I know of few lonelier occupations than belaying when one is cold; one's partner is out of sight, and all one can gauge his progress by is the slow paying out of the rope. At least I could watch Don, this time, though the absence of my glasses made it hard to see what he was doing. At last, at the end of an hour, he had gained a ledge forty feet up. He put in a piton, attached a fixed rope; then we descended. All the way up the route we were to leave these light, cheap ropes in, since it was the only way to make reasonably safe all the difficult pitches we would have to climb again with loads, several times each. We had brought nearly 7,000 feet of fixed rope; we eventually used it all.

When we got back to the col we found Matt and

Ed at work on our cave. It looked very good, with a combination hall and foyer inside the door, and the beginnings of a bedroom to the right. Even when it was sunny outside, though, a perpetual cold reigned within the cave, for the subsurface snow never warms, much less melts, in Alaska. Don and I went down to base camp; Matt and Ed would spend that night in the cave in order to get a good start on the route the next day.

That evening Sheldon flew over a half-dozen times, circling low over our tent at base camp. He also flew over the gap of the col, so he probably saw our steps leading up there and perhaps also signs of digging around the snow cave. Don and I waved at Sheldon, and wondered if he was trying to tell us something. But what could he possibly tell us? If the world had declared war, if New York City were gone, we wouldn't find out till after the expedition.

Around 1:30 A.M. I woke from a drowsy sleep to hear faint shouts. My first thought, given substance by a bad dream I had been having, was "They are in trouble." As I shook off the sleepiness I realized that the shouts were simply their belay signals yelled back and forth. That was good—it meant they were off to an early start and should get a lot of the Stegosaur climbed today. But later, when Don and I arrived at the col, we found that Matt and Ed, despite a full day's work, had been unable to place more than two new pitches. Ed's pitch, our fifth, was especially difficult. He climbed a cliff of the steepest ice we had yet found (about 80 degrees), directly beneath a prow of rock he deftly bypassed. Six pitches in three days— less than half the Stegosaur, less than a fourth of the ridge, less than a—what?—tenth? of the whole route. So far, moreover, the climbing had been difficult; yet the face above was bound to be even harder. We were beginning to get discouraged.

Don and I had enlarged the snow cave with a bedroom on the left, and that night all four of us slept in it for the first time. The plan was for Don and me to advance the route that night, while Matt and Ed brought a load up from base camp. But when Don and I got up to go there was a white-out. It was warm, but a wind blew stinging snow over the col: insidious weather, the worst possible for the route. We went back to bed. Later, all four of us descended to base camp and brought up heavy loads in the horrible, sloppy snow that the unusual warmth was making of our icefall route. As we neared the cave again, we could hear the hiss of wet piles of snow sliding off the ridge above, effacing the steps it had taken us so long to chop and kick.

That night, July 8–9, we resolved to make the strongest possible attack on the route, one pair starting at midnight, the other relieving them four hours later. But the weather, still poor, began to get worse. When Matt and Don awoke at midnight it was actually raining. They could hear, but not see, structures collapsing not only on our route but all over the basin. Going would have been pointless and quite dangerous. At

4:00 A.M. Ed and I had a look, but things were as bad as before. So we declared our first rest day and tried to enjoy it. During the day, the temperature rose higher than we were to record again for the balance of the expedition, to an incredible 46° F. But at the same time it was a chilly 16° F. in the cave. Still, the amount of space we had in it was a virtue no usable tent possesses; each of the two bedrooms was roughly the size and shape of the inside of a small car. What was more, we didn't have to keep it clean. We read a lot, wrote in our diaries, cooked delicacies, like stewed banana flakes, and broke open our one recreational luxury—a Monopoly set. We propped the board on some food boxes in the kitchen so that we could easily play from the bedrooms; only the banker ever had to sit up. It would have been hard to play Monopoly in our tent except by remote control, and then the possibilities for cheating would have been irresistible. I like to think we had other reasons for building the cave, but this turned out to be its greatest advantage.

Perhaps, though, the cave was a way for us to hide from the route. At the time we might have felt such an urge; and the cave's isolation was certainly total. We could barely hear an airplane flying by, even straining; someone shouting at the top of his voice could not be heard outside more than thirty feet away. The snow let some light through, but most of our illumination came from the door; yet only from a single angle could one see anything out the door but a patch of sky. But the cave engendered in us no claustrophobia. Perhaps we

▲ 279

did want to hide. It has since intrigued me to think of the cave—sealed up by winter snows shortly after we left it, an empty tomb gradually sinking within the glacier, intact, as the new snows of each successive year pile above it; some three hundred cubic feet of space, once a place that briefly housed four men's fears and hopes; whose walls once absorbed laughter, the rattle of dice, the roar of a stove, the nervous swish of a pencil writing; where still lie a few discarded books, an empty food can, a sock with a hole in the toe, a Monopoly set—that will never be seen again by any man. We lived there for a month as alert to the few things we chose for a while to make our lives as we were oblivious to all the rest. The snow cave was cold as a freezer, west of our mountain—so we called it the Westing House. As we lay within it the only visible sign of our presence from outside would have been the small hole in the snow that served as our door. Had an avalanche swept over us, we would have slept through it, never awakening. Had the Battle of Gettysburg been fought just below us on the Tokositna, we might have heard the occasional faint pop of the cannon. An existentialist dream (or nightmare), our cave, the perfect realization of man's essential solitude, which was discovered in the twentieth century among the crowds in Paris and New York, though men have been as alone as glaciers and galaxies since they learned to think. Yet the cave did not oppress us; with a grunt we could communicate. There was no telephone to answer, the supermarket was just outside the door, and the library at the foot of the sleeping bag was open twenty-four hours a day. For a while we were self-sufficient; but that is all one can say, anyway, since men die. No Utopia, our snow cave; ours was no society, or, if one, its only stratum was the ruling class, four smug kings. No spiritual pilgrimage, our snowshoe hike up there; no quest of truth more apocalyptic than a handhold, our climbing above. At least it is easy to say that; but at the last disavowal I want to hesitate. After all, it would be nice to believe that climbing could somehow be a search for truth as well as for a summit. Or, if one assumes that life itself is that kind of search, it would be nice to believe that climbing could actually find something. It would somehow justify the effort. This part of Mount Huntington was, of course, a new place on the earth, and in the age that has doomed the geographical unknown, mountaineering can be regarded as a final twist of exploration. The sides of steep mountains are perhaps the hardest places on the earth to reach. But is a two-inch crack in a granite slab in the middle of an economically useless cliff even of geographical interest? Yet we, the four of us, could thrill to see even a one-inch crack. As long as men had been confined to the earth's surface, there was still the allure of hidden places; there were still "Shangri-La's" and "Golden West's" in their minds, at least. But the airplane ended that; it proved that the world looks pretty much the same all over; big places and cold places exist, of course, but the pattern is the same: there are only seas and deserts,

▲ 281

jungles and forests, plains and mountains, swamps and icecaps. The airplane proved, above all, that you didn't have to be there to find out what a place was like. There are still plenty of square miles of land on which no man has ever stood; but before someone does, he will probably consult a map that can tell him where to dig for tungsten, or how many feet, give or take a few, the rain that falls there must roll to reach the sea. No, the place for explorers now is space; what mountain wall can stir the exploratory imagination as can the Plutonian desert?

There are on mountains, of course, summits. But the only pot of gold is at the end of the Pikes Peak Hill Climb. The summits one may now visit before anyone else looks remarkably like other parts of their mountains. The air is the same as, if a little thinner than, that at the bottom; the snow there would melt in one's hand to the same dreary water that flows from its foot. No ladder leads into the sky, and to try to get higher would be as futile for the climber as it was for Icarus. Men, among them mountaineers, have claimed that the only discovery one can make by climbing is that of oneself. But there must be easier ways; and anyway, is that discovery as important as others we might attempt with the same effort? Will it cure loneliness? Will it make death sweet? Yet I have come down from mountains comprehending no better who I am or why I climbed than when I set out, and still been happy. Climbers take risks, and to climb is so all-involving that it temporarily approximates life. If the old question, the one Mallory tried to answer is a valid one, I have given up trying to meet it rationally. Perhaps, if one were immortal, he would feel prompted to ask an ordinary person "Why do you live?" How well could that embarrassed mortal answer? Beyond the neatness of any rationale for life lies its untranslatable glory, the elemental courage of wanting to live. Climbing is serious, because it is like life for us who do it, not like a sport; perhaps we betray it by trying to explain our reasons.

The next night, July 9–10, only Don and I planned to climb. We got off an hour late, but surprisingly both the weather and the condition of the snow were superb. Thanks to the fixed ropes, we reclimbed the six pitches without belaying in only one hour. I led our first new pitch, on which we ran into the first of many "chute-tops," the steep upper bowls of the funnel-like gullies, whose treacherous snow had to be traversed in order to reach the next tower of rock. We were on a more or less level stretch now; the Stegosaur wound its tortuous way ahead of us, spine after spine gapped by the chute-tops. We were always tempted to climb on the sure, solid rock, but we knew that once we had steps placed in the snow and ice they would be much easier to follow with loads than pitches on the difficult rock. The climbing became spectacular, without being terribly difficult; but the unusualness of the terrain made us uneasy. Always beneath us gaped that incredible gulf, which, in good weather, we could see was made of ice-plated rock and steep, plastered snow scarred by the grooves of avalanches and the dents of falling rocks. After two more pitches we grew optimistic about finishing the Stegosaur in a day or two. But we had to turn back, then; despite our fine time, we were beginning to get far enough above the cave so that it took too long to cross the previous pitches in order to start the next ones. We had to find a camp site soon, but so far nothing had looked remotely usable. Bivouacs, or tentless camps, tend to be a last resort in Alaska because of the arctic cold and the danger of getting caught in a long storm.

The weather stayed clear all day. We decided to try the shift system that night. Don and Matt tried to get to sleep early, but Ed and I could bask in the sun outside. We were sitting on two food cans reading when Sheldon flew over. We stood up and waved; to our surprise he responded by dropping a box out his window.

Excitedly we waited for it to land. It looked at first as if it would hit somewhere below us in the middle of the icefall. I started to complain about having to hike down to pick it up, but Ed said, "No, look, it's sailing up toward us."

After a moment I said, "Yeah, you're right. Wouldn't it be funny if it sailed right on over the col?"

With a whoosh the box flew over our heads and disappeared just beyond the col. Ed howled with disappointment. We ran up to the col. I thought I could pick out a scrape in the snow, just twenty feet below the crest, where the box must have hit before taking

Above: Mt. Huntington from the northwest: the French Ridge (center); the west face (right profile). *Below:* The west face of Mt. Huntington. The route is marked in the solid line, with camps I (Snow Cave), II (Alley Camp), III (Nose Camp), and IV (Bivouac). The French route is the left-hand sky line.

Above: The upper basin of the Tokositna Glacier from the 38th pitch. *Left:* Matt Hale beside the high camp, pitched under the direct-aid ceiling. *Right:* The author coming up the fixed ropes on the Stegosaur.

Matt Hale standing beneath the Nose. Note the fixed rope indicating where the overhang was climbed.

Ed Bernd belaying at the top of the 38th pitch.

Above: Ed Bernd on the 26th pitch (this is where the accident happened on the descent). *Right:* Walking the level part of the summit ridge; Matt Hale (nearer) and Ed Bernd. *Far right:* The author, just three pitches below the summit, on the descent.

Left: Ed Bernd at the bivouac tent on the summit icefield, the afternoon before the summit push. *Below:* Left to right: Matt Hale, Don Jensen, Dave Roberts, Ed Bernd at the start of the climb.

the 3,000-foot plunge. We returned to the cave, waking Don and Matt to complain about the tragedy.

"What if it was the radio?" Matt blurted sleepily. I had a vision of trying to explain it to the rental company, as a squad of private detectives held guns on us to make us sign away five years' labor to pay it off. Sheldon, of course, couldn't be held responsible. After the expedition we found out our sympathetic pilot had tried to supply us with a gallon of ice cream. "Marshmallow ripple, too," he said wistfully.

Despite the excitement, Don and Matt got off by midnight. The weather was deteriorating. When Ed and I arose four hours later, a gray cloud bank was blowing in from the south. Before we caught up with the other two, we heard their shouted signals, mingled with the unnerving sound of big rocks crashing down. When we got nearer, we could see Matt leading across a dike of black, basaltic rock, the only bad rock on our route. The patch of red, Matt's parka, against the blackness seemed tiny and ineffectual, especially because Don's belay spot was hidden around a corner so it looked, though we knew better, as if Matt were going it alone. They had four new pitches placed by the time we caught them; more important, they had finished the Stegosaur. Ed and I took over the lead at the bottom rim of the Lower Park. Climbing on a smooth expanse of steep snow, though easy, rattled me at first. The protective solidity the rock had offered was gone. After bringing Ed up the first pitch, I asked him if I could lead the next one as well. Since I weighed about fifty pounds less than he, it would be safer that way. He was very generous. As I led off and glanced back, nothing could have looked solider than that rock of a belayer. More than his size, his cheerfulness gave him that look of strength that I relied on. That cheerfulness was an element we would have totally lacked without him; it was one element Don and I had missed on Deborah. There Ed stood now, facing into the wind, shivering, but he was grinning. He was enjoying it.

Ed seemed born for that sort of contradictory challenge, for battlefields bigger than those his will could rule. His uncharacteristic depression in our first week on the glacier, or the long hours on the road he had insisted on staying awake, watching, brooding in the night, as if his life were bound to be short and had to be lived hard, as if sleep were its betrayal, seemed to resolve now into the happiness he could find only in climbing. I knew how he felt; I felt as he did the sting of the cold, knowing as he did that the cold could not really get to us, and that in the face of the gray storm that was approaching we could continue to climb, for a while at least, each footstep penetrating farther into a place man had never gone. I knew the wild, close feeling in his heart that welcomed even the wind; the very act of standing before it a declaration that this was part of what he was meant to live for—or if not meant (if there had been no intention in his creation), then at least it was one of those few things that he could momentarily devote all of himself to, body, heart, mind, without the need for anything else. But I could also hear with him the mind's whispered warning not to climb too bravely or too far, which seemed to echo from the spiritless gulf beneath our feet. I knew all this, but only because I felt it, too. The rest of Ed, how he differed from me, I could scarcely glimpse.

The Lower Park had some bad snow on it. The top of the fourteenth pitch was the first belay spot where we couldn't place a rock piton. I had tried to use one of the special long aluminum daggers we had made for soft ice and snow, but only after burying it and waiting for it to freeze in did I feel confident of its stability. We placed a total of two and a half new pitches before the wind, rising to a gale and flinging snow in our faces, forced us to return. It had been our best day yet. Together, the four of us had got nearly seven new pitches in. As we reached the cave, our hair and eyelashes crusted with ice, Ed and I felt a tired satisfaction. But we had still seen no camp site above and we had to have one soon.

We learned that Don, in descending, had banged his head on his ice ax quite hard. He suffered headaches and spells of seeing double for several weeks afterward; but if he had a concussion, it didn't hinder his climbing. The storm increased that day and the temperature rose. There was no chance of climbing again the next night, so we got all our clothes as dry as we could in the cave. Our consciences wouldn't let us waste a day, so we descended to base camp for a load in the morning, getting our clothes soaked again. The cave was particularly miserable to enter wet; it must have been a little like going into a walk-in freezer after a shower.

The encouragement of our good day waned and died, as a four-day storm besieged us. Every night we woke and prepared to climb, but the weather and warmth frustrated all our efforts. On July 14 Ed and Matt started at 3:00 A.M. Don and I were going to follow later, but the other two made terribly slow progress, getting wet and tired rechopping all the steps. They managed to climb only the first four pitches. They left their loads there, but it was a wasted day. Don and I never started.

Two days later the weather seemed to improve, and the temperature dropped to 26° F. We had begun to feel the time pressure; we were way behind schedule, and we couldn't hold out much beyond August 10. Therefore we decided we had to force things. Don and I started out first to clear the route. Matt and Ed followed with the bare minimum of a camp, determined to pitch it somewhere above. All the steps were gone; the four-day storm had filled them up or avalanched them off. But despite the slow going, the snow was at last crisp again. Don and I reached our previous high point in four hours, and after two more we had placed our eighteenth and nineteenth pitches, almost to the end of the Lower Park. On the way down we passed Ed and Matt, who were bringing up their camp. Though we didn't know it then, the four of us would never camp together again, and we would never climb together until the summit day. The clear weather that seemed in the offing had deteriorated; as we continued down, the snow began to fall heavily. Near the bottom one of my crampons broke; as the last straw, our spare pair was at base camp, which we'd hoped not to have to visit again. Now there was no choice but to make another wet trip down the icefall the next day.

Meanwhile Matt and Ed had reached the top of our highest pitch. There was a possibility there for a camp site, but a poor one. Leaving their loads, they pushed the route higher to look for a better spot. At the top of the Lower Park Matt led into the steep ice chute of the Alley, then nicely around the corner onto the Upper Park. They were exhilarated by the easy going above; quickly they stormed up five more pitches, but the steep slope never relented. Disappointed, they gave up the search and went back down. They were getting tired after a long day, and the storm's fury continued to increase. At last, in the afternoon, they reached their packs again. They set to work chopping a tent platform out of the 45-degree ice. It was frightfully slow work. After five hours they had a ledge large enough to accommodate the small tent, though for safety they had to pass ropes that were anchored to pitons around it and prop a rock under one of the outside corners. At midnight, near exhaustion after nineteen straight hours of work, they piled into the tent. They had four days of food there, and hoped to push the route further, but they absolutely depended on support from below.

Down in the cave, Don and I were getting discouraged. The storm continued. We spent the next day, as anticipated, retrieving the extra crampons, but the snow conditions were so poor we couldn't have climbed anyway. On July 18 we started up with a load. Don, leading, had to plow away deep masses of sticky snow. We were trying to climb continuously, but this was not possible while the snow prevented us from seeing each other. As Don led, the rope between us would bite into the new snow and stick. Don would feel the rope taut behind him and stop, thinking that I was on a hard stretch. I would see the rope cease to move above me and stop also, assuming Don was on a difficult move or clearing away some snow. So we would both stand there until one of us would impatiently shout, "Are you climbing?"

After a pause the other voice would trickle back: "No! Are you on a hard move?"

"No."

"Climb, then!"

"The rope is stuck!"

"Where?"

The situation was impossible. The shouting only made us irritable with each other. We gave up on the fourth pitch, tied our loads to a piton and returned to the cave. Waiting there was even worse. We kept worrying about Matt and Ed. For all we knew they'd never been able to pitch a tent, but were huddled miserably somewhere, tied to some rock, waiting out the storm. The natural gloominess of the cave enhanced our fears. Matt and Ed were out of sight, out of earshot, and apparently out of safe climbing distance so long as the storm continued. They had only four days of food. We knew they would start to ration it, if necessary, but it wouldn't stretch much beyond six days. Having to ration, moreover, was the first step toward emergency.

In addition, we were getting nowhere on the route. Always present in our minds was the experience of Don and me on Deborah, when day after day of storms, during which we couldn't leave the tent, ate away our chances until, when the weather finally cleared, there was no hope left. Yet that year after twenty days we were halfway up. We had been on Huntington twenty days, but now we were less than a third of the way to the top, with all the real difficulties ahead of us.

On July 19 we forced ourselves to reach Matt and Ed. All the steps needed replacing, even those we had chopped the day before. Our progress was extremely slow; with 40-pound packs we had to make brutal efforts to climb some of the pitches. The snow was still falling. When, leading on the seventeenth pitch, I caught sight of the little triangle of orange above, seemingly tacked to the wall, I felt a thrill of relief. By the time we reached the tent it seemed silly ever to have worried.

Matt and Ed, however, had been unable to get out of their camp since pitching it. The exposure was fantastic. The front door looked straight across the face to the ghostly south ridge of Huntington, and inches from the door the slope swept sheer almost 4,000 feet to the lower glacier. Anything dropped out of the tent apparently went all the way; we lost a pot that way when somebody nudged it.

But their achievement in the face of all these problems cheered us up. Don stayed with Ed in the tent, while Matt descended with me. The weather got steadily better, and the sun actually peeked out occasionally. As we passed the ninth pitch I looked over the side of the ridge where a cornice had broken back to the bare ice. I'd had a hunch that it might be less than a full rope-length down to a high tongue of glacier below. If so, we could set up a rappel rope here for descending, and, on the way up, climb the rope by the prusik technique, thereby short-cutting the first nine pitches. We dropped a rope over the edge. It reached with thirty feet to spare! Soon the thing was set up, and we had an easy descent to the cave. The next day we prusiked up the rope and hauled our packs. The slope was about 70 degrees, made of hard blue ice over which the packs slid smoothly. We reached the tent with our loads and deposited them. We could hear Ed and Don climbing above the Upper Park. We were particularly anxious to know how they were doing, because at last they were confronting the face itself. On our way down we came in sight of them. They looked very small against the towering wall above. As we watched, it became obvious from their painfully slow movement that the climbing was truly severe. Don had to belay from one spot, a cold and dangerous ledge, for more than three hours.

Just before getting to camp, Matt and I saw a lenticular cloud cap forming on the summit of McKinley, the kind that almost inevitably presages a storm. Therefore, even though it was a fine clear day, we were pessimistic. The pattern proved true to form, for soon a blanket of cloud had enveloped us and snow had begun to fall. The storm continued without change for three days. The long hours in the cave slowly passed with nothing for Matt and me to do but wait and talk. The monotony of the softly falling snow made us wonder if it would ever stop. The storm seemed to be the final blow to our chances, if the intrinsic difficulties Ed and Don had begun to explore hadn't been. In despair Matt and I discussed other possibilities, even that of abandoning the route altogether and trying to salvage something for the summer, like a new route on Hunter. But the dream would be gone. All those months in Cambridge thinking about what would be the hardest route ever done in Alaska, if only we could pull it off, seemed wasted. In the depth of gloom I looked around for someone, something to blame, but all that I had was the exasperating feeling of our inadequacy. The cave always seemed too big for two people; Monopoly had lost its interest, and we spent the long hours reading our soggy books or simply thinking.

At last the storm ended. On July 23 we set out for the Alley Camp, as we had begun to call the tent Don and Ed were occupying. The snow had covered our steps again, and a coating of ice had to be scraped off the rope as we prusiked up. We had hoped Don and Ed might be climbing today, but as we approached the tent it became obvious they were still in it. We met them just as they were getting dinner cooked. They had spent twenty hours desperately trying to fix their stove, which had broken, and at last had got it working again. But if we were to trade places, they had to descend right away. With more than gallantry, they left the cooked dinner for us and packed to go down. The weather, which I'd hoped would at last hold clear for a while, had turned foul again. Snow was falling in a slight wind. As they got ready to leave, Matt and I asked them about their progress on the face. They'd managed only two and a half new pitches in their four days; those had been extreme and strenuous, harder by far than anything on the ridge.

I saw no reason to be encouraged. But Ed was inexplicably enthusiastic. "The climbing's beautiful up there," he said. "We'll make it, Dave. You wait and see." I got annoyed. It irritated me that he didn't see how poor our chances were; I thought it was evidence of poor judgment. Only months later, after the expedition, did I think of that moment again; only then was I reminded of it by recalling that, after all, I had been wrong and Ed right. And only then did I realize how important Ed's enthusiasm, his refusal to give up, had been to all of us. I gradually pieced together again how we had felt at the time, and it became apparent to me that, actually, Ed had been no more optimistic than any of us; without the experience of other expeditions, the difficulties we were facing must have seemed overwhelming to him. I saw that Ed had realized all this, but had sensed the faltering of our morale, and had done the one thing he could to bolster it, had put on the only mask of encouragement we wouldn't see through. It was so characteristic of him, of his almost magical way of understanding people, of his rare talent for knowing when to use tact instead of honesty without being dishonest. I felt empty, realizing this, because it was all too late, because I hadn't told him I understood and thanked him for it. Because I hadn't understood. . . . All he had said was, "We'll make it, Dave."

6 ▲ Blue Sky and Hope

The snow didn't let up on July 24. Matt and I, glad
at last to be out of the chilly cave, began to get used
to the cramped and careful existence the Alley Camp
demanded. We couldn't climb that day; we were getting high enough now so that we could push the route
ahead only in good weather, because of the cold and
the difficulty of the climbing. We shifted to a daytime
schedule for the same reason.

The twenty-fifth dawned perfectly clear. I had no
inkling of the fact until I stuck my head out the door
and saw blue sky above the savage pinnacles of the

south ridge. We got started as quickly as we could, after a hurried breakfast. All our water came from chunks of ice we chopped off the tent platform. Just as we got ready to go, the sun hit the tent. The effect wildly rejuvenated our spirits. We had almost given up believing that the sun ever shone. Now the tent warmed like a greenhouse to a comfortable room temperature, even though it was only 25° F. outside.

As we started up the Alley, we saw how much work we'd have to do simply to restore the easy pitches. The steps had vanished. Only the fixed ropes, which hadn't been placed throughout, showed where the route went. Fortunately Matt remembered the details of the pitches from his first trip up nine days before. We found that by kicking under the new snow we could find the old steps, still pretty solid.

Soon we had crossed the Upper Park. Above us loomed a vertical inside corner of rock, the twenty-sixth pitch, the first one of the face. Don had led it on July 20, climbing the rock free in crampons. When Matt and I tried to reclimb the pitch with 25-pound packs, we realized what an incredible performance Don's had been. We had to take the packs off to climb the pitch, then haul them up when we got to the top. And even though we relied heavily on the fixed rope they'd left, the pitch was a strenuous effort.

Nor was the next one much easier. Ed had led this, also in crampons, up 70-degree slabs that plated the core of the mountain. The intricate pitch wandered off to the left, then back directly over the belayer. This had been where Ed was climbing when we had seen Don belaying from his cold perch for so long. Every bit of ice Ed had to chop out of the cracks had bombarded Don below. Again I found it impossible to carry the light pack over the pitch, even with the help of a fixed rope. The four days of storm between our efforts had coated not only the rock but the ropes with rime-ice and feathers of frost. All of it had to be cleared away. My crampons scraped and slipped on the smooth rock. At one point, I stuck the pick of my ax in a crack above my head and tried to do a pull-up on the ax. Finally, after making the kind of effort that would leave us tired for a day, we had our loads up to Don's and Ed's previous high point. It had taken six hours. Here Ed had hoped for a camp site, but the possibilities looked very poor to me. We had time only for a tentative half-pitch more before we had to descend. From our highest point we saw Ed and Don far below, climbing on the ridge. But they were on the lower part of the Stegosaur. Matt and I couldn't figure it out. Were they stubbornly refusing to use our short cut? We yelled to them; because the air was perfectly still, we could understand what they yelled back:

"We're cleaning the first nine pitches."

Thus we learned that Don and Ed were ascending the first pitches a last time to remove the pitons and fixed ropes from them. If we got a chance for the summit, we would need all the equipment above. It was a thankless chore, especially on a beautiful day. But they had had the lead for a while; now they were supporting us.

Matt and I returned to the tent, our muscles sore and tired. The weather was still perfect; we had enjoyed finally getting high on a day when we could see all the way to the horizon. But the fact that it had taken us six hours simply to repeat the previous pitches was pretty discouraging. We could attribute a lot of our slowness to the accumulation of snow and ice from the recent storm. But we would have to go a lot faster the next time to have a hope of putting in any new route.

It was beginning to get dark at night now, not pitch dark, but too dark to read in the tent for a few hours around midnight. Now that we were on a daytime schedule, the darkness helped re-establish for us a diurnal regularity. Because we were still quite pessimistic, though, and because we were tired from the day before, we half hoped for a storm the next day, as an excuse to rest.

But the twenty-sixth also dawned astonishingly clear, and the air stood still around us. We got moving by 10:30 A.M. We decided to carry only the bare minimum of pitons and ropes we would need to put in the route; no extra food, no camp, no equipment for farther up. The snow, thanks to the sun on it yesterday and the night's freeze, was in beautiful shape. We flew over the ten old pitches in two hours, only a third of what it had taken us yesterday. Matt led the rest of the new pitch we'd taken a stab at before. It forced him into a steep, ice-filled chimney. Sometimes I could see a foot or a hand; sometimes only the rope disappearing into the chimney. Matt was having trouble with it, espe-

▲ 307

cially because of the ice. Near the top he ran into a bulge that stuck out over his head, barring further progress. At last he managed to hammer a piton into it, hang a little rope ladder, called a "stirrup," from the piton, and climb past the bulge. Only the next day, when we found the piton loose, did we realize that he'd hammered it not between rock and rock, but between rock and ice; the ice had since melted under the pressure and sun.

Matt's lead was a fine one, but it had taken most of an hour. At this rate we couldn't get much farther, unless we were willing to climb late into the night. But my lead went easier. Though we were climbing now on 60-degree rock and ice, with a 4,500-foot drop below us, the going was not as hard as it had been. For the first time on the expedition, at least for me, the climbing had become an unmixed pleasure.

At times like those, the mind does not wander, nor does it really think, except to make the almost automatic judgments of route, piton, and rope the climbing calls for. One's actions seem to take on something of a pagan ritual: the feet develop sensitivities one would have never thought them capable of; the hands and eyes control one's being. I tend to remember that day, July 26, in these mindless, immediate terms. My memories still rest in my nerve endings, as if in recalling our climbing I could turn my body inside out to examine it under colder light than the sun's. While I was leading that day, I was most acutely aware of the pleasure of contrast in my fingers between the cold give of the snow

and the warm dryness of the rock, between the smooth
ice and the rough granite. More than to anything else,
my fingers were sensitive to the rock; they moved
quickly over it, learning its shape better than my eyes
could, settling instinctively in the right grip. While
I belayed Matt, only my fingers handled the rope
through muffling mittens; then the pleasure was visual:
all our belay spots allowed us to look outward. No
perusal could exhaust the teeming wealth of that sight
of the Tokositna Glacier and the mountains across it
as no one had ever seen them before. Flutings, flashing
in the sun, crowded my view; crevasses scored the glacier below like wrinkles on old skin; even the sky
seemed less rich than those mountains. I could tilt my
head back to watch Matt above, and while I did so
I could feel with his fingers, know with his brain how
far he could lean or reach without losing the precious
edge of balance.

But this kind of remembrance numbs the mind's conscious part, the part that wants to understand as well
as sense. It cannot explain why the touch and strain of
ice and rock under my hands should send pleasure as
well as blood surging through my veins. When most
of our lives are spent dulling our senses in order to
think, ignoring pain in order to tolerate it, how then
could Matt or I wish for a chance only to feel? It
would not have satisfied us, obviously, to sit on some
safe sundeck idly pawing a few chunks of rock and ice
for our sensual amusement. The mind can never really
feel, nor can it stop thinking. Nor was my mind numb

then, I know; in fact, part of the breathless urgency of that day's climbing for me came from another kind of awareness, a detached knowledge that came only from my mind; a sense that the universe was looking over our shoulders, even though all we could see looking back at it was the blank sky's blueness. I tried, then, momentarily to abstract the sensual splendor of our climbing by standing at some metaphorical distance from it. And the farther I got, the more discomforting its smallness and ours seemed. Huntington itself, huge enough only for our minds to encompass, occupied but a little plot of earth in the sprawl of Alaska, which in turn began to cover only a patch on a globe we have made aeronautically puny without figuring out how to leave it. Suppose, however, that we do figure that out; can we ever stand on the sun? The earth would span only an average sun-spot; Huntington less than a speck in the sun-spot; someone climbing Huntington not even a speck on the speck. Yet none of our fondest fantasies, granting us a star's strength or size, seem to realize what we could do with that power. Even our wish for immortality only betrays the limits of our imagination. Matt and I felt a kind of power that day, climbing well in the sun, yet we would be vaporized to a wisp of gas in one instantaneous flick of one infinitesimal tongue of the sun's fire. And the sun, for all its brilliance, is a mediocre star, as stars go (and they are definitely going). Compared even to its prodigal size, moreover, there is so much emptiness around it that the sun might run wild all its life looking for friends, and never bump into another sol. Even this appalling emptiness might leave room for us to proclaim our purpose, since all the stars we can see at night, and quite a few more, belong to one happy galactic society. They all revolve, in orderly paths in the same direction, about the old kings in the center. We might then be no more than the serfs of serfs, but we should know our rulers. But someone had to find out about forty years ago (and the world hasn't been the same since) that some of the things up there were foreigners, apparently oblivious to our galaxy. All of a sudden someone else realized that there were lots of them, and that each of them was not simply an uninvited outlaw, but a whole galaxy of its own. It got worse and worse, as knowledge tends to. It soon became obvious that the distances between galaxies dwarfed the distances between the stars into comparative inches. And, as if space were still not big enough for them, the galaxies seemed to be running away from each other. There is not even a known center; it is not as if all the other galaxies were running away from us; we too are getting out of here as fast as we can.

This is not important, perhaps; it is merely true. Perhaps it should even be comforting, for it tends to indicate that loneliness is not simply our mistake, but the condition of the universe. Think, then, of the lost paradise when, as astronomers (fanciful men) would have us believe, everything (because what is flying apart must once have been together), every grain of dust and star, even the atoms that now make us live, was crammed, let us say ten billion years ago, into a primeval ball that would fit nicely in your pocket next to the penknife.

But if we must take it seriously, it is frightening. Perhaps there is no point laying one's soul open to the universe. The sky is blue, trees and grass grow, men live; what more do we need to know? Let us declare, then, that we will ignore the universe—after all, it ignores us.

If on July 26 my eye saw, metaphorically speaking, beyond the dazzling walls of the Tokositna basin into a raw cosmic night, it did not stop me from climbing with Matt that day. The trouble with the deep end of awareness, the honest vision of a soundless everywhere in which there is no up or down, is that everything human shrinks to nothingness before it. Nothing man does will last forever, granted; but still there is something to say about it. People will listen, if no one else will. Someone will see, for instance, a picture of two men beneath a mountain wall, roped together, apparently trying to climb it, and will thrill somewhat as the climbers themselves did, and wonder what it was like for them. The men in those pictures, so calm and proficient they seem to take on some of the mountain's own implacable cold, still are men, men afraid to die and capable of love. Hooded, gaunt, they have their dreads and wishes. For them motion is life, as much as for anyone. The pictures can paralyze only their balanced grace, suspending something that words, which move as they moved, lose. But the men themselves had to move. Climbing is defined by a purposed completion, the summit; yet the best of it is never that final victory, for after that there is only the descent. The best moments lurk in the tension just before success.

That was what then animated Matt and me. For once, we were moving as perfectly as we knew how. For the first time the summit dared whisper in our ears. It might depend on how far we could get that day, on what we should find in the next few hours.

We faced now three choices, alternatives we had known about from the route photos before we came. Matt and I were just below the hardest part of the whole face, no matter which route we took. On the right (we could just see it now) lay a remarkable hollow, a cave within a cave, sheltered by nested overhangs. If we could get there, we might camp in it and eventually traverse even farther right, beyond and above it, heading at last toward the summit along a thin rock rib. But getting to the double cave looked very difficult, and we knew the traverse beyond might be seriously threatened by avalanches. Directly above us rose a long, smooth slab, averaging a frightening 80 degrees. There would be no possibility of climbing it free. But we could see that the pencil-thin cracks in it tended to peter out, leaving blank gaps of smooth rock into which we should not even be able to get pitons. We had expansion bolts, which as a last resort can substitute for pitons, but even so the going would be slow and difficult, maybe impossible. On the left we could see our third alternative. A steep ice gully led up three hundred feet, stopping under a huge "ceiling," an overhang that split the face without a break. Imagine an ant climbing a wall inside a room, then heading out, upside down, across the ceiling. That is what would be required of us for fifty feet, with the aid, of course, of pitons we might hammer into a crack, if there was one in the ceiling.

Those were the choices. After a short discussion Matt and I chose the left-hand route. The ceiling might be the most difficult of all the problems embodied in all three choices, but at least it was a short, one-pitch problem, not a matter of sustained severity. Three pitches took us up the ice gully. As we neared the ceiling, which we had begun to call the "Nose," we could see that something like a crack, perhaps too wide a crack, split it from bottom to top. When we reached the Nose, it was Matt's turn to lead.

He took off his crampons. Fortunately I had been able to get an extraordinarily solid piton in. I felt secure, which, of course, made Matt feel better too. Without much trouble, he pitoned up the wall beneath the ceiling. Then he found that the crucial crack was six inches wide: wider than any of our pitons. A series of small cracks we hadn't been able to see from below offered an alternative; Matt was able to get our smaller pitons in them. I could watch everything simply by looking straight up, where Matt was dangling like a spider over me. It reminded me of ceilings we'd climbed together in New Hampshire and New York, good "practice" climbs we'd called them, on those cider-sweet autumn days or those spring-thaw afternoons.

This was the real thing, now. Matt was climbing skillfully, calmly, but he knew as well as I that the pitch he was leading was the key to the whole face. It was a matter of simply doing what he knew how to, one piton after the other. Soon he was at the lip of the ceiling; then I saw him step out of his last stirrup and disappear above. In a few minutes he was anchored, and yelled for me to come up.

By the time I reached him, we had already been climbing for eight hours, so it was past the time we should have turned back. The sun lay low in the distance over Mount Foraker, and its flawless light tinged the rock above a brownish-gold. Nothing above us looked as difficult as the Nose. It was still a long way to the summit, but it all seemed possible now. Still, we were reluctant to go down, to end our first perfect climbing day, one of the few in our lives. Always we felt as if the hours of sheer splendid sky and sun were shortly numbered; if we slept, the storms, like thieves, could sneak upon us.

We spoke quietly, discussing the route and our chances rather than the bursting sense of triumph we were beginning to feel. Matt was never one to proclaim his feelings; whether out of a residual shyness or simply to counter my often vocal enthusiasm, he always hid his exultation. But he couldn't disguise his intensity; I felt now, in the silence, an electric tension between us, the charged excitement we occasionally got climbing together, as we had in the last few pitches, from a kind of communication in which the motions of our climbing were more eloquent than words, on which, realizing this, we obtruded only the shouted signals we needed for belaying. Neither of us could have reached this place in the sky alone; if we could have, the excitement would have been fraught with loneliness. Because we shared the pleasure now, neither of us could feel lonely. All that was visible of the pleasure in Matt's face was its intensity, the almost haggard gauntness, as if his body itself were ravaged rather than fed by that intensity. I had seen it first on that beginners' climb in New York, again out of a wild storm in New Hampshire, once glowing through a fever on a sharp summit in Colorado, now where it belonged, on a big mountain, a mountain that could match his intensity with cold massiveness.

But we had to go down. We rappelled off the Nose, dangling for the last seventy feet completely in the air, connected only to the rope. Then we descended the long ice gully; we could watch our shadows, projected on the rock wall a hundred feet away, climbing down beside us like a pair of phantom imitators. Then the sun set, and we continued down into the dusk.

On the Upper Park, as it was getting really dark, we met Ed and Don. They were terribly excited. They had seen us climbing way above, but hadn't realized that we'd actually passed the Nose. They intended to go on up that night, looking for a place to camp somewhere above. We assured them there were no good sites until the Nose. They compromised, pitching our other tent at the top of the Upper Park, having to work far into the night to build a platform. Matt and I descended the six pitches to the Alley Camp. We arrived after a twelve-and-a-half-hour day, very tired, very happy.

The next morning an early mist surprised us. But it lifted, revealing another superb day. We had to have another camp above, maybe two, before we could assault the summit. The plan was for Matt and me to carry loads up to the top of the gully just beneath the Nose, where Ed and Don, following, would try to pitch a camp. Matt and I got off in the late morning, but we were still tired, and moved lethargically. We passed Ed and Don as they were starting to take down their tent. Above the twenty-ninth pitch, where Matt and I had left our loads two days before, we picked up the two food boxes and continued. We couldn't wear our packs in the ice-filled chimney; but the set-up of the pitch was so awkward that it took two hours to work out a hauling system on it. Above, things went faster. We got the loads to the Nose at 6:20 P.M. An hour later, going down, we crossed ropes with Ed and Don as they ascended to set up their high camp. The meeting had an emotionality about it that none of our others had had. We all felt a tense joy now that things were working; moreover, as we got higher, the strange and beautiful country of vertical ice and rock more exclusively involved us. Matt and I knew we might not see the other two again before they had reached the summit. We knew, also, that Ed and Don might be the only ones who would have a chance of getting to the top. It didn't matter. Any kind of success, after the storms and dulled hopes of the last months, would fill us with gratitude. As we passed them in the dying sunlight, we couldn't tell them how much our desires went with them; instead we breathlessly described every detail of the route and every item of strategy we thought might aid them. They couldn't tell us how proud and thankful they were for our work getting past the Nose; so they arranged plans for the next few days when we would be out of contact. Thus the meeting, like so many human confrontations, passed in confused inarticulateness, for which only the joy in my throat compensated. I wanted to sit for hours with them, but co-operation now depended on our contrary paths. So Matt and I climbed down into the dusk again as Ed and Don went up into the pure sky.

The next day, July 28, we woke to find the weather still holding, though clouds had begun to build far to the northwest behind McKinley and Foraker. In a short but strenuous day, Matt and I went down to the ninth pitch and retrieved, in one horrible 55-pound load each, the pitons, rope, and food we would need to take up to Don and Ed for the assault above the Nose. That day we never saw or heard them, so we couldn't tell what they had accomplished.

It turned out that the platform beneath the Nose had taken them a very long time to chop, their efforts complicated by finishing in the midnight darkness. The platform was never really adequate for the tent, which had to be pitched narrower than usual. Nor could they get very good pitons into the smooth wall above to anchor the tent. But at least the projecting eave of the Nose above guarded the tent from falling rocks. The front door overlooked the spectacular western drop to the Tokositna basin, and the sun set that night almost in line with the door. Inches beyond its outside wall, the steep snow slope plunged toward vertical rock. Don and Ed were camped above a 5,000-foot drop, down which an object might fall with only five or six bounces. Everything outside the tent—food boxes, fixed ropes, hard hats, hammers—had to be tied to the wall.

Because they hadn't finished the job until early morning, Don and Ed couldn't accomplish much on the twenty-eighth. Don placed a fixed line of stirrups on the Nose, though, so that it could be climbed with less effort than leading it had taken. They needed further support from us below, however. But they were ready the next day to push the route above the Nose, as far as they could, maybe to a point in reach of the summit. If only the weather held. . . .

7 ▲ The Summit

July 29 dawned clear. Our fifth perfect day in a row, it was almost more than we could believe. Don and Ed got moving by 7:30 A.M. Quickly over the Nose, from there on, they faced unclimbed rock and ice. Ed started to lead the first new pitch. Suddenly he remembered he'd forgotten his ice ax in the rush to get started. It was down by the tent.

"What a dumb thing to do," he said to Don. "You think we should go back for it?"

"No. It would take too much time. We can make do with an icelite."

So Don and Ed took turns leading with Don's ax,

while the second man used one of our aluminum daggers for balance and purchase. Although it was awkward, it seemed to work.

To make things more unsettling, they had only five or six fixed ropes and about a dozen pitons. Matt and I had not yet been able to bring up supplies to them; they could expect us to reach the tent sometime today with more of everything, but the beautiful weather couldn't be wasted. They would go as high as they reasonably could.

Ed led the next pitch, a traverse on steep, crunchy snow, quickly and well, needing only a piton at the top to belay from. Don managed the same economy on the next, our thirty-seventh pitch, though the snow was becoming ice in which he had to chop steps. At the top of the 55-degree pitch he found a protruding block of granite, but there didn't seem to be any good cracks in it. At last he hammered a short, stubby piton in about three-quarters of an inch, tied a loop around its blade to minimize the torque if a pull should come on it, and belayed Ed up. The pitch above required another steep traverse, again on the shallow snow-ice that lay uncomfortably close to the rock beneath. Ed led it carefully. Don could see him silhouetted against the sky all the way. The sun was beginning to hit the face, and they welcomed it after their first pitches in cold shadow. To be sure, sooner or later the sun might loosen the snow, but it would be very hard to climb difficult rock without its warmth. And it looked as if they would have to climb a steep cliff very soon.

They left fixed ropes on the first three pitches, then

decided to save their few remaining ones, placing them only on the worst pitches, where they would be most helpful on the descent. Don led another pitch, their easiest yet. With excitement he realized at the top of it that he was standing beside the large smooth pillar we had noticed in the Washburn pictures, and which he knew marked the beginning of the last rock barrier. Ed led into a steep couloir, now hard blue ice in which he laboriously and precariously had to chop steps. But he reached rock on the opposite side where he could get in a good anchor. So far they had used only five pitons in five pitches—the absolute minimum, certainly fewer than they would have used had they had plenty to spare. But they had climbed fast. The snow was still solid, but the rock was warming up. It looked as if they might be able to climb the 70-degree cliff above them barehanded. They certainly couldn't climb all of it with mittens on.

Don began the cliff. At least it had a few fine, sharp-edged holds. Trying to save the pitons, he went forty feet before he put one in. It rang solidly as he pounded it—thank God for the fine rock on this route! Thirty feet above that he was faced by a blank section, unclimbable, free. He hammered in a poor piton, one that wouldn't go all the way in, but vibrated noisily as he hit it. But at last it would hold his weight, and with a stirrup he surmounted the blank stretch. Difficult as it was, the climbing exhilarated him, especially knowing, as both Ed and he did, that above the cliff lay only the long, steep summit ice field. Don climbed into a wide chimney, moved up fifteen feet, and found the top blocked by a little ceiling. There was a way out to the left if there was even one handhold at the top of his reach. Except for a thin crack, though, there was nothing. Choosing his smallest piton, he was able to hammer it in about half an inch. He tested it cautiously, putting a carabiner through the piton's eye to hold on to. It felt insecure, but didn't budge; it would probably hold. He was forty feet above the bad piton, seventy feet above his good one. Moving delicately, putting as little weight on the piton as possible, he swung himself up and around the corner. Ed, watching tensely, saw Don step onto the snow above the highest rock. The cliff was climbed. Don quickly brought Ed up. Ed led a short pitch of crusty snow above, which seemed to lie just below the edge of something. Topping the rim, he looked ahead in amazement. The smooth expanse of the summit ice field lay above him, swooping upward at an unbroken 50-degree angle to the summit. After a month of climbing among jagged towers, inside chimneys, up enclosed couloirs, the summit ice field looked nightmarishly bare. It was like hacking one's way out of a jungle suddenly to stand on the edge of an empty desert.

It meant that they might have a chance for the summit that very day. Ed finished the pitch and brought Don up. Together they planned their attack. It was early afternoon, and going for the summit would undoubtedly require a bivouac. Four hundred feet above them stood the only bit of rock in the whole expanse, an outcrop about ten feet high. They decided to aim for it.

Four quick pitches on the unnervingly open slope brought them to it. The last fifty feet before the rock were steeper, and the sun had started to undermine the ice. They reached the rock with a feeling of relief, and agreed that the snow conditions would get worse for the next few hours. Choosing the one small ledge the rock offered, they chopped a little platform on it and pitched the tiny two-man bivouac tent Don had made. It was crowded inside, but consequently warm. Holding a stove on their laps, they could melt ice chips to make water. It was about five in the afternoon. They decided to wait for night, then go all out for the summit. It was still a long way, perhaps five more hours if things went well. But it was within reach. There was still not a cloud in the sky, no wind to disturb even a grain of snow. The afternoon sun gleamed on the mountains around them as they sat, drunk with the excitement of height, looking over the wilderness below them. For the first time they could see all of the Tokositna Glacier, even the dirty tongue sprawled on the tundra in the hazy distance, whose last ice Belmore Browne had crossed sixty years before. . . .

Matt and I had started at 11:15 A.M. from the Alley Camp. On a hunch, I had suggested that we take our down jackets and an extra lunch, as well as the ropes and pitons we were relaying up to Don and Ed. We made very good time, reaching their tent beneath the Nose in only three and a half hours. It was still early;

it seemed pointless to go down at once. We decided to climb above the Nose; at least we could put in extra rope and pitons to safeguard the route behind the leaders for their descent. We were encouraged by the fact that we couldn't hear their shouts; they must be far above.

As we were preparing to climb the Nose, Matt noticed Ed's ax beside the tent. That was very strange; why hadn't he taken it? Unable to think of a more ominous reason, we assumed he had simply forgotten it as he climbed the difficult ceiling and, once above, had decided it wasn't worth going back for. Matt put the ax in his pack so that we could give it to Ed if we caught them, or at least leave it hanging from a piton where they couldn't help finding it on their way down.

At the top of the Nose we saw the newly placed fixed rope stretching around the corner. Without much trouble we followed their steps. Matt led the first pitch, I the second. It was about 3:30 P.M.; the snow was just beginning to deteriorate in the sun. The steps they had chopped in the ice, therefore, occasionally seemed uncomfortably small; we enlarged a few of them. At the top of the thirty-seventh pitch I saw that the anchor piton was a poor one and looked around for a place to put a new one. About five minutes later I gave up and tied in to the eye of the piton. Since I wasn't sure how long the piton's blade was, I had no way of judging how far into the crack it had been hammered. But there was a fixed rope leading above to the next piton, so it seemed reasonably safe.

Matt started to lead, holding the fixed rope wrapped around his left arm. Only four feet above me he stopped on a steep ice-step to tighten his right crampon, which seemed to be coming off. As he pulled on the strap his foot slipped and he fell on top of me. Not alarmed, I put up a hand to ward off his crampon, holding him on belay with the other. As his weight hit me, I felt the snow platform I had stomped for my feet collapse. But I was tied in with only a foot or two of slack, and I knew that the anchor would catch me immediately, and I would have no trouble catching Matt a foot or two below me. Yet we were sliding suddenly, unchecked. I realized the piton must have pulled out, but wondered in a blur why the fixed rope wasn't holding me; had it come loose, too? We were falling together, gaining speed rapidly. Matt was on top of me. We began to bounce, and each time we hit I had the feeling, without any pain, that I was being hurt terribly. Everything was out of control. I was still probably holding the rope in a belay, but I could do nothing to stop us. The mountain was flashing by beneath us, and with detachment I thought, This is what it's like. . . .

Suddenly we stopped. Matt was sitting on top of me. For an instant we didn't dare breathe. Then we carefully tried to stand on the steep ice.

"Don't move yet!" I said. "We could start going again!"

Now the fear, which we hadn't had time to feel as we fell, swept over us.

"Are you all right?" Matt asked urgently.

I couldn't believe those bounces hadn't broken any bones. I could move all right and I didn't seem to be bleeding. "I think so. Are you?"

"I guess. I lost my ice ax, though."

Then I realized my glasses were missing. As I looked around I saw them balanced on the tip of my boot. I grabbed them and put them on.

"We've got to get a piton in immediately," I said.

I managed to hammer in several poor ones. We could relax a little now, but trying to relax only made us more frightened. Matt had lost the crampon he was adjusting and both mittens. I had lost the dark clip-ons to my glasses. My right crampon had been knocked off, but it hung from my ankle by the strap. We were bruised but otherwise unhurt. The fall seemed to have been selectively violent.

What had stopped us? Matt still had his hand wrapped around the fixed rope, yet we had been falling without any apparent retardation. I looked up. The fixed rope, no longer attached to the anchor I had been belaying from, still stretched in one long chain to the anchor on the next pitch beyond. We saw Matt's ax, too, planted in the ice where his fall had started. Then we saw that the climbing rope had snagged above us on a little nubbin of rock. That was apparently what had stopped us.

It was safer, at least at first, to go up than to go down. I led, soon getting a very good piton in. I traversed back into our steps. As I passed the nubbin that had caught the rope, I looked at it. It was rounded, no bigger than the knuckle of one of my fingers.

Finally I got to a safe anchor above the bad one. As Matt came up, I tried to figure out what had happened. Just after we stopped falling, I had noticed the piton dangling at my feet, still tied to me, but unconnected to the fixed rope. I realized that I had attached myself to the piton's eye, while the fixed ropes had been tied around its blade. When the piton came out, we were no longer connected to the fixed ropes, except by the grasp of Matt's left hand.

We were extremely shaken. We discussed whether to go back or go on. I wanted to go on. The accident, though it had scared us badly, shouldn't affect our general resolve, I said. I had the feeling, too, that if we went back now we might develop an overwhelming, irrational fear and never want to go above the Nose. Matt reluctantly agreed. Fortunately, I had an extra pair of mittens for him. I could get along without the dark glasses, since it was growing late; but the loss of Matt's crampon was more serious. If I led the rest of the pitches, though, enlarging the right-foot steps for him, we thought it would work.

We continued, still shaky and nervous. Now we deliberately overpitoned the route, making it as safe as was humanly possible. As we climbed, we regained confidence. Soon we no longer had Ed's and Don's fixed ropes to follow, but their steps were clear. Wondering where they had climbed the cliff, I caught sight of a fixed rope dangling. The sight was more than exciting; it was reassuring as well.

I led the cliff, marveling at the difficulties Ed and Don had overcome with only three pitons. I put in about five more. As the sun passed over Foraker, low to the west, I emerged on the summit ice field. There was still no sign of Don and Ed, but as I belayed Matt up, I heard Ed shout to us from somewhere above.

"Where are you?" I yelled back.

"In the rock outcrop!"

We couldn't see them, but hearing their voices again was thrilling. Matt and I hurried up the steep ice to join them. The conditions were at their worst now, even though it was 8:00 P.M. Twice I had to hammer rock pitons into the ice for anchors, never a dependable technique.

At last we were reunited. It was wonderful to see them. Ed said at once, "You didn't happen to bring my ice ax up, did—you did? What a couple of buddies!" Then, trying not to overstate it, we described our near-accident. Ed, especially, seemed disturbed; but the safety of numbers and the realization that now we could go to the summit together, as a rope of four, made up for all our misgivings. We ate a few candy bars as the sun set behind McKinley and the mountains faded into the dusky pallor of early night. Around 10:00 P.M. we started.

Since we had only two ropes, we had to tie in at 90-foot intervals instead of the usual 140. Don went first, I second, Matt third, while Ed brought up the rear. In order to save time, I belayed Don above me with one rope and one hand and Matt below me with the other simultaneously. It was growing dark rapidly.

▲ 329

Soon I could see Don only as a faint silhouette in the sky, seeming to walk toward Cassiopeia. We were getting tired; the darkness made our effort seem more private, more detached from the mountain beneath us. After five pitches, at half-past midnight, we reached the summit ridge. We could scarcely tell we were there, except by the gradual leveling of the steep slope. We knew the far side was festooned with cornices overhanging the Ruth Glacier, so we didn't go all the way up to the ridge's level crest.

Now all that remained was the quarter-mile across to the summit, a narrow, airy walkway with a 5,000-foot drop on the left and a 6,000-foot drop on the right. This was the first and only part of our climb that coincided with the French route. Although it was such a short distance to the top, we knew we couldn't afford to underestimate it, for it had taken the French four and a half hours to reach the summit from here a year and a month before. For 600 feet we moved continuously, a ghostly walk in the sky. The night seemed to muffle all sound, and I had the illusion for an instant that we were the only people alive in the world. Soon we faced two flutings, short walls of vertical snow carved and crusted by the incessant wind, which spared the ridge only a few days each year. Perhaps we had been lucky enough to hit one of them. Here it was imperative that the four of us spread as far apart as possible. Don started up toward the first fluting as I belayed from a not very solid ice ax. Traversing high, he stuck his foot through the cornice and quickly pulled it back. Through the hole he could see the dull blueness of the Ruth Glacier below. He returned to my belay spot near exhaustion from the tension and exertion of a whole day of leading. We traded places and I started for the fluting, approaching it lower. The light was returning; an orange wall of flame lit the tundra north of McKinley. I could see the contours of the nearby snow now, glimmering palely. As I neared the bottom of the first wall, I thought I saw something sticking out of the snow. I climbed over to it. Stretched tight in the air, a single, frail foot of thin rope emerged from the ice. I pulled on it, but it was stuck solid. The sight was strangely moving. It testified, in a way, both to the transience and to the persistence of man. That bit of French fixed rope was the only human thing not our own that we had found during the whole expedition. It even seemed to offer a little security. I clipped in to it although I knew it was probably weather-rotten.

It seemed best to attack the fluting high, probably even on top of the cornice. If it broke off, at least there would be the weight of the other three on the opposite side of the ridge to hold me. The snow was terrible, made more out of air than anything else. I used one of our longest aluminum daggers in my left hand, my ax in the right, trying to plant something in the snow I could hold on to. At last, by hollowing a kind of trough out of the fluting, I could half climb, half chimney up. Just beyond its top the second fluting began. Don came up to belay me for the new obstacle. It was a little harder, but with a last spurt of energy I got over it. Though things seemed to be happening quickly to me, I took a long time on each fluting, and Matt and Ed grew cold waiting at the other end of the rope. Eventually all four of us were up, however. Then there were only three pitches left, easy ones, and suddenly I stood on top, belaying the others up. The summit itself was a cornice, so we had to remain a few feet below it, but our heads stood higher.

It was 3:30 A.M. We'd been going for sixteen hours without rest. Now we were too tired even to exult. The sun had just risen in the northeast; a hundred and thirty miles away we could see Deborah, only a shadow in the sky. As Don looked at it I said, "This makes up for a lot." He nodded.

There was no one to tell about it. There was, perhaps, nothing to tell. All the world we could see lay motionless in the muted splendor of sunrise. Nothing stirred, only we lived; even the wind had forgotten us. Had we been able to hear a bird calling from some pine tree, or sheep bleating in some valley, the summit stillness would have been familiar; now it was different, perfect. It was as if the world had held its breath for us. Yet we were so tired . . . the summit meant first of all a place to rest. We sat down just beneath the top, ate a little of our lunch, and had a few sips of water. Ed had brought a couple of firecrackers all the way up; now he wanted to set one off, but we were afraid it would knock the cornices loose. There was so little to do, nothing we really had the energy for, no gesture appropriate to what we felt we had accomplished: only a numb happiness, almost a languor. We photographed each other and the views, trying even as we took the pictures to impress the sight on our memories more indelibly than the cameras could on the film. If only this moment could last, I thought, if no longer than we do. But I knew even then that we would forget, that someday all I should remember would be the memories themselves, rehearsed like an archaic dance; that I should stare at the pictures and try to get back inside them, reaching out for something that had slipped out of my hands and spilled in the darkness of the past. And that someday I might be so old that all that might pierce my senility would be the vague heart-pang of something lost and inexplicably sacred, maybe not even the name Huntington meaning anything to me, nor the names of three friends, but only the precious sweetness leaving its faint taste mingled with the bitter one of dying. And that there were only four of us (four is not many), and that surely within eighty years and maybe within five (for climbing is dangerous) we would all be dead, the last of our deaths closing a legacy not even the mountain itself could forever attest to.

We sat near the summit, already beginning to feel the cold. I got up and walked a little bit beyond, still roped, down the top of the east ridge, which someday men would also climb. From there I could see the underside of the summit cornice and tell that we had judged right not to step exactly on top. We had touched it with our ice axes, reaching out, but it might not have borne our weight.

Ed, who was normally a heavy smoker, had sworn

off for the whole expedition. Now, out of his inexhaustible pockets, he pulled three cigarettes. He had no trouble lighting them; after smoking two, though, he felt so light-headed he had to save the third. One of the things he must have looked forward to, I realized, was that ritual smoke on the summit, partly because of the surprise he knew it would cause. But that was only one of Ed's reasons for being there, a minor one. I thought then, much as I had when Matt and I sat on the glacier just after flying in, that I wanted to know how the others felt and couldn't. Trying to talk about it now would have seemed profane; if there was anything we shared, it was the sudden sense of quiet and rest. For each of us, the high place we had finally reached culminated ambitions and secret desires we could scarcely have articulated had we wanted to. And the chances are our various dreams were different. If we had been able to know each others', perhaps we could not have worked so well together. Perhaps we would have recognized, even in our partnership, the vague threats of ambition, like boats through a fog: the unrealizable desires that drove us beyond anything we could achieve, that drove us in the face of danger; our unanswerable complaints against the universe— that we die, that we have so little power, that we are locked apart, that we do not know. So perhaps the best things that happened on the summit were what we could see happening, not anything beneath. Perhaps it was important for Don to watch me walk across the top of the east ridge; for Matt to see Ed stand with a cigarette in

his mouth, staring at the sun; for me to notice how Matt
sat, eating only half his candy bar; for Ed to hear Don
insist on changing to black-and-white film. No one
else could see these things; no one else could even ask
whether or not they were important. Perhaps they were
all that happened.

It was getting a little warmer. We knew we had to
get down before the sun weakened the snow, especially
on the summit ice field. Each of us as we left took a
last glance back at the summit, which looked no different than when we had come, but for the faint footprints
we had left near it.

We put fixed ropes in on all the difficult pitches, refusing to let up or get careless now that we were so
tired. For the same reason we didn't take dexedrine
tablets, though we carried them. When we reached the
bivouac tent, we split into pairs to continue down. Ed
and I went first, while Don and Matt packed up the
little camp before following us. The sun, high in a still
perfect sky, had taken the magic out of the mountain's
shapes. Only the soft early light and the tension of our
expectancy could have left it as beautiful as it had been.
At last, after twenty-five straight hours of technical
climbing, we rappelled off the Nose and piled, all four
together, into the tent.

Now we could relax at last, but the tent was far too
crowded. We felt giddy, and laughed and shouted as
the edge of our alertness wore off. We had brought up
our pint of victory brandy—blackberry-flavored—and
now indulged in a few sips, toasting everything from

Washburn to Kalispell. Each of us managed to doze off at some time or other, with someone else's foot or elbow in his face. In the afternoon it grew unbearably hot and stuffy inside, and the Nose began to drip (appropriately enough), pouring water through the roof of the tent. We cooked all our favorite delicacies, robbing the two food boxes rapaciously. By 6:00 P.M. it had started to cool again, and we saw that, finally, the weather might be turning bad, after six consecutive perfect days, a spell almost unheard of in Alaska. It was as if the storms had politely waited for us to finish our climb. We slept a little more, but still couldn't get comfortable. Around 9:00 P.M. Ed suggested that he and I go down in the night to the Alley Camp. We were still tired, but it wouldn't be a difficult descent. Once he and I got to the Camp, moreover, all four of us could rest in luxurious comfort, a sleeping bag each, room to stretch out full length, and plenty of food to wait out any storm. We dressed and were ready to go by 9:40 P.M.

8 ▲ The Accident

The snow was in poorer condition than we liked; it hadn't refrozen yet, and might not that night since a warm wind was coming in. I knew the pitches below better than Ed, having been over them five times to his one, so I tried to shout instructions to him when the route was obscure. It got to be too dark to see a full rope-length. I went down the twenty-ninth pitch, our ice-filled chimney, feeling rather than seeing the holds. But the fixed ropes helped immensely, and since I came last on the two hard pitches (twenty-ninth and twenty-seventh), Ed didn't have to worry so much about not knowing the moves. Despite the conditions, we were moving efficiently.

At the top of the twenty-sixth pitch, the vertical inside corner Don had led so well in crampons, we stopped to rappel. We stood, side by side, attached to the bottom of the fixed rope we had just used on the pitch above. In the dark, we could discern only the outlines of each other's faces. Under our feet, we felt our crampons bite the ice. Just below the little ledge we stood on, the rock shrank vertically away, and empty space lurked over the chasm below. It was too dark to see very far down. Above us, the steepest part of the face, which we had just descended, loomed vaguely in the night. Up there, on another ledge, Don and Matt were probably sleeping. Beside us, in the mild darkness, icicles dripped trickles of water that splashed on the rocks. The fixed rope was wet; here and there ice, from the splashing, had begun to freeze on it.

We didn't have an extra rope, so we untied and attached ourselves to the fixed line, setting up a rappel with the climbing rope. Ed attached a carabiner to the anchor, through which he clipped the climbing rope, so that we could pull it down from the bottom. He wrapped the rope around his body and got ready to rappel. We were tired, but were getting down with reasonable speed. It was ten minutes before midnight.

"Just this tough one," I said. "Then it's practically walking to camp."

"Yeah," Ed answered.

He leaned back. Standing about five feet from him,

338 ▲

I heard a sharp scraping sound. Suddenly Ed was flying backward through the air. I could see him fall, wordless, fifty feet free, then strike the steep ice below.

"Grab something, Ed!" But even as I shouted, he was sliding and bouncing down the steep ice, tangled in the rappel rope. He passed out of sight, but I heard his body bouncing below. From the route photos I knew where he had fallen; there wasn't a chance of his stopping for 4,000 feet.

Perhaps five seconds had passed. No warning, no sign of death—but Ed was gone. I could not understand. I became aware of the acute silence. All I could hear was the sound of water dripping near me. "Ed! Ed! Ed!" I shouted, without any hope of an answer. I looked at the anchor—what could have happened? The piton was still intact, but the carabiner and rope were gone with Ed. It made no sense.

I tried to shout for help to Matt and Don. But they were nearly 1,000 feet above, hidden by cliffs that deflected and snow that absorbed my voice. I realized they couldn't hear me. Even the echo of my shouts in the dark seemed tiny. I couldn't just stand there; either I must go up or I must go down. It was about an equal distance either way, but the pitches above were more difficult. I had no rope. There was no point going up, because there was nothing we could do for Ed. His body lay now, as far as anyone could ever know, on the lower Tokositna, inaccessible. An attempt even by the three of us to descend the 4,000 feet to look for him would be suicidally dangerous, especially since we would have only one rope for all of us. If I went up, I should eventually have to go down again. All it could do was add to the danger. I realized these things at the time. Yet the instinct, in my isolation, to try to join Matt and Don was so compelling that for a while I didn't even consider the other possibility. But it became obvious I had to go down.

At least the fixed ropes were still in. I used two carabiners to attach myself to them, then began to climb down the steep pitch we had started to rappel. I moved jerkily, making violent efforts, telling myself to go more slowly. But I had to use the adrenaline that was racing through me now; it was the only thing that could keep the crippling fear and grief temporarily from me.

I managed to get down the hard pitch. The snow on the Upper Park was in poor condition. I broke steps out beneath me, but held my balance with the fixed rope. I realized that I was going far too fast for safety, but slowing down was almost impossible. As I traversed to the Alley, I was sure the weak snow would break under my feet, but it held. At last I arrived at the tent. The seven pitches had taken eighteen minutes, dangerously fast. But I was there; now there was nothing to do but wait alone.

I crawled into the tent. It was full of water. Matt and I had left the back door open! In the dark I sponged it out, too tired to cry, in something like a state of shock. I took two sleeping pills and fell asleep.

In the morning I gradually woke out of a gray stupor. It seemed to be snowing lightly. I felt no sudden pang about the accident; even in sleep I must have remained aware of it. I forced myself to cook and eat a breakfast, for the sake of establishing a routine, of occupying myself. I kept thinking, *What could have happened?* The carabiner and rope were gone; nothing else had been disturbed. Perhaps the carabiner had flipped open and come loose; perhaps it had broken; perhaps Ed had clipped in, in such a way that he wasn't really clipped in at all. Nothing seemed likely. It didn't matter, really. All that mattered was that our perfect expedition, in one momentary mechanical whim, had turned into a trial of fear and sorrow for me, as it would for Matt and Don when they learned, and into sudden blankness for Ed. His death had come even before he could rest well enough to enjoy our triumph.

The time passed with terrible slowness. I knew Matt and Don would be taking their time now that it was snowing. I grew anxious for their arrival, afraid of being alone. I tried to relax, but I caught myself holding my breath, listening. Occasionally a ball of snow would roll up against the tent wall. I was sure each time that it was one of them kicking snow down from above. I would stick my head out the tent door, looking into the empty whiteness for a sign of them. My mind magnified even the sound of snowflakes hitting the tent into their distant footsteps.

I made myself eat, write in my diary, keep the tent dry, keep a supply of ice near the door. But I began to worry about Matt and Don, too. I knew there was no reason to expect them yet, but what if they had had an accident, too?

There were some firecrackers in the tent. We had

tentatively arranged on the way up to shoot them off in an emergency. I might have done that now, but there was no emergency. It would be more dangerous to communicate with them than not to, because in their alarm they might abandon caution to get down fast.

I began to wonder what I would do if they didn't come. What if I heard them calling for help? I would have to go up, yet what could I do alone? I calculated that they had at most five days' food at the Nose Camp. I had enough for twenty days at the Alley Camp. I would wait five or six days, and if there was no sign of them, I would try to finish the descent alone. At the cave I could stamp a message for Sheldon; if he flew over, he would see it. If he didn't, I would eventually start to hike out, seventy miles down an unknown glacier, across rivers, through the tundra. . . .

But these were desperate thoughts, the logical extremes of possible action I might have to take; I forced myself to consider them so that no potential course of events could lurk unrealized among my fears.

Already I had begun to miss Ed in a way separate from the shock and loneliness. I longed for his cheeriness, that fund of warmth that Matt, Don, and I lacked. I had wanted so much to relax in the tent, talking and joking with him, reliving the long summit day. I hadn't climbed with him since July 11. Now it was the last day of the month, and he was gone.

I went outside the tent only to urinate. Each time, I tied a loop around my waist and clipped in to a piton outside, not only because I was afraid but because I

couldn't be sure that the sleeping pills and the shock
(if it was actually shock) were not impairing my judgment or balance. I felt always tense, aware that I was
waiting, minute by minute. I could think of very little
but the accident; I couldn't get the sight of Ed falling,
sudden and soundless, out of my head.

The snow continued to fall lightly, but the tent got
warmer as the hidden sun warmed the air. In the afternoon I began to hear a high, faint whining sound. It
was like nothing human, but I couldn't place it. Could
it be some kind of distress signal from Matt or Don?
Impossible. . . . Could it be the wind blowing through
a carabiner somewhere above? But there was almost
no wind. Was it even real? I listened, holding my
breath, straining with the effort to define the sound.
I couldn't even tell if it was above the camp or below.
I sang a note of the same pitch to convince myself the
sound was real. It seemed to stop momentarily, but I
couldn't be sure I hadn't merely begun to ignore it.
Finally I noticed that when I went outside the tent, I
couldn't hear it. Therefore the sound had to come from
inside. At last I found it—vaporized gas, heated by
the warmth of the day, was escaping from the stove's
safety valve! I felt silly but measurably relieved.

I tried to relive every moment Ed and I had had
together the last day, as if doing so could somehow
salvage something from the tragedy. My recollections
had stuck on a remark he had made in the Nose Camp
as we rested after the summit. I had told him that it
had been the best day I'd ever had climbing. Ed had

▲ 343

said, "Mine too, but I don't know if I'd do the whole thing again."

I thought he was still upset about Matt's and my near-accident, and suggested so. Ed thought a moment, then said, "No. It's not only that."

We hadn't pursued it, but his attitude had seemed strange to me. For me, there was no question but that it would have been worth doing all over again. Nor for Don. And I thought Matt would have said so, too. But Ed had climbed less than we had; perhaps he wasn't so sure that climbing was the most important thing in his life, as we would have said it was in ours.

Now his remark haunted me. The accident, ultimately inexplicable beyond its mechanical cause, which itself we would never be sure of, seemed that much more unfair in view of what Ed had said. It would have been better, fairer, perhaps, had it happened to me. Yet not even in the depth of anguish could I wish that I had died instead. And that irreducible selfishness seemed to prove to me that beyond our feeling of "commitment" there lay the barriers of our disparate self-love. We were willing to place our lives in each other's hands, but I wouldn't have died for Ed. What a joke we played on ourselves—the whole affair of mountaineering seemed a farce then. But the numbness returned; I told myself to wait, to judge it all in better perspective, months, years from now.

By that night there had still been no sign of Matt or Don. I took another sleeping pill and finally dozed off. Sometime in the night, on the edge of sleeping and waking, I had a vision of Ed stumbling, bloody, broken, up to the tent, yelling out in the night, "Why didn't you come to look for me?" I woke with a jolt, then waited in the dark for the dream to dissolve. I hadn't considered, after the first moments, trying to look for Ed's body. For me alone, without a rope, to try to descend the 4,000 feet would certainly have been suicide. Yet because there was nothing to do, and because I hadn't seen Ed's dead body, a whisper of guilt had lodged in my subconscious, a whisper that grew to Ed's shout in my nightmare.

I took a sip of water and fell asleep again. In the morning I discovered my watch had stopped. An unimportant event, it hit me with stunning force. It was as if one more proof of reality were gone, one more contact with the others, Matt and Don first of all, everyone else alive in the world eventually. I set the watch arbitrarily and shook it to get it started.

That day, August 1, dragged by as the last one had. I was no more relaxed than I had been before. The weather was good for a few minutes in the morning, then clouded up again; but at least it had stopped snowing. I felt surer now that Matt and Don would get to me, but I began to dread their arrival, for it would open the wounds of shock in them, and I would have to be the strong one, at first.

I thought of how rarely an expedition is both successful and tragic, especially a small expedition. Something like 95 per cent of the dangers in a climb such as ours lay in the ascent. But we had worked for thirty-one days, many of them dangerous, on the route without a serious injury before finally getting to the summit. Going down should have taken only two or three days, and it is usually routine to descend pitches on which fixed ropes have been left. I was reminded of the first ascent of the Matterhorn, when only hours after its conquest the climbing rope broke, sending four of Edward Whymper's seven-man party to their deaths. Then I realized that the Matterhorn had been climbed one hundred years, almost to the day, before our ascent. I thought, also, of the ascent of Cerro Torre in Patagonia in 1959, still regarded by many as the hardest climb ever done. On its descent Toni Egger, one of the best mountaineers in the world, had fallen off a cold rappel to his death, leaving only Cesare Maestri to tell of their victory. But thinking of those climbs explained ours no better. I knew that Whymper, after the Matterhorn, had been persecuted by the public, some of whom even suggested he had cut the rope. I knew that, even in an age that understands mountaineering a little better than the Victorians did, vague suspicions still shrouded the Cerro Torre expedition. But even if we could explain Ed's death to mountaineers, how could we ever explain it to those who cared more about him than about any mountain?

Around 4:00 P.M. I heard the sound of a plane, probably Sheldon's, flying near the mountain. I couldn't see anything through the mist, but perhaps his very presence meant that it was clear up above, possibly that he could see our steps leading to the summit.

Around 10:00 P.M. I thought I heard a shout. I

looked out of the tent, but saw nothing, and was starting to attribute the sound to a random noise of the
mountain, ice breaking loose somewhere or a rock falling, when suddenly Matt came in sight at the top of
the Alley. He let out a cheery yell when he saw me.
I couldn't answer, but simply stared at him. Pretty
soon Don came in sight and yelled, "How are things
down there?" I pretended I couldn't hear him. Matt
said later that they had seen our tracks from high on
the mountain and therefore known that Ed and I
hadn't completed the descent to the cave. This had
disturbed them a little, and their mood had acquired
gloominess during the treacherous last descent, on steps
covered by new snow, using ice-coated fixed ropes, once
belaying in a waterfall that had frozen their parkas
stiff. But as they approached, Matt had seen my head
poking out of the tent and for an instant had thrown
off his worries. Yet my silence made him uneasy again;
then, before he got to the tent, he saw that there was
only one pack beside it. Then I said, "Matt, I'm alone."

He belayed Don all the way down before either of
us said anything to him. When Matt told him, Don
stood there frozen momentarily, looking only at the
snow. Then, in a way I cannot forget, he seemed to
draw a breath and swallow the impact of the shock.
He said, "All right. Let's get inside the tent." His
voice, calm as ever, was heavy with a sudden fatigue.
But once they knew, once I saw that they were taking it
without panic, being strong, I felt an overwhelming
gratitude toward them: out of my fear, an impulse
like love.

9 ▲ Remnants

We spent a crowded, uncomfortable night. The tent platform had begun to slope downhill, and it was too small for all of us. We had planned to finish the descent when the weather became good. But the next day it was storming, probably the worst day we had had. We began to worry about the pitches below getting unclimbably dangerous; perhaps even the fixed ropes might be buried. Although it was only August 2, winter was arriving: the days were growing not only shorter but noticeably colder.

We spent most of the day waiting for a let-up, but

our crowded situation was too unpleasant. As long as we had the rest of the descent before us we could not relax. We decided to go in the late afternoon despite the storm. We got dressed and moved outside the tent. A bitter wind whistled across the ridge, chilling us at once. We had a difficult time taking down the tent, because we got in each other's way trying to maneuver around the platform while staying tied in to our pitons. Moreover, the tent's back corner had frozen into the ice. At last we half chopped, half ripped it out. Our hands lost their feeling almost immediately when we had to take our mittens off; our toes grew numb after the first few minutes.

We were ready to leave by 7:30 P.M. We thought it should take about two hours to get down to the cave. In good weather we had done it in little more than one hour. Now we faced the problem of descending, three on a rope, pitches that were made for only two. Since Matt had just one crampon, he had to go in the middle. Don started off, while I waited to descend last.

The snow conditions were terrible, by far the worst we had yet run into. A full foot of loose powdery snow overlay our steps; often the steps themselves had melted out, leaving only the slick surface of the ice beneath. We went continuously at first, but at a pace slower than a snail's. Don had to rechop steps under the snow, reaching awkwardly down with his ax. The fixed ropes were coated with ice, sometimes in a solid sheath a quarter-inch thick. Moreover, since we were only seventy feet apart, two of us were often relying on the same section of fixed rope at the same time, threatening to pull each other off. Matt, despite his missing crampon, had to use the ropes as little and as gently as possible, because I, coming last, could not afford to fall, and Don wouldn't have been able to replace the steps without holding on to something.

But we seemed to move all right on the comparatively easy, rock-free pitches of the Lower Park. At least, once we got going we were all three in motion most of the time, and our feet and hands began to warm up a little.

On the thirteenth pitch, the one which joined the Stegosaur to the Lower Park, Don suddenly shouted, "Falling!" Matt and I braced ourselves, but the pull never came. Don had managed to hold himself with the fixed rope. The pitch was in terrible shape. We had to traverse awkwardly on steep ice that was coated with a rime-frost that looked solid until stepped on. Matt fell at the same spot Don had, but caught himself the same way. Gamely, he went back to rechop the steps so that I might get down safely. When I reached the spot, I found the fixed rope was of no use for balance, but I had to hold on to it in case of a slip. Even with the improved steps, I came as near falling as I ever have without coming off. Matt and Don had stopped to belay me. There were only three and a half more pitches above the rappel, but we realized we had to belay each one of them carefully. The rock added a factor of difficulty that made it too dangerous to travel continuously. First we tried tying Matt in only five feet above Don, while I belayed both of them from a solid stance. They crept down the twelfth pitch. I got very cold again, and begged the rope to pay out faster, since that was all I could see of their progress. Finally one of them yelled, "On belay!" and I could descend. The pitch was far more difficult than it ever had been on the way up. I was afraid that the fixed rope might have weathered enough to be dangerously weak, but I had to rely on it anyway. When I reached them, Don and Matt said the system was no good. They had kept getting in each other's way, pulling each other off; it was an impossible effort to co-ordinate their movements.

We moved Matt back to the middle of the rope. I went first, while Don, already quite cold, had to stand in the same spot for a much longer time to belay us ahead. It was starting to get really dark; it must have been near midnight. The darkness intensified my nervousness. Even in the best psychological state, that kind of climbing would make one very uneasy. Now, under the pall of fear Ed's death had imposed, the descent became, for me at least, a nightmarish episode. In addition, the cold and the biting wind increased our clumsiness and tended to isolate us further, because it was hard to hear our shouts against the wind and unpleasant to hold one's face into it in order to watch. Within a few minutes, it was too dark to see each other very far apart anyway.

I was glad at first to lead, to be rid of the responsibility of coming last. But I began to appreciate what a job it was to replace the steps. We couldn't take off our mittens, but I needed to scrape and chop the snow off holds whose location I only dimly recalled. Finally I would get to a piton, and Matt could start moving. It was still a while before Don could begin, though. When he shouted, his voice shook with the cold.

It grew almost pitch dark. The lower we got on the mountain, the darker it got, and the enclosed recesses between the towers of the Stegosaur shut out the faint light from the north, if not the wind.

At last we were getting down. We decided to go continuously again, for we were so cold we couldn't stand the immobility of belaying, and the rope now passed over fingers of rock between us that would catch a fall as well as would any belay we might make. At one point Don and I stood on top of two towers while Matt climbed in the gap between. The rope stuck; I yelled at Matt, but there was no answer. Don and I could hear each other's shouts perfectly, but Matt seemed oblivious. I started to go back for him, but at last Matt heard Don and answered. His voice sounded as far away as if he were on a different mountain.

I finally got within a few feet of the top of the rappel, but I couldn't reach it. Matt was stuck in an incredible tangle at the last piton. I heard him swearing at the ropes, then suddenly a frightened cry from Don as he fell. Again, the fixed rope caught him, but he couldn't find any of the steps. I felt annoyed because we were climbing so poorly. But it was so cold, and I felt the tiredness seeping even into the edge of nervousness I had known for three days. We were almost down; then there would be no more hard climbing. For eighteen days we had hung every minute, over that abyss, never less than 3,000 feet above its hidden floor: the place where Ed's body now lay.

At last Matt got the tangle straightened out. I reached the piton and belayed them down. We were together again. It almost seemed too great an effort to tie the two ropes together so that we could pull them down after we had rappelled. The rope we had left there had frozen in at the bottom so that we could scarcely pull up enough slack to pass around our bodies. But finally we managed to set the thing up. I stepped over the side of the ridge with a conscious sense of relief and quickly rappelled down, knocking the ice off the rope we had left. Matt and Don followed. Then we pulled the ropes down, cutting ourselves off for good from our route, from the far, frozen summit. We staggered back to the cave, arriving at 3:30 A.M. It had taken us eight hours to descend what we had expected to complete in two. It was the day of climbing I should least ever want to repeat.

We found the cave shrunk in size, but otherwise unchanged. The storm continued for three days. We went outside around noon on the third to stamp a sign, "Fly out," in the snow. Sheldon would see this if he flew over, we were pretty sure. There was no emergency now, no reason to call for help. If Sheldon didn't see our sign within ten days or so, we would begin to hike out.

We saw no point in searching for Ed's body. Any search we could make, even plane-assisted, would be dangerous. We would have to scour the bottom of a 6,000-foot avalanche chute, down which constantly spilled rocks and ice. After the five days of storm, his body was likely to be covered by new snow, and the chances were good that that snow wouldn't melt before winter. The body, for all we knew, had been crushed and torn in the fall. We did not want to offend its dignity by salvaging a mutilated, unrecognizable corpse. All that was mortal of Ed would freeze into an unknown glacier. Within a year there would be no part of him near its surface. Gradually the remnants of his being would sink within the Tokositna, locked in unfathomable ice. None of our words would ever stir the air above his tomb; never would anyone in that place lie about why he had died. No one would ever say there that it was right. If the unconcerned glacier should someday spill Ed's body out on the gravel bar at its mouth, rocks would still cover it; no one would ever know. Mysteries lie with Ed; but the most important of them, perhaps, could not be solved. Ed kept a diary. He had written more than a hundred pages in it in red ink, but it fell with him. That diary might have offered some clue to him, some clue to the urge that he, who made things come so easily, who understood people so well and cared about them, could have felt for an unwitnessable challenge in an inhuman place. But he had never been at rest within himself; he struggled to believe, to explain his fears and joys. The diary wouldn't have answered for those who loved him the pained question, "Why did he have to go there?"

But for Matt, Don, and me there was all of life to anticipate. We wanted to get back, but we dreaded it, too. I could picture, even then, the reception we had to expect from those who had last seen us, exuberant and eager, going off (for all some of them knew) on a pleasant summer outing. I knew even then the taste of transmitted grief that would be our duty. Already I heard the stunned, empty silence over the phone from Pennsylvania, saw the bloodshot eyes drained of hope, felt the friend's stifled wince. A remark Ed's father had made when we had stopped at their house in early June stuck in my mind now. He had said, "It's hard for you boys to understand how parents can worry about this kind of thing." I had simply agreed—it *was* hard for us to understand. Now it was tragically easier.

In the snow cave we could relax, in a sense. We no longer had to hold on to something when we went outside the tent; we no longer felt the threat of empty space beneath us. But in the absence of the tension that had bound us together, a dull feeling of loss set in. We had been robbed not only of Ed, but of all but a few hours of exultation, and would never again recall our triumph with pleasure unmitigated by pain. Now there was only another wait. To make things worse, we began to feel some of the antagonisms which our common dependence had, for the last two weeks, obliterated. We couldn't agree on a few things. I wanted to hike out in eight days or so; Don preferred to wait as long as we could. Don wanted to climb the little peak west of Huntington to get pictures of the route. I had no enthusiasm for the idea and would have felt fear on the ridge again. Matt was indifferent, but agreed to accompany Don if there was time and good weather. Don wanted to arrange, if possible, to have more food dropped in to continue climbing in our basin. I wanted to get out to face notifying Ed's parents, and Matt had to get out for a job commitment. We had talked the accident dry. All our conversation could do now was attempt to recover the sense of joy we had begun to feel as we rested at the Nose Camp after the summit. We were able, in our few days in the cave, to regain a sense of pride. I felt a strong passion, a loyalty, toward our accomplishment, but I knew it wasn't joy. We wasted time methodically, waiting for Sheldon.

On August 6 the weather cleared. We spent most of the day outside in the sun. We hoped for Sheldon, but knew the chances were good he wouldn't fly by. After all, he had been over only once since July 20, even during the long spell of good weather we had had. The new snow had plastered our route, making it look cold and splendid. In the early evening the sun lit high, ribbed clouds above McKinley, and cast a brown warmth on the rock of the face, reflected in ghostly radiance on the shadowed floor of the glacier. Never had the mountain seemed more beautiful, not even in its first untouched magic. Sheldon didn't come, however. As it got dark, we lit the few candles we had brought and set them up in the snow cave to read and write by. When I went outside, I could see the warm glow diffused through the snow of the cave's roof, and I felt an old, childish fear of the dark. The cave seemed the only island of safety in a limitless sea of night.

After we extinguished the candles, I lay awake thinking. I was trying to imagine how I could tell Ed's parents. I thought of the things that, sooner or later, people would say about Ed's death, as attempts at consolation. There were three things, especially, that would be said, things that had been said before, by me as well as others, about men who had been killed mountaineering; but now, none of them seemed to offer real consolation. It would be said that Ed died doing what he enjoyed most, that his last conscious moments were happy ones. But he did not want to die; every part of him that was aware he was falling did not want that to be, but was powerless. There was never enough happiness to last as long as we would have it. It would be said that the way he died was somehow "right." But he did not have to die; to die young is never right. It would be said that, at least, he never had time to feel pain or even fear. But, though I could not have wanted Ed to die suffering, dying without pain or fear seems to me the equivalent of living without joy. Let us be aware of our end, because life is all we have. Yet, though I could not find consolation in these thoughts, and knew they would be little consolation to his parents, I could not rid my mind of some image of beauty connected with Ed's death, as if his fall without a sound had owned, for an instant, a freedom no one ever knew in life.

At 4:00 A.M. I woke, hearing the faint hum of an

▲   357

airplane. I put my boots on and ran out of the cave. It was Sheldon. Don and Matt, awake now also, joined me as we tried to point at our sign in the snow. Sheldon seemed to see it, acknowledged us by circling, then dropped a note. It landed in the crevasse below camp, but we roped up and went to get it. He instructed us to proceed to the floor of the glacier. We packed rapidly, then left the cave, looking back as we descended the icefall for the last time. A few hours later Sheldon returned, landing easily on the hard glacier. Matt and I got in the plane first. In a second load he could pick up Don and the rest of our equipment. Sheldon had seen our tracks to the summit five days before, and Matt and Don in the Nose Camp, but he had no idea that anything had gone wrong. He couldn't quite believe Ed's death. We made several passes near the bottom of the avalanche chute, but could see no sign of anything human. Then we headed out over the tundra.

Sheldon kept saying, "Boy, that's rough. What happened?" All I could do was explain the facts of the accident. I couldn't explain beyond that; I couldn't tell him the urgency of our happiness before. Huntington faded behind us; I couldn't explain. We had spent forty days alone there, only to come back one man less, it seemed. We had found no answers to life: perhaps only the room in which to look for them.

In Talkeetna the grass smelled damp and sweet. Flies swarmed, buzzing around us as we put down our packs, and the air blazed with fireweed.

Epilogue ▲

From Talkeetna I called Ed's parents to break the news. His father's first words were, "Is this some kind of a joke?" A week later, I flew to Philadelphia to visit them for three days, in hopes of bringing solace through some explanation of our climb. The effort was a dismal failure: they didn't want to hear about Huntington, and their grief was deeper than I could fathom. Fourteen years later, I wrote about that painful visit, in an essay called "Moments of Doubt."

Our climb gained a lot of attention in the climbing world, in part, because of its tragic conclusion. Shortly after our return, we got a letter from Bradford Washburn;

he had received a letter from Lionel Terray, the great French climber who the year before us had led the first ascent of Huntington by the northwest ridge. Terray did not believe that four unheralded Americans could have climbed the west face; could it be a hoax, he asked Washburn?

Terray was a tremendous hero to both Don and me. No book had stirred our psyches more powerfully than his autobiography, *Conquistadors of the Useless*. The sterling partnership between Terray and Louis Lachenal, forged on the Eiger and Annapurna, seemed to us a mystic brotherhood. We identified so strongly with that pair, in fact, that we sometimes called each other "Louis" or "Lionel." Don, with his strong, solid determination, was Terray; I, with my quicksilver impatience, was Lachenal. With the youthful japery that bespeaks the highest homage, Don or I would shout out in the middle of a climb a quotation from some Terray epic: "Guido, the sardine tin!" say, from the first ascent of Fitzroy.

At once we wrote back to Washburn, promising to send Terray any proof he might require that we had indeed climbed the west face. But before Washburn could forward our offer, Terray was killed in a mysterious fall on a cliff in the South of France. Tied to him in the fatal plunge was Marc Martinetti, also a veteran of Huntington.

Don and I climbed together again at Christmas, in the Palisades of the Sierra Nevada. The weather was atrocious; we climbed nothing, and the grim tent-bound days in the snow were all too reminiscent of Deborah.

After that, slowly, we began to grow apart. I am still

not sure why: perhaps when it came down to it, we were simply too different from one another. In 1967 we both went back to Alaska, but on separate expeditions. Don, who had never purged Deborah from his innermost thoughts, gathered together a very strong party, including John Hudson, Art Gran, and Pete Carman, to make another attempt on the east ridge. I was not interested in a second try myself. Don acknowledged his own ambivalence, writing me shortly before his departure, "In wakefulness it sometimes looks like a jolly good climb . . . but in the subconscious it has always been cruel."

Don's team flew in to the West Fork Glacier, obviating the laborious hike-in that we had made in 1964. They quickly climbed to the col at 9,400 feet, where they received an airdrop from their pilot. Splendidly established, they saw their chances deteriorate with the weather. They held out for twenty-five days on the col, surviving an earthquake, but were able to climb only about 100 feet higher than Don and I had on the first expedition. Don himself had bad bronchitis throughout the trip and did no climbing above the col.

Meanwhile, 250 miles to the southwest of Deborah, I was climbing with five friends, including Matt, in an unexplored range that we named the Revelation Mountains. Over the course of fifty-two days, we made nine first ascents, but all of the hardest peaks thwarted us. The summer of 1967 was perhaps the stormiest in a generation in the Alaska mountains. We managed barely to hold our own at base camp, fighting to keep our tents pitched in the worst blizzards I have ever seen. At the same time on Mount McKinley, seven members of the Wilcox party were dying of hypothermia above 17,000 feet.

In 1969 Don and I met in Banff. For several weeks we hung out together, but we were in opposite climbing moods. With two other friends, I had ambitions for a big new route; eventually we climbed the north face of Temple and nearly killed ourselves in the process. Don would talk vaguely of things he wanted to climb, but resisted our invitations. While the three of us talked routes, he conspicuously spread papers across the picnic table and immersed himself in the math equations that had become his grad-school passion. I wondered if he were trying to quit climbing.

Not so. In subsequent years, he did hard routes in Canada, the Alps, and California, including many first ascents. One summer in Chamonix, Don and Matt ran into each other by accident; both in great shape, they got halfway up the Walker Spur on the Grandes Jorasses in very fast time before being stormed off. I was never sure exactly what Don had accomplished in the Ramparts or High Sierra. He was offhand in his letters, and in his whole life he never wrote a journal article about any climb he did. He kept tinkering with gear and invented a revolutionary pack design for climbs like Deborah. Marketed briefly as the Jensen Pack, it was a prototype for the frameless rucksacks the best alpinists use today. During the same years, I kept climbing in Alaska, stringing together expeditions in the Kichatna Spires, the Arrigetch, the Ruth Gorge, and other ranges.

Don and I each married, and that contributed to our

drift in different directions. I started teaching in western Massachusetts, where Sharon and I adopted urban predilections. Our idea of a good time was to drive into Boston for a Red Sox game or a concert, then dinner in a good restaurant. Don was teaching, too, but he and Joan longed for an ascetic, pastoral life. They contemplated chucking it all and homesteading in the Yukon; the plan was serious enough that they made a reconnaissance and bought land.

One day in November 1973 I learned that Don had been killed in a bicycling accident in Scotland, where he was teaching. We had grown apart, to be sure, but his death hit me with devastating force. For the first time, I made my own acquaintance with real grief. I was on my way to Los Angeles when I got the news, and after my business was done I flew to San Francisco to visit Don's parents.

His mother was in a strange state. Later I would realize that Alzheimer's disease had set in, even though she was barely in her sixties. She seemed to know what had happened to Don, but then she would forget and ask her husband, "Is Dave here to go climbing with Don?" Mortified, he would scold her in the other room; then I heard him weeping quietly by himself.

The unraveling of Don's family was the stuff of Greek tragedy. His mother died not long afterwards of her terrible illness, and then Don's father learned that he had incurable cancer. A hunter all his life, he ended it with his own gun.

In 1972 came the third ascent of Huntington, by a

five-man team on a new route, the east ridge. Within a year thereafter, two members of that team had been killed climbing. There was even talk of a Huntington jinx: with Don's death, in only nine years after the first ascent, seven of the seventeen men who had climbed Huntington had been killed, in six different accidents.

The east ridge of Deborah was finally climbed in 1983 by two teams that met by chance on the mountain and joined forces. The crux pitches high on the route were solved by two of the strongest mountaineers in North America, Carl Tobin and Dave Cheesmond. One of the Deborah climbers, Englishman John Barry, later wrote a vivid account of the ascent in a book called *The Great Climbing Adventure*. It gratified me to come across these words (though the omission of Don's name was unfortunate): "Often, on the way up, we would stand amazed at Roberts' efforts. All those years ago."

After Huntington Matt and I stayed the closest of friends, climbing with each other in the East, Wyoming, Colorado, Canada, the Alps, and Alaska. In later years we have traveled much together, to such places as Spain and Italy, Kashmir and Ladakh, Guatemala and Mali. We still talk on the phone every other week or so, and often share the holidays.

On the twentieth anniversary of our summit day on Huntington, Matt and I met at his apartment in Washington, D.C. We got good and drunk, projected our Huntington slides on the screen once more, and told ourselves what bold fellows we had been in the recklessness of youth. We talked about Don and Ed, and there, in the cozy apartment, with the beer bottles strewn across the floor, the last slide still glowing on the screen, we missed them both a lot.

Glossary

aid or direct aid — any sort of climbing that uses mechanical means (pitons, slings, stirrups) for holds or balance, instead of merely for safety.

belay — to secure one's partner against possible fall by passing the rope around the body.

bivouac tent — a two-man tent, little bigger than two men's bodies, that can be pitched on the slightest of ledges and the steepest of slopes, for a minimal camp; usually used in a final assault.

carabiner — a metal, oval snap-link that attaches the climbing rope to the piton.

chimney — an unusually steep, narrow gully.

climbing rope — the main rope, connecting a pair of climbers.

col — a gap in a ridge; a pass.

continuous climbing — both climbers moving together, roped, but without belay.

cornice — an overhanging lip of snow, formed along the top of a ridge by the wind.

couloir — a steep gully, usually filled with ice or snow.

crampons — metal spikes attached to the sole of the boot, for use on ice or hard snow.

expansion bolts — a nail or screw sleeve that is driven into the rock by means of hand drill and hammer; used as a last resort where there are no natural cracks adequate for pitons.

fixed ropes — ropes left in place to facilitate load-carrying and reclimbing a pitch.

free climbing — climbing without reliance on pitons; opposed to "aid" climbing.

ice ax — the ice climber's chief tool: a wooden or metal shaft about 2½ feet long, whose head has a pointed metal pick on one end, a flat adze on the other; it looks much like a miner's pick.

icefall — a steep, crevassed section of glacier.

icelite — a long, pointed, barbed, L-section aluminum ice piton, invented by Don Jensen specifically for Alaskan conditions; especially useful where the ice is too rotten to hold a shorter ice screw.

ice screw — a type of piton, with a corkscrew blade, that is screwed, rather than hammered, into an ice cliff.

pitch — one rope's length on the mountain.

piton — a metal peg hammered into cracks in the rock; a carabiner is attached to the head, or eye, of the piton, and the climbing rope is clipped into the carabiner, thus reducing the length of the leader's possible fall.

prusik — a means of climbing a rope that has been left in place on a steep pitch; waist- and foot-loops are tied to the main rope with a prusik knot, which slides freely up or down normally but grips and holds when one's weight is put on it.

rappel — to descend by sliding down a rope that has been attached to a piton or prong of rock.

stirrup — a three- or four-step rope ladder made of nylon webbing attached to a piton in direct-aid climbing, when there are no possible natural holds; by using several in sequence, the climber can climb pitch after pitch without a natural hold.

THE MOUNTAINEERS, founded in 1906, is a non-profit outdoor activity and conservatin club, whose mission is "to explore, study, preserve and enjoy the natural beauty of the outdoors . . ." Based in Seattle, Washington, the club is now the third largest such organization in the United States, with 15,000 members and five branches throughout Washington State.

The Mountaineers sponsors both classes and year-round outdoor activities in the Pacific Northwest, which include hiking, mountain climbing, ski-touring, snowshoeing, bicycling, camping, kayaking and canoeing, nature study, sailing, and adventure travel. The club's conservation division supports environmental causes through educational activities, sponsoring legislation, and presenting information programs. All club activities are led by skilled, experienced volunteers, who are dedicated to promoting safe and responsible enjoyment and preservation of the outdoors.

The Mountaineers Books, an active, non-profit publishing program of the club, produces guidebooks, instructional texts, historical works, natural history guides, and works on environmental conservation. All books produced by The Mountaineers are aimed at fulfilling the club's mission.

If you would like to participate in these organized outdoor activities or the club's programs, consider a membership in The Mountaineers. For information and an application, write or call The Mountaineers, Club Headquarters, 300 Third Avenue West, Seattle, Washington 98119; (209) 284-6310.

▲ About the Author

David Roberts is a freelance writer for *National Geographic*, *Outside*, *Smithsonian*, *Atlantic Monthly*, and other magazines. He is the author of many books, most recently *Iceland: Land of the Sagas* (Harry N. Abrams) and *Jean Stafford: A Biography* (Little, Brown). Roberts, a Cambridge, Massachusetts, resident, began climbing as a Harvard undergraduate in the 1960s. He has been on thirteen expeditions in Alaska and the Yukon.